I0378126

लक्ष्मी पूजा Lakṣmī Pūjā and Thousand Names

by Devi Mandir Publications
5950 Highway 128
Napa, CA 94558 USA
Communications: Phone and Fax 1-707-966-2802
E-Mail swamiji@shreemaa.org
Please visit us on the World Wide Web at
http://www.shreemaa.org

ISBN 978-1-877795-05-3
Library of Congress Catalog Card Number
CIP 2001 126165

लक्ष्मी पूजा Lakṣmī Pūjā and Thousand Names
Swami Satyananda Saraswati
1. Hindu Religion. 2. Worship. 3. Spirituality.
4. Philosophy. I. Saraswati, Swami Satyananda;
Saraswati, Swami Vittalananda

Saṁskṛta and Computer Layout
by Swami Vittalananda and Swami Adaityananda Saraswati

Table of Contents

yantra	1
Introduction	2
devatā praṇām	3
dhyānam	5
ācamana	14
saṅkalpa	18
gaṇeśa pūjā	23
puṇyā havācana, svasti vācana	26
gāyatrī viddhi	34
sāmānyārghya	46
puṣpa śuddhi	49
kalaśa sthāpana	50
prāṇa pratiṣṭhā	60
viśeṣārghya	68
bhūta śuddhi	72
kara śuddhi	73
bhūtāpsāraṇa	74
aghamārṣaṇa	75
agni prajvālitaṁ	76
mātṛkā pūjā	83
nava durgā pūjā (1)	91
nava patrikā pūjā	98
nava durgā pūjā (2)	102
yantra pūjā	106
sarvato bhadramaṇḍala devatā sthāpanam	114
aṣṭāśakti pūjā	129
nava grahaṇa pūjā	133
yogiṇī pūjā	138
astra pūjā	146
bāhya mātrikā nyāsa	151
mātṛkā nyāsa	157
aṅga pūjā	163
pīṭha nyāsa	166
āvāhaṇa	171
prāṇa pratiṣṭhā	173
stapana	177
pūjā naivedya	180
lakṣmī pūjā	196
lakṣmī sahasranāmastotram	204
lakṣmī sahasranāmavali	225
śrī lakṣmī cālīsā	352
shree maa pūjā	362

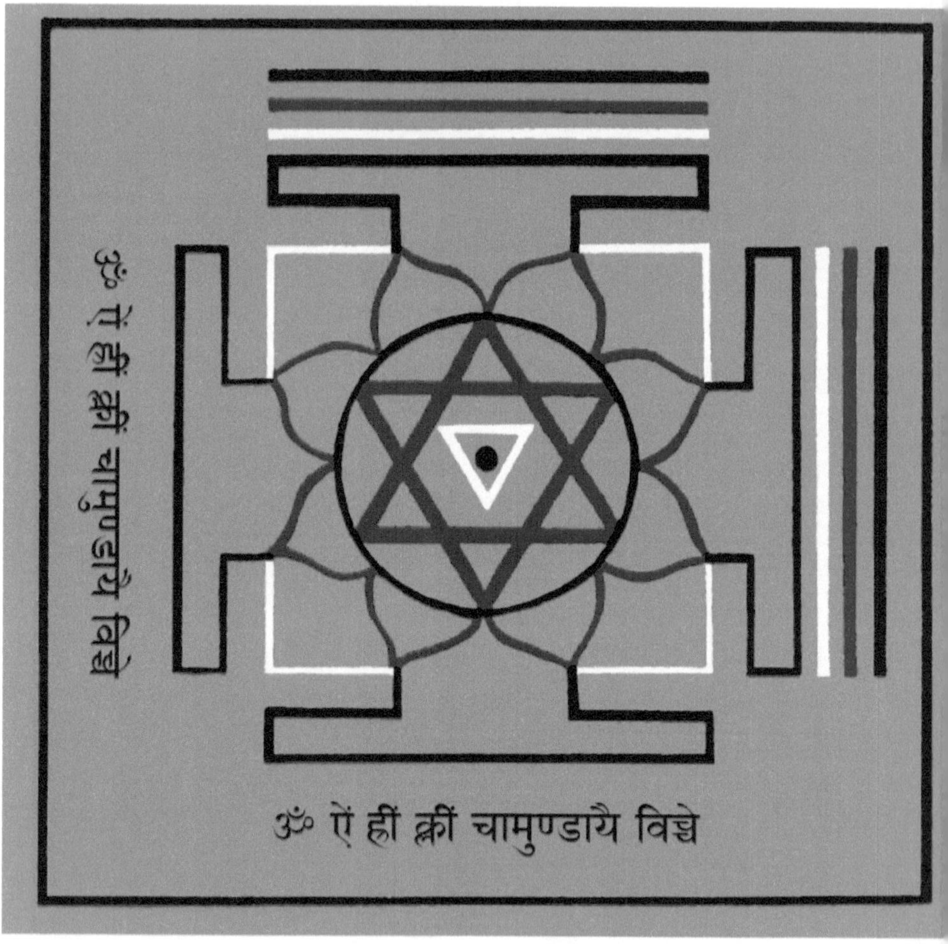
ॐ ऐं ह्रीं क्लीं चामुण्डायै विच्चे
ॐ ऐं ह्रीं क्लीं चामुण्डायै विच्चे

Introduction

Lakśya means the goal. Lakṣmī manifests the goal, every aim in existence. What our goals are, are what we value; that which we value is our wealth. And it is in this sense that Lakṣmī is the Goddess of Wealth, our goals, our values, our aspirations.
Śrī means the Highest Respect. Śa means peace. Ra means the mind, ī means your heart or intuition. The Highest Respect is peace in the mind and peace in the heart. When we can experience life with peace in our minds and peace in our hearts, we are offering our respect.

One of Lakṣmī's names is Śrī. In this text a thousand other names are given, along with Her pūjā, japa and nyāsa. When we worship, we focus our attention. That is what worship is. As we practice to achieve greater intensities of focus, greater degrees of absorption, we find greater efficiency in our actions and greater peace in our minds and in our hearts.

That is Lakṣmī's promise: "Whoever will pursue their goals with peace, they will find the wealth." May Lakṣmī bless us all with Her wealth, with Her peace and with fulfillment of our every aspiration in life.

Swami Satyananda Saraswati
Devi Mandir, 2001

देवता प्रणाम्
devatā praṇām

श्रीमन्महागणाधिपतये नमः

śrīmanmahāgaṇādhipataye namaḥ
We bow to the Respected Great Lord of Wisdom.

लक्ष्मीनारायणाभ्यां नमः

lakṣmīnārāyaṇābhyāṁ namaḥ
We bow to Lakṣmī and Nārāyaṇa, The Goal of all Existence and the Perceiver of all.

उमामहेश्वराभ्यां नमः

umāmaheśvarābhyāṁ namaḥ
We bow to Umā and Maheśvara, She who protects existence, and the Great Consciousness or Seer of all.

वाणीहिरण्यगर्भाभ्यां नमः

vāṇīhiraṇyagarbhābhyāṁ namaḥ
We bow to Vāṇī and Hiraṇyagarbha, Sarasvatī and Brahmā, who create the cosmic existence.

शचीपुरन्दराभ्यां नमः

śacīpurandarābhyāṁ namaḥ
We bow to Śacī and Purandara, Indra and his wife, who preside over all that is divine.

मातापितृभ्यां नमः

mātāpitṛbhyāṁ namaḥ
We bow to the Mothers and Fathers.

इष्टदेवताभ्यो नमः

iṣṭadevatābhyo namaḥ
We bow to the chosen deity of worship.

कुलदेवताभ्यो नमः
kuladevatābhyo namaḥ
We bow to the family deity of worship.

ग्रामदेवताभ्यो नमः
grāmadevatābhyo namaḥ
We bow to the village deity of worship.

वास्तुदेवताभ्यो नमः
vāstudevatābhyo namaḥ
We bow to the particular household deity of worship.

स्थानदेवताभ्यो नमः
sthānadevatābhyo namaḥ
We bow to the established deity of worship.

सर्वेभ्यो देवेभ्यो नमः
sarvebhyo devebhyo namaḥ
We bow to all the Gods.

सर्वेभ्यो ब्राह्मणेभ्यो नमः
sarvebhyo brāhmaṇebhyo namaḥ
We bow to all the Knowers of divinity.

dhyānam

खड्गं चक्रगदेषुचापपरिघाञ्छूलं भुशुण्डीं शिरः
शङ्खं संदधतीं करैस्त्रिनयनां सर्वाङ्गभूषावृताम् ।
नीलाश्मद्युतिमास्यपाददशकां सेवे महाकालिकां
यामस्तौत्स्वपिते हरौ कमलजो हन्तुं मधुं कैटभम् ॥

khaḍgaṁ cakra gadeṣu cāpa
parighāñ chūlaṁ bhuśuṇḍīṁ śiraḥ
śaṅkhaṁ saṁdadhatīṁ karai
strinayanāṁ sarvāṅga bhūṣāvṛtām |
nīlāś madyutimāsya pāda
daśakāṁ seve mahākālikāṁ
yāmastaut svapite harau
kamalajo hantuṁ madhuṁ kaiṭabham ||

Bearing in Her ten hands the sword of worship, the discus of revolving time, the club of articulation, the bow of determination, the iron bar of restraint, the pike of attention, the sling, the head of egotism and the conch of vibrations, She has three eyes and displays ornaments on all Her limbs. Shining like a blue gem, She has ten faces. I worship that Great Remover of Darkness whom the lotus-born Creative Capacity praised in order to slay Too Much and Too Little when the Supreme Consciousness was asleep.

अक्षस्रक्परशुं गदेषुकुलिशं पद्मं धनुः कुण्डिकां
दण्डं शक्तिमसिं च चर्म जलजं घण्टां सुराभाजनम् ।
शूलं पाशसुदर्शने च दधतीं हस्तैः प्रसन्नाननां
सेवे सैरिभमर्दिनीमिह महालक्ष्मीं सरोजस्थिताम् ॥

akṣasrak paraśuṁ gadeṣu
kuliśaṁ padmaṁ dhanuḥ kuṇḍikāṁ
daṇḍaṁ śaktīm asiṁ ca carma
jalajaṁ ghaṇṭāṁ surābhājanam |
śūlaṁ pāśa sudarśane ca
dadhatīṁ hastaiḥ prasannānanāṁ
seve sairibha mardinī
miha mahālakṣmīṁ sarojasthitām ||

She with the beautiful face, the Destroyer of the Great Ego, is seated upon the lotus of Peace. In Her hands She holds the rosary of alphabets, the battle axe of good actions, the club of articulation, the arrow of speech, the thunderbolt of illumination, the lotus of peace, the bow of determination, the water-pot of purification, the staff of discipline, energy, the sword of worship, the shield of faith, the conch of vibrations, the bell of continuous tone, the wine cup of joy, the pike of concentration, the net of unity and the discus of revolving time named Excellent Intuitive Vision. I worship that Great Goddess of True Wealth.

घण्टाशूलहलानि शङ्खमुसले चक्रं धनुः सायकं
हस्ताब्जैर्दधतीं घनान्तविलसच्छीतांशुतुल्यप्रभाम् ।
गौरीदेहसमुद्भवां त्रिजगतामाधारभूतां महा-
पूर्वामत्र सरस्वतीमनुभजे शुम्भादिदैत्यार्दिनीम् ॥

ghaṇṭā śūla halāni śaṅkha
musale cakraṁ dhanuḥ sāyakaṁ
hastābjair dadhatīṁ ghanānta
vilasacchītāṁ śutulya prabhām ।
gaurīdeha samudbhavāṁ
trijagatām ādhārabhūtāṁ mahā-
pūrvāmatra sarasvatīm
anubhaje śumbhādi daityārdinīm

Bearing in Her lotus hands the bell of continuous tone, the pike of concentration, the plow sowing the seeds of the Way of Truth to Wisdom, the conch of vibrations, the pestle of refinement, the discus of revolving time, the bow of determination and the arrow of speech, whose radiance is like the moon in autumn, whose appearance is most beautiful, who is manifested from the body of She Who is Rays of Light, and is the support of the three worlds, I worship that Great Goddess of All-Pervading Knowledge, who destroyed Self-Conceit and other thoughts.

या चण्डी मधुकैटभादिदैत्यदलनी या माहिषोन्मूलिनी
या धूम्रेक्षणचण्डमुण्डमथनी या रक्तबीजाशनी ।
शक्तिः शुम्भनिशुम्भदैत्यदलनी या सिद्धिदात्री परा
सा देवी नवकोटीमूर्तिसहिता मां पातु विश्वेश्वरी ॥

yā caṇḍī madhukaiṭabhādidaityadalanī yā māhiṣonmūlinī
yā dhūmrekṣaṇacaṇḍamuṇḍamathanī yā raktabījāśanī
śaktiḥ śumbhaniśumbhadaityadalanī yā siddhidātrī parā
sā devī navakoṭīmūrtisahitā māṁ pātu viśveśvarī

That Caṇḍī, who slays the negativities of Too Much and Too Little and other Thoughts; Who is the origin of the Great Ego, and the Destroyer of Sinful Eyes, Passion and Anger, and the Seed of Desire; the Energy that tears asunder Self-Conceit and Self-Deprecation, the Grantor of the highest attainment of perfection: may that Goddess who is represented by ninety million divine images, the Supreme Lord of the Universe, remain close and protect me.

ॐ अग्निर्ज्योतिर्ज्योतिरग्निः स्वाहा ।
सूर्यो ज्योतिर्ज्योतिः सूर्यः स्वाहा ।
अग्निर्वर्चो ज्योतिर्वर्चः स्वाहा ।
सूर्यो वर्चो ज्योतिर्वर्चः स्वाहा ।
ज्योतिः सूर्यः सूर्यो ज्योतिः स्वाहा ॥

oṁ agnir jyotir jyotir agniḥ svāhā
sūryo jyotir jyotiḥ sūryaḥ svāhā
agnir varco jyotir varcaḥ svāhā
sūryo varco jyotir varcaḥ svāhā
jyotiḥ sūryaḥ sūryo jyotiḥ svāhā

oṁ The Divine Fire is the Light, and the Light is the Divine Fire; I am One with God! The Light of Wisdom is the Light, and the Light is the Light of Wisdom; I am One with God! The Divine Fire is the offering, and the Light is the Offering; I am One with God!
The Light of Wisdom is the Offering, and the Light is the Light of Wisdom; I am One with God!

(Wave light)

ॐ अग्निर्ज्योती रविर्ज्योतिश्चन्द्रो ज्योतिस्तथैव च ।

ज्योतिषामुत्तमो देवि दीपोऽयं प्रतिगृह्यताम् ॥

एष दीपः ॐ श्रीं लक्ष्मयै नमः ॥

oṁ agnirjyotī ravirjyotiścandro jyotistathaiva ca
jyotiṣāmuttamo devi dīpo-yaṁ pratigṛhyatām
eṣa dīpaḥ oṁ śrīṁ lakṣmyai namaḥ

oṁ The Divine Fire is the Light, the Light of Wisdom is the Light, the Light of Devotion is the Light as well. The Light of the Highest Bliss, Oh Goddess, is in the Light which we offer, the Light which we request you to accept. With the offering of Light Oṁ I bow to the Goddess Lakṣmī.

(Wave incense)

ॐ वनस्पतिरसोत्पन्नो गन्धात्ययी गन्ध उत्तमः ।

आघ्रेयः सर्वदेवानां धूपोऽयं प्रतिगृह्यताम् ॥

एष धूपः ॐ श्रीं लक्ष्मयै नमः ॥

oṁ vanaspatirasotpanno gandhātyayī gandha uttamaḥ
āghreyaḥ sarvadevānāṁ dhūpo-yaṁ pratigṛhyatām
eṣa dhūpaḥ oṁ śrīṁ lakṣmyai namaḥ

oṁ Spirit of the Forest, from you is produced the most excellent of scents. The scent most pleasing to all the Gods, that scent we request you to accept. With the offering of fragrant scent Oṁ I bow to the Goddess Lakṣmī.

ārātrikam

ॐ चन्द्रादित्यौ च धरणी विद्युदग्निस्तथैव च ।

त्वमेव सर्वज्योतीषिं आरात्रिकं प्रतिगृह्यताम् ॥

ॐ श्रीं लक्ष्मयै नमः आरात्रिकं समर्पयामि

oṁ candrādityau ca dharaṇī vidyudagnistathaiva ca
tvameva sarvajyotīṣiṁ ārātrikaṁ pratigṛhyatām
oṁ śrīṁ lakṣmyai namaḥ ārātrikaṁ samarpayāmi

All knowing as the Moon, the Sun and the Divine Fire, you alone are all light, and this light we request you to accept. With the offering of light Oṁ I bow to the Goddess Lakṣmī.

ॐ पयः पृथिव्यां पय ओषधीषु
पयो दिव्यन्तरिक्षे पयो धाः ।
पयःस्वतीः प्रदिशः सन्तु मह्यम् ॥

oṁ payaḥ pṛthivyāṁ paya oṣadhīṣu
payo divyantarikṣe payo dhāḥ
payaḥsvatīḥ pradiśaḥ santu mahyam

oṁ Earth is a reservoir of nectar, all vegetation is a reservoir of nectar, the divine atmosphere is a reservoir of nectar, and also above. May all perceptions shine forth with the sweet taste of nectar for us.

ॐ अग्निर्देवता वातो देवता सूर्यो देवता चन्द्रमा देवता
वसवो देवता रुद्रो देवता ऽदित्या देवता मरुतो देवता विश्वे
देवा देवता बृहस्पतिर्देवतेन्द्रो देवता वरुणो देवता ॥

oṁ agnirdevatā vāto devatā sūryo devatā candramā devatā vasavo devatā rudro devatā-dityā devatā maruto devatā viśve devā devatā bṛhaspatirdevatendro devatā varuṇo devatā

oṁ The Divine Fire (Light of Purity) is the shining God, the Wind is the shining God, the Sun (Light of Wisdom) is the shining God, the Moon (Lord of Devotion) is the shining God, the Protectors of the Wealth are the shining Gods, the Relievers of Sufferings are the shining Gods, the Sons of the Light are the shining Gods; the Emancipated seers (Maruts) are the shining Gods, the Universal Shining Gods are the shining Gods, the Guru of the Gods is the shining God, the Ruler of the Gods is the shining God, the Lord of Waters is the shining God.

ॐ भूर्भुवः स्वः ।
तत् सवितुर्वरेण्यम् भर्गो देवस्य धीमहि ।
धियो यो नः प्रचोदयात् ॥

oṁ bhūr bhuvaḥ svaḥ
tat savitur vareṇyam bhargo devasya dhīmahi
dhiyo yo naḥ pracodayāt

oṁ the Infinite Beyond Conception, the gross body, the subtle body and the causal body; we meditate upon that Light of Wisdom which is the Supreme Wealth of the Gods. May it grant to us increase in our meditations.

ॐ भूः

oṁ bhūḥ

oṁ the gross body

ॐ भुवः

oṁ bhuvaḥ

oṁ the subtle body

ॐ स्वः

oṁ svaḥ

oṁ the causal body

ॐ महः

oṁ mahaḥ

oṁ the great body of existence

ॐ जनः

oṁ janaḥ

oṁ the body of knowledge

ॐ तपः

oṁ tapaḥ

oṁ the body of light

ॐ सत्यं

oṁ satyaṁ
oṁ the body of Truth

ॐ तत् सवितुर्वरेण्यम् भर्गो देवस्य धीमहि ।
धियो यो नः प्रचोदयात् ॥

oṁ tat savitur vareṇyam bhargo devasya dhīmahi dhiyo yo naḥ pracodayāt
oṁ we meditate upon that Light of Wisdom which is the Supreme Wealth of the Gods. May it grant to us increase in our meditations.

ॐ आपो ज्योतीरसोमृतं ब्रह्म भूर्भुवस्स्वरोम् ॥

oṁ āpo jyotīrasomṛtaṁ brahma bhūrbhuvassvarom
May the divine waters luminous with the nectar of immortality of Supreme Divinity fill the earth, the atmosphere and the heavens.

ॐ मां माले महामाये सर्वशक्तिस्वरूपिणि ।
चतुर्वर्गस्त्वयि न्यस्तस्तस्मान्मे सिद्धिदा भव ॥

oṁ māṁ māle mahāmāye sarvaśaktisvarūpiṇi catur vargas tvayi nyastas tasmān me siddhidā bhava
oṁ My Rosary, The Great Measurement of Consciousness, containing all energy within as your intrinsic nature, give to me the attainment of your Perfection, fulfilling the four objectives of life.

ॐ अविघ्नं कुरु माले त्वं गृह्णामि दक्षिणे करे ।
जपकाले च सिद्ध्यर्थं प्रसीद मम सिद्धये ॥

oṁ avighnaṁ kuru māle tvaṁ gṛhṇāmi dakṣiṇe kare japakāle ca siddhyarthaṁ prasīda mama siddhaye
oṁ Rosary, You please remove all obstacles. I hold you in my right hand. At the time of recitation be pleased with me. Allow me to attain the Highest Perfection.

ॐ अक्षमालाधिपतये सुसिद्धिं देहि देहि
सर्वमन्त्रार्थसाधिनि साधय साधय सर्वसिद्धिं परिकल्पय
परिकल्पय मे स्वाहा ॥

oṁ akṣa mālā dhipataye susiddhiṁ dehi dehi sarva mantrārtha sādhini sādhaya sādhaya sarva siddhiṁ parikalpaya parikalpaya me svāhā
oṁ Rosary of rudrākṣa seeds, my Lord, give to me excellent attainment. Give to me, give to me. Illuminate the meanings of all mantras, illuminate, illuminate! Fashion me with all excellent attainments, fashion me! I am One with God!

एते गन्धपुष्पे ॐ गं गणपतये नमः

ete gandhapuṣpe oṁ gaṁ gaṇapataye namaḥ
With these scented flowers oṁ we bow to the Lord of Wisdom, Lord of the Multitudes.

एते गन्धपुष्पे ॐ आदित्यादिनवग्रहेभ्यो नमः

ete gandhapuṣpe oṁ ādityādi navagrahebhyo namaḥ
With these scented flowers oṁ we bow to the Sun, the Light of Wisdom, along with the nine planets.

एते गन्धपुष्पे ॐ शिवादिपञ्चदेवताभ्यो नमः

ete gandhapuṣpe oṁ śivādipañcadevatābhyo namaḥ
With these scented flowers oṁ we bow to Śiva, the Consciousness of Infinite Goodness, along with the five primary deities (Śiva, Śakti, Viṣṇu, Gaṇeśa, Sūrya).

एते गन्धपुष्पे ॐ इन्द्रादिदशदिक्पालेभ्यो नमः

ete gandhapuṣpe oṁ indrādi daśadikpālebhyo namaḥ
With these scented flowers oṁ we bow to Indra, the Ruler of the Pure, along with the Ten Protectors of the ten directions.

एते गन्धपुष्पे ॐ मत्स्यादिदशावतारेभ्यो नमः
ete gandhapuṣpe oṁ matsyādi daśāvatārebhyo namaḥ
With these scented flowers oṁ we bow to Viṣṇu, the Fish, along with the Ten Incarnations which He assumed.

एते गन्धपुष्पे ॐ प्रजापतये नमः
ete gandhapuṣpe oṁ prajāpataye namaḥ
With these scented flowers oṁ we bow to the Lord of All Created Beings.

एते गन्धपुष्पे ॐ नमो नारायणाय नमः
ete gandhapuṣpe oṁ namo nārāyaṇāya namaḥ
With these scented flowers oṁ we bow to the Perfect Perception of Consciousness.

एते गन्धपुष्पे ॐ सर्वेभ्यो देवेभ्यो नमः
ete gandhapuṣpe oṁ sarvebhyo devebhyo namaḥ
With these scented flowers oṁ we bow to All the Gods.

एते गन्धपुष्पे ॐ सर्वाभ्यो देवीभ्यो नमः
ete gandhapuṣpe oṁ sarvābhyo devībhyo namaḥ
With these scented flowers oṁ we bow to All the Goddesses.

एते गन्धपुष्पे ॐ श्री गुरवे नमः
ete gandhapuṣpe oṁ śrī gurave namaḥ
With these scented flowers oṁ we bow to the Guru.

एते गन्धपुष्पे ॐ ब्राह्मणेभ्यो नमः
ete gandhapuṣpe oṁ brāhmaṇebhyo namaḥ
With these scented flowers oṁ we bow to All Knowers of Wisdom.

Tie a piece of string around right middle finger or wrist.

ॐ कुशासने स्थितो ब्रह्मा कुशे चैव जनार्दनः ।

कुशे ह्याकाशवद् विष्णुः कुशासन नमोऽस्तु ते ॥

oṁ kuśāsane sthito brahmā kuśe caiva janārdanaḥ
kuśe hyākāśavad viṣṇuḥ kuśāsana namo-stu te

Brahmā is in the shining light (or kuśa grass), in the shining light resides Janārdana, the Lord of Beings. The Supreme all-pervading Consciousness, Viṣṇu, resides in the shining light. Oh Repository of the shining light, we bow down to you, the seat of kuśa grass.

आचमन

ācamana

ॐ केशवाय नमः स्वाहा

oṁ keśavāya namaḥ svāhā

We bow to the one of beautiful hair.

ॐ माधवाय नमः स्वाहा

oṁ mādhavāya namaḥ svāhā

We bow to the one who is always sweet.

ॐ गोविन्दाय नमः स्वाहा

oṁ govindāya namaḥ svāhā

We bow to He who is one-pointed light.

ॐ विष्णुः ॐ विष्णुः ॐ विष्णुः

oṁ viṣṇuḥ oṁ viṣṇuḥ oṁ viṣṇuḥ

oṁ Consciousness, oṁ Consciousness, oṁ Consciousness.

ॐ तत् विष्णोः परमं पदम् सदा पश्यन्ति सूरयः ।

दिवीव चक्षुराततम् ॥

oṁ tat viṣṇoḥ paramaṁ padam sadā paśyanti sūrayaḥ
divīva cakṣurā tatam

oṁ That Consciousness of the highest station, who always sees the Light of Wisdom, give us Divine Eyes.

ॐ तद् विप्र स पिपानोव जुविग्रन्सो सोमिन्द्रते ।
विष्णुः तत् परमं पदम् ॥

oṁ tad vipra sa pipānova juvigranso somindrate
viṣṇuḥ tat paramaṁ padam
oṁ That twice-born teacher who is always thirsty for accepting the nectar of devotion, Oh Consciousness, you are in that highest station.

ॐ अपवित्रः पवित्रो वा सर्वावस्थां गतोऽपि वा ।
यः स्मरेत् पुण्डरीकाक्षं स बाह्याभ्यन्तरः शुचिः ॥

oṁ apavitraḥ pavitro vā sarvāvasthāṁ gato-pi vā
yaḥ smaret puṇḍarīkākṣaṁ sa bāhyābhyantaraḥ śuciḥ
oṁ The Impure and the Pure reside within all objects. Who remembers the lotus-eyed Consciousness is conveyed to radiant beauty.

ॐ सर्वमङ्गलमाङ्गल्यम् वरेण्यम् वरदं शुभं ।
नारायणं नमस्कृत्य सर्वकर्माणि कारयेत् ॥

oṁ sarva maṅgala māṅgalyam
vareṇyam varadaṁ śubhaṁ
nārāyaṇaṁ namaskṛtya sarvakarmāṇi kārayet
All the Welfare of all Welfare, the highest blessing of Purity and Illumination, with the offering of respect we bow down to the Supreme Consciousness who is the actual performer of all action.

ॐ सूर्य्यश्चमेति मन्त्रस्य ब्रह्मा ऋषिः प्रकृतिश्छन्दः आपो देवता आचमने विनियोगः ॥

oṁ sūryyaścameti mantrasya brahmā ṛṣiḥ
prakṛtiśchandaḥ āpo devatā ācamane viniyogaḥ
oṁ these are the mantras of the Light of Wisdom, the Creative Capacity is the Seer, Nature is the meter, the divine flow of waters is the deity, being applied in washing the hands and rinsing the mouth.

Draw the asana yantra with some drops of water and/or sandal paste at the front of your seat. Place a flower on the bindu in the middle.

ॐ आसनस्य मन्त्रस्य मेरुपृष्ठ ऋषिः सुतलं छन्दः कूर्म्मो
देवता आसनोपवेशने विनियोगः ॥

oṁ āsanasya mantrasya merupṛṣṭha ṛṣiḥ sutalaṁ chandaḥ kūrmmo devatā āsanopaveśane viniyogaḥ

Introducing the mantras of the Purification of the seat. The Seer is He whose back is Straight, the meter is of very beautiful form, the tortoise who supports the earth is the deity. These mantras are applied to make the seat free from obstructions.

एते गन्धपुष्पे ॐ ह्रीं आधारशक्तये कमलासनाय नमः ॥

ete gandhapuṣpe oṁ hrīṁ ādhāraśaktaye kamalāsanāya namaḥ

With these scented flowers oṁ hrīṁ we bow to the Primal Energy situated in this lotus seat.

ॐ पृथ्वि त्वया धृता लोका देवि त्वं विष्णुना धृता ।
त्वञ्च धारय मां नित्यं पवित्रं कुरु चासनम् ॥

oṁ pṛthvi tvayā dhṛtā lokā devi tvaṁ viṣṇunā dhṛtā tvañca dhāraya māṁ nityaṁ pavitraṁ kuru cāsanam

oṁ Earth! You support the realms of the Goddess. You are supported by the Supreme Consciousness. Also bear me eternally and make pure this seat.

ॐ गुरुभ्यो नमः

oṁ gurubhyo namaḥ

oṁ I bow to the Guru.

ॐ परमगुरुभ्यो नमः

oṁ paramagurubhyo namaḥ

oṁ I bow to the Guru's Guru.

ॐ परापरगुरुभ्यो नमः

oṁ parāparagurubhyo namaḥ
oṁ I bow to the Gurus of the lineage.

ॐ परमेष्ठिगुरुभ्यो नमः

oṁ parameṣṭhigurubhyo namaḥ
oṁ I bow to the Supreme Gurus.

ॐ गं गणेशाय नमः

oṁ gaṁ gaṇeśāya namaḥ
oṁ I bow to the Lord of Wisdom.

ॐ अनन्ताय नमः

oṁ anantāya namaḥ
oṁ I bow to the Infinite One.

ॐ ऐं ह्रीं क्लीं चामुण्डायै विच्चे

oṁ aiṁ hrīṁ klīṁ cāmuṇḍāyai vicce
oṁ Creation, Circumstance, Transformation are known by Consciousness.

ॐ नमः शिवाय

oṁ namaḥ śivāya
oṁ I bow to the Consciousness of Infinite Goodness.

Clap hands 3 times and snap fingers in the ten directions (N S E W NE SW NW SE UP DOWN) repeating

ॐ श्रीं लक्ष्म्यै नमः

oṁ śrīṁ lakṣmyai namaḥ
Oṁ I bow to the Goddess Lakṣmī.

सङ्कल्प
saṅkalpa

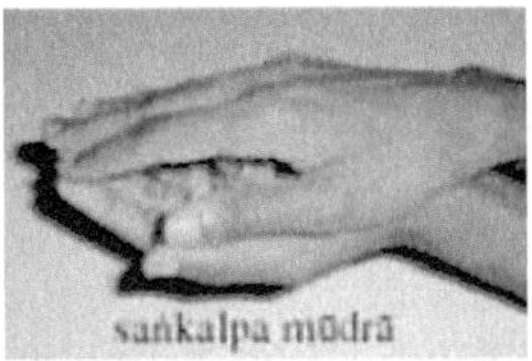

विष्णुः ॐ तत् सत् । ॐ अद्य जम्बूद्वीपे ( ) देशे ( ) प्रदेशे ( ) नगरे ( ) मन्दिरे ( ) मासे ( ) पक्षे ( ) तिथौ ( ) गोत्र श्री ( ) कृतैतत् श्रीलक्ष्मी कामः पूजाकर्माहं करिष्ये ॥

viṣṇuḥ oṁ tat sat oṁ adya jambūdvīpe (Country) deśe (State) pradeśe (City) nagare (Name of house or temple) mandire (month) māse (śukla or kṛṣṇa) pakṣe (name of day) tithau (name of) gotra śrī (your name) gotra śrī (your name) kṛtaitat śrī lakṣmī kāmaḥ pūjā karmāhaṁ kariṣye

The Consciousness Which Pervades All, oṁ That is Truth. Presently, on the Planet Earth, Country of (Name), State of (Name), City of (Name), in the Temple of (Name), (Name of Month) Month, (Bright or Dark) fortnight, (Name of Day) Day, (Name of Sādhu Family), Śrī (Your Name) is performing the worship for the satisfaction of the Respected Lakṣmī.

ॐ यज्जाग्रतो दूरमुदेति दैवं तदु सुप्तस्य तथैवैति ।
दूरङ्गमं ज्योतिषां ज्योतिरेकं तन्मे मनः शिवसङ्कल्पमस्तु ॥

oṁ yajjāgrato dūramudeti
daivaṁ tadu suptasya tathaivaiti
dūraṅgamaṁ jyotiṣāṁ jyotirekaṁ
tanme manaḥ śiva saṅkalpamastu

May our waking consciousness replace pain and suffering with divinity as also our awareness when asleep. Far extending be our radiant aura of light, filling our minds with light. May that be the firm determination of the Consciousness of Infinite Goodness.

या गुङ्गूर्या सिनीवाली या राका या सरस्वती ।
ईन्द्राणीमह्व ऊतये वरुणानीं स्वस्तये ॥

yā guṅgūryā sinīvālī yā rākā yā sarasvatī
īndrāṇīmahva ūtaye varuṇānīṁ svastaye

May that Goddess who wears the Moon of Devotion protect the children of Devotion. May that Goddess of All-Pervading Knowledge protect us. May the Energy of the Rule of the Pure rise up. Oh Energy of Equilibrium grant us the highest prosperity.

ॐ स्वस्ति न इन्द्रो वृद्धश्रवाः स्वस्ति नः पूषा विश्ववेदाः ।
स्वस्ति नस्तार्क्ष्यो अरिष्टनेमिः स्वस्ति नो बृहस्पतिर्दधातु ॥

oṁ svasti na indro vṛddhaśravāḥ
svasti naḥ pūṣā viśvavedāḥ
svasti nastārkṣyo ariṣṭanemiḥ
svasti no bṛhaspatirdadhātu

The Ultimate Prosperity to us, Oh Rule of the Pure, who perceives all that changes; the Ultimate Prosperity to us, Searchers for Truth, Knowers of the Universe; the Ultimate Prosperity to us, Oh Divine Being of Light, keep us safe; the Ultimate Prosperity to us, Oh Spirit of All-Pervading Delight, grant that to us.

ॐ गणानां त्वा गणपतिꣳ हवामहे
प्रियाणां त्वा प्रियपतिꣳ हवामहे
निधीनां त्वा निधिपतिꣳ हवामहे वसो मम ।
आहमजानि गर्भधमा त्वमजासि गर्भधम् ॥

oṁ gaṇānāṁ tvā gaṇapati guṁ havāmahe
priyāṇāṁ tvā priyapati guṁ havāmahe
nidhīnāṁ tvā nidhipati guṁ havāmahe vaso mama
āhamajāni garbbhadhamā tvamajāsi garbbhadham

We invoke you with offerings, Oh Lord of the Multitudes; we invoke you with offerings, Oh Lord of Love; we invoke you with offerings, Oh Guardian of the Treasure. Sit within me, giving birth to the realm of the Gods within me; yes, giving birth to the realm of the Gods within me.

ॐ गणानां त्वा गणपतिꣳ हवामहे
कविं कवीनामुपमश्रवस्तमम् ।
ज्येष्ठराजं ब्रह्मणां ब्रह्मणस्पत
आ नः शृण्वन्नूतिभिः सीद सादनम् ॥

oṁ gaṇānāṁ tvā gaṇapati guṁ havāmahe
kaviṁ kavīnāmupamaśravastamam
jyeṣṭharājaṁ brahmaṇāṁ brahmaṇaspata
ā naḥ śṛnvannūtibhiḥ sīda sādanam

We invoke you with offerings, Oh Lord of the Multitudes, Seer among Seers, of unspeakable grandeur. Oh Glorious King, Lord of the Knowers of Wisdom, come speedily hearing our supplications and graciously take your seat amidst our assembly.

ॐ अदितिर्द्यौरदितिरन्तरिक्षमदितिर्माता स पिता स
पुत्रः । विश्वे देवा अदितिः पञ्च जना
अदितिर्जातमदितिर्जनित्वम् ॥

oṁ aditir dyauraditirantarikṣamaditirmātā
sa pitā sa putraḥ
viśve devā aditiḥ pañca janā
aditirjātamaditirjanitvam

The Mother of Enlightenment pervades the heavens; the Mother of Enlightenment pervades the atmosphere; the Mother of Enlightenment pervades Mother and Father and child. All Gods of the Universe are pervaded by the Mother, the five forms of living beings, all Life. The Mother of Enlightenment, She is to be known.

ॐ त्वं स्त्रीस्त्वं पुमानसि त्वं कुमार अत वा कुमारी ।
त्वं जिर्नो वन्देन वञ्चसि त्वं जातो भवसि विश्वतोमुखः ॥

oṁ tvaṁ strīstvaṁ pumānasi
tvaṁ kumāra ata vā kumarī
tvaṁ jirno vandena vañcasi
tvaṁ jāto bhavasi viśvatomukhaḥ

You are Female, you are Male; you are a young boy, you are a young girl. You are the word of praise by which we are singing; you are all creation existing as the mouth of the universe.

ॐ अम्बेऽम्बिकेऽम्बालिके न मा नयति कश्चन ।
ससस्त्यश्वकः सुभद्रिकां काम्पीलवासिनीम् ॥

oṁ ambe-ambike-mbālike na mā nayati kaścana
sasastyaśvakaḥ subhadrikāṁ kāmpīlavāsinīm

Mother of the Perceivable Universe, Mother of the Conceivable Universe, Mother of the Universe of Intuitive Vision, lead me to that True Existence. As excellent crops (or grains) are harvested, so may I be taken to reside with the Infinite Consciousness.

ॐ शान्ता द्यौः शान्तापृथिवी शान्तमिदमुर्वन्तरिक्षम् ।
शान्ता उदन्वतिरापः शान्ताः नः शान्त्वोषधीः ॥

oṁ śāntā dyauḥ śāntā pṛthivī śāntam idamurvantarikṣam
śāntā udanvatirāpaḥ śāntāḥ naḥ śāntvoṣadhīḥ

Peace in the heavens, Peace on the earth, Peace upwards and permeating the atmosphere; Peace upwards, over, on all sides and further; Peace to us, Peace to all vegetation;

ॐ शान्तानि पूर्वरूपाणि शान्तं नोऽस्तु कृताकृतम् ।
शान्तं भूतं च भव्यं च सर्वमेव शमस्तु नः ॥

oṁ śāntāni pūrva rūpāṇi śāntaṁ no-stu kṛtākṛtam
śāntaṁ bhūtaṁ ca bhavyaṁ ca sarvameva śamastu naḥ

Peace to all that has form, Peace to all causes and effects; Peace to all existence, and to all intensities of reality including all and everything; Peace be to us.

ॐ पृथिवी शान्तिरन्तरिक्षं शान्तिर्द्यौः
शान्तिरापः शान्तिरोषधयः शान्तिः वनस्पतयः शान्तिर्विश्वे मे
देवाः शान्तिः सर्वे मे देवाः शान्तिर्ब्रह्म शान्तिरापः शान्तिः
सर्वं शान्तिरेधि शान्तिः शान्तिः सर्व शान्तिः सा मा शान्तिः
शान्तिभिः ॥

**oṁ pṛthivī śāntir antarikṣaṁ śāntir dyauḥ
śāntir āpaḥ śāntir oṣadhayaḥ śāntiḥ vanaspatayaḥ śāntir
viśve me devāḥ śāntiḥ sarve me devāḥ śāntir brahma
śāntirāpaḥ śāntiḥ sarvaṁ śāntiredhi śāntiḥ śāntiḥ sarva
śāntiḥ sā mā śāntiḥ śāntibhiḥ**

Let the earth be at Peace, the atmosphere be at Peace, the heavens be filled with Peace. Even further may Peace extend, Peace be to waters, Peace to all vegetation, Peace to All Gods of the Universe, Peace to All Gods within us, Peace to Creative Consciousness, Peace be to Brilliant Light, Peace to All, Peace to Everything, Peace, Peace, altogether Peace, equally Peace, by means of Peace.

ताभिः शान्तिभिः सर्वशान्तिभिः समया मोहं यदिह घोरं
यदिह क्रूरं यदिह पापं तच्छान्तं
तच्छिवं सर्वमेव समस्तु नः ॥

**tābhiḥ śāntibhiḥ sarva śāntibhiḥ samayā mohaṁ yadiha
ghoraṁ yadiha krūraṁ yadiha pāpaṁ tacchāntaṁ
tacchivaṁ sarvameva samastu naḥ**

Thus by means of Peace, altogether one with the means of Peace, Ignorance is eliminated, Violence is eradicated, Improper Conduct is eradicated, Confusion (sin) is eradicated, all that is, is at Peace, all that is perceived, each and everything, altogether for us,

ॐ शान्तिः शान्तिः शान्तिः ॥

oṁ śāntiḥ śāntiḥ śāntiḥ

oṁ Peace, Peace, Peace

गणेश पूजा

gaṇeśa pūjā

worship of gaṇeśa

ॐ विश्वेशं माधवं ढुण्ढिं दण्डपाणिं च भैरवम् ।
वन्दे काशीं गुहां गङ्गां भवानीं मणिकर्णिकाम् ॥

oṁ viśveśaṁ mādhavaṁ ḍhuṇḍhiṁ
daṇḍapāṇiṁ ca bhairavam
vande kāśīṁ guhāṁ gaṅgāṁ
bhavānīṁ maṇikarṇikām

Oṁ the Lord of the Universe, Lord Viṣṇu Mādhava, who holds the club in his hand and is fearless, worships He Who dwells in the cave at Benaris, who holds aloft the Gaṅgā, who is the Lord of the Universe, He who wears jeweled earrings.

gaṇeśa gāyatrī

ॐ तत् पुरुषाय विद्महे वक्रतुण्डाय धीमहि ।
तन्नो दन्ती प्रचोदयात् ॥

oṁ tatpuruṣāya vidmahe vakratuṇḍāya dhīmahi
tanno dantī pracodayāt

Oṁ we meditate on that Perfect Consciousness, we contemplate the One with a broken tooth. May that One with the Great Tusk grant us increase.

एते गन्धपुष्पे ॐ गं गणपतये नमः

ete gandhapuṣpe oṁ gaṁ gaṇapataye namaḥ

With these scented flowers oṁ we bow to the Lord of Wisdom, Lord of the Multitudes.

gaṇeśa dhyānam
meditation

ॐ सुमुखश्चैकदन्तश्च कपिलो गजकर्णकः ।
लम्बोदरश्च विकटो विघ्ननाशो विनायकः ॥

oṁ sumukhaścaika dantaśca kapilo gaja karṇakaḥ
lambodaraśca vikaṭo vighnanāśo vināyakaḥ

Oṁ He has a beautiful face with only one tooth (or tusk), of red color with elephant ears; with a big belly and a great tooth he destroys all obstacles. He is the Remover of Obstacles.

धूम्रकेतुर्गणाध्यक्षो भालचन्द्रो गजाननः ।
द्वादशैतानि नामानि यः पठेच्छृणुयादपि ॥

dhūmraketurgaṇādhyakṣo bhāla candro gajānanaḥ
dvādaśaitāni nāmāni yaḥ paṭhecchṛṇu yādapi

With a grey banner, the living spirit of the multitudes, having the moon on his forehead, with an elephant's face. Whoever will recite or listen to these twelve names

विद्यारम्भे विवाहे च प्रवेशे निर्गमे तथा ।
संग्रामे संकटे चैव विघ्नस्तस्य न जायते ॥

vidyārambhe vivāhe ca praveśe nirgame tathā
saṁgrāme saṁkate caiva vighnastasya na jāyate

at the time of commencing studies, getting married, or on entering or leaving any place; on a battlefield of war, or in any difficulty, will overcome all obstacles.

शुक्लाम्बरधरं देवं शशिवर्णं चतुर्भुजम् ।
प्रसन्नवदनं ध्यायेत् सर्वविघ्नोपशान्तये ॥

śuklāmbaradharaṁ devaṁ śaśivarṇaṁ caturbhujam
prasannavadanaṁ dhyāyet sarvavighnopaśāntaye

Wearing a white cloth, the God has the color of the moon and four arms. That most pleasing countenance is meditated on who gives peace to all difficulties.

अभीप्सितार्थसिद्ध्यर्थं पूजितो यः सुरासुरैः ।
सर्वविघ्नहरस् तस्मै गणाधिपतये नमः ॥

abhīpsitārtha siddhyartham pūjito yaḥ surā suraiḥ
sarvavighna haras tasmai gaṇādhipataye namaḥ

For gaining the desired objective, or for the attainment of perfection, he is worshipped by the Forces of Union and the Forces of Division alike. He takes away all difficulties, and therefore, we bow down in reverance to the Lord of the Multitudes.

वक्रतुण्ड महाकाय सूर्यकोटिसमप्रभ ।
अविघ्नं कुरु मे देव सर्वकार्येषु सर्वदा ॥

vakratuṇḍa mahākāya sūrya koṭi samaprabha
avighnaṁ kuru me deva sarva kāryeṣu sarvadā

With a broken (or bent) tusk, a great body shining like a million suns, make us free from all obstacles, Oh God. Always remain (with us) in all actions.

एकदन्तं महाकायं लम्बोदरं गजाननम् ।
विघ्ननाशकरं देवं हेरम्बं प्रणामाम्यहम् ॥

ekadantaṁ mahākāyaṁ lambodaraṁ gajānanam
vighnanāśakaraṁ devaṁ herambaṁ praṇāmāmyaham

With one tooth, a great body, a big belly and an elephant's face, he is the God who destroys all obstacles to whom we are bowing down with devotion.

मल्लिकादि सुगन्धीनि मालित्यादीनि वै प्रभो ।
मयाऽहृतानि पूजार्थं पुष्पाणि प्रतिगृह्यताम् ॥

mallikādi sugandhīni mālityādīni vai prabho
mayā-hṛtāni pūjārthaṁ puṣpāṇi pratigṛhyatām

Various flowers, such as mallikā and others of excellent scent, are being offered to you, Our Lord. All these flowers have come from the devotion of our hearts for your worship. Please accept them.

एते गन्धपुष्पे ॐ गं गणपतये नमः
ete gandhapuṣpe oṁ gaṁ gaṇapataye namaḥ
With these scented flowers oṁ we bow to the Lord of Wisdom, the Lord of the Multitudes.

puṇyā havācana, svasti vācana
proclamation of merits and eternal blessings

ॐ शान्तिरस्तु
oṁ śāntirastu
oṁ Peace be unto you.

ॐ पुष्टिरस्तु
oṁ puṣṭirastu
oṁ Increase or Nourishment be unto you.

ॐ तुष्टिरस्तु
oṁ tuṣṭirastu
oṁ Satisfaction be unto you.

ॐ वृद्धिरस्तु
oṁ vṛddhirastu
oṁ Positive Change be unto you.

ॐ अविघ्नमस्तु
oṁ avighnamastu
oṁ Freedom from Obstacles be unto you.

ॐ आयुष्यमस्तु
oṁ āyuṣyamastu
oṁ Life be unto you.

ॐ आरोग्यमस्तु
oṁ ārogyamastu
oṁ Freedom from Disease be unto you.

ॐ शिवमस्तु

oṁ śivamastu
oṁ Consciousness of Infinite Goodness be unto you.

ॐ शिवकर्माऽस्तु

oṁ śivakarmā-stu
oṁ Consciousness of Infinite Goodness in all action be unto you.

ॐ कर्मसमृद्धिरस्तु

oṁ karmasamṛddhirastu
oṁ Progress or Increase in all action be unto you.

ॐ धर्मसमृद्धिरस्तु

oṁ dharmasamṛddhirastu
oṁ Progress and Increase in all Ways of Truth be unto you.

ॐ वेदसमृद्धिरस्तु

oṁ vedasamṛddhirastu
oṁ Progress or Increase in all Knowledge be unto you.

ॐ शास्त्रसमृद्धिरस्तु

oṁ śāstrasamṛddhirastu
oṁ Progress or Increase in Scriptures be unto you.

ॐ धन-धान्यसमृद्धिरस्तु

oṁ dhana-dhānyasamṛddhirastu
oṁ Progress or Increase in Wealth and Grains be unto you.

ॐ इष्टसम्पदस्तु

oṁ iṣṭasampadastu
oṁ May your beloved deity be your wealth.

ॐ अरिष्टनिरसनमस्तु

oṁ ariṣṭanirasanamastu
oṁ May you remain safe and secure, without any fear.

ॐ यत्पापं रोगमशुभमकल्याणं तद्दूरे प्रतिहतमस्तु

oṁ yatpāpaṁ rogamaśubhamakalyāṇaṁ taddūre pratihatamastu
oṁ May sin, sickness, impurity, and that which is not conducive unto welfare, leave from you.

ॐ ब्रह्म पुण्यमहर्यच्च सृष्ट्युत्पादनकारकम् ।
वेदवृक्षोद्भवं नित्यं तत्पुण्याहं ब्रुवन्तु नः ॥

oṁ brahma puṇyamaharyacca sṛṣṭyutpādanakārakam vedavṛkṣodbhavaṁ nityaṁ tatpuṇyāhaṁ bruvantu naḥ
The Creative Capacity with the greatest merit, the Cause of the Birth of Creation, eternally has its being in the tree of Wisdom. May His blessing of merit be bestowed upon us.

भो ब्राह्मणाः ! मया क्रियमाणस्य लक्ष्मीपूजनाख्यस्य कर्मणः पुण्याहं भवन्तो ब्रुवन्तु ॥

bho brāhmaṇāḥ! mayā kriyamāṇasya lakṣmīpūjanākhyasya karmaṇaḥ puṇyāhaṁ bhavanto bruvantu
Oh Brahmiṇs! My sincere effort is to perform the worship of Lakṣmī. Let these activities yield merit.

ॐ पुण्याहं ॐ पुण्याहं ॐ पुण्याहं ॥

oṁ puṇyāhaṁ oṁ puṇyāhaṁ oṁ puṇyāhaṁ
oṁ Let these activities yield merit.

ॐ अस्य कर्मणः पुण्याहं भवन्तो ब्रुवन्तु ॥

oṁ asya karmaṇaḥ puṇyāhaṁ bhavanto bruvantu
oṁ Let these activities yield merit.

ॐ पुण्याहं ॐ पुण्याहं ॐ पुण्याहं ॥

oṁ puṇyāhaṁ oṁ puṇyāhaṁ oṁ puṇyāhaṁ
oṁ Let these activities yield merit (3 times).

पृथिव्यामुद्धृतायां तु यत्कल्याणं पुरा कृतम् ।
ऋषिभिः सिद्धगन्धर्वैस्तत्कल्याणं ब्रुवन्तु नः ॥

pṛthivyāmuddhṛtāyāṁ tu yatkalyāṇaṁ purā kṛtam
ṛṣibhiḥ siddha gandharvaistatkalyāṇaṁ bruvantu naḥ
With the solidity of the earth, let supreme welfare be. May the Ṛṣis, the attained ones and the celestial singers bestow welfare upon us.

भो ब्राह्मणाः ! मया क्रियमाणस्य लक्ष्मीपूजनाख्यस्य कर्मणः
कल्याणं भवन्तो ब्रुवन्तु ॥

bho brāhmaṇāḥ! mayā kriyamāṇasya
lakṣmīpūjanākhyasya karmaṇaḥ kalyāṇaṁ
bhavanto bruvantu
Oh Brahmiṇs! My sincere effort is to perform the worship of Lakṣmī. Let these activities bestow welfare.

ॐ कल्याणं ॐ कल्याणं ॐ कल्याणं

oṁ kalyāṇaṁ oṁ kalyāṇaṁ oṁ kalyāṇaṁ
oṁ Let these activities bestow welfare (3 times).

सागरस्य तु या ऋद्धिर्महालक्ष्म्यादिभिः कृता ।
सम्पूर्णा सुप्रभावा च तामृद्धिं प्रब्रुवन्तु नः ॥

sāgarasya tu yā ṛddhirmahālakṣmyādibhiḥ kṛtā
sampūrṇā suprabhāvā ca tāmṛddhiṁ prabruvantu naḥ
May the ocean yield Prosperity, as it did when the Great Goddess of True Wealth and others were produced; fully and completely giving forth excellent lustre, may Prosperity be unto us.

भो ब्राह्मणाः ! मया क्रियमाणस्य लक्ष्मीपूजनाख्यस्य कर्मणः

ऋद्धिं भवन्तो ब्रुवन्तु ॥

bho brāhmaṇāḥ! mayā kriyamāṇasya lakṣmīpūjanākhyasya karmaṇaḥ ṛddhiṁ bhavanto bruvantu

Oh Brahmiṇs! My sincere effort is to perform the worship of Lakṣmī. Let these activities bestow Prosperity.

ॐ कर्म ऋध्यताम् ॐ कर्म ऋध्यताम् ॐ कर्म ऋध्यताम्

oṁ karma ṛdhyatām oṁ karma ṛdhyatām oṁ karma ṛdhyatām

oṁ Let these activities bestow Prosperity (3 times).

स्वस्तिरस्तु याविनाशाख्या पुण्यकल्याणवृद्धिदा ।

विनायकप्रिया नित्यं तां च स्वस्तिं ब्रुवन्तु नः ॥

svastirastu yā vināśākhyā puṇya kalyāṇa vṛddhidā vināyakapriyā nityaṁ tāṁ ca svastiṁ bruvantu naḥ

Let the Eternal Blessings which grant changes of indestructible merit and welfare be with us. May the Lord who removes all obstacles be pleased and grant to us Eternal Blessings.

भो ब्राह्मणाः ! मया क्रियमाणस्य लक्ष्मीपूजनाख्यस्य कर्मणः

स्वस्तिं भवन्तो ब्रुवन्तु ॥

bho brāhmaṇāḥ! mayā kriyamāṇasya lakṣmīpūjanākhyasya karmaṇaḥ svastiṁ bhavanto bruvantu

Oh Brahmiṇs! My sincere effort is to perform the worship of Lakṣmī. Let these activities bestow Eternal Blessings.

ॐ आयुष्मते स्वस्ति ॐ आयुष्मते स्वस्ति

ॐ आयुष्मते स्वस्ति

oṁ āyuṣmate svasti oṁ āyuṣmate svasti oṁ āyuṣmate svasti

oṁ May life be filled with Eternal Blessings (3 times).

ॐ स्वस्ति न इन्द्रो वृद्धश्रवाः स्वस्ति नः पूषा विश्ववेदाः ।
स्वस्ति नस्तार्क्ष्यो अरिष्टनेमिः स्वस्ति नो बृहस्पतिर्दधातु ॥

oṁ svasti na indro vṛddhaśravāḥ
svasti naḥ pūṣā viśvavedāḥ
svasti nastārkṣyo ariṣṭanemiḥ
svasti no bṛhaspatirdadhātu

The Eternal Blessings to us, Oh Rule of the Pure, who perceives all that changes; the Eternal Blessings to us, Searchers for Truth, Knowers of the Universe; the Eternal Blessings to us, Oh Divine Being of Light, keep us safe; the Eternal Blessings to us, Oh Spirit of All-Pervading Delight, grant that to us.

समुद्रमथनाज्जाता जगदानन्दकारिका ।
हरिप्रिया च माङ्गल्या तां श्रियं च ब्रुवन्तु नः ॥

samudramathnājjātā jagadānandakārikā
haripriyā ca māṅgalyā tāṁ śriyaṁ ca bruvantu naḥ

Who was born from the churning of the ocean, the cause of bliss to the worlds, the beloved of Viṣṇu and Welfare Herself, may Śrī, the Highest Respect, be unto us.

भो ब्राह्मणाः ! मया क्रियमाणस्य लक्ष्मीपूजनाख्यस्य कर्मणः
श्रीरस्त्विति भवन्तो ब्रुवन्तु ॥

bho brāhmaṇāḥ! mayā kriyamāṇasya
lakṣmīpūjanākhyasya karmaṇaḥ śrīrastviti
bhavanto bruvantu

Oh Brahmiṇs! My sincere effort is to perform the worship of Lakṣmī. Let these activities bestow the Highest Respect.

ॐ अस्तु श्रीः ॐ अस्तु श्रीः ॐ अस्तु श्रीः

oṁ astu śrīḥ oṁ astu śrīḥ oṁ astu śrīḥ

oṁ Let these activities bestow the Highest Respect (3 times).

ॐ श्रीश्च ते लक्ष्मीश्च पत्न्यावहोरात्रे पार्श्वे नक्षत्राणि
रूपमश्विनौ व्यात्तम् । इष्णन्निषाणामुं म इषाण
सर्वलोकं म इषाण ॥

oṁ śrīśca te lakṣmīśca patnyāvahorātre pārśve nakṣatrāṇi rūpamaśvinau vyāttam iṣṇannisāṇāmuṁ ma iṣāṇa sarvalokaṁ ma iṣāṇa

oṁ the Highest Respect to you, Goal of all Existence, wife of the full and complete night (the Unknowable One), at whose sides are the stars, and who has the form of the relentless search for Truth. Oh Supreme Divinity, Supreme Divinity, my Supreme Divinity, all existence is my Supreme Divinity.

मृकण्डसूनोरायुर्यद्ध्रुवलोमशयोस्तथा ।
आयुषा तेन संयुक्ता जीवेम शरदः शतम् ॥

mṛkaṇḍasūnorāyuryaddhruvalomaśayostathā
āyuṣā tena saṁyuktā jīvema śaradaḥ śatam

As the son of Mṛkaṇḍa, Mārkaṇḍeya, found imperishable life, may we be united with life and blessed with a hundred autumns.

शतं जीवन्तु भवन्तः

śataṁ jīvantu bhavantaḥ

May a hundred autumns be unto you.

शिवगौरीविवाहे या या श्रीरामे नृपात्मजे ।
धनदस्य गृहे या श्रीरस्माकं साऽस्तु सद्मनि ॥

śiva gaurī vivāhe yā yā śrīrāme nṛpātmaje
dhanadasya gṛhe yā śrīrasmākaṁ sā-stu sadmani

As the imperishable union of Śiva and Gaurī, as the soul of kings manifested in the respected Rāma, so may the Goddess of Respect forever be united with us and always dwell in our house.

ॐ अस्तु श्रीः ॐ अस्तु श्रीः ॐ अस्तु श्रीः

oṁ astu śrīḥ oṁ astu śrīḥ oṁ astu śrīḥ

May Respect be unto you.

प्रजापतिर्लोकपालो धाता ब्रह्मा च देवराट् ।
भगवाञ्छाश्वतो नित्यं नो वै रक्षन्तु सर्वतः ॥

prajāpatirlokapālo dhātā brahmā ca devarāṭ
bhagavāñchāśvato nityaṁ no vai rakṣantu sarvataḥ
The Lord of all beings, Protector of the worlds, Creator, Brahmā, Support of the Gods; may the Supreme Lord be gracious eternally and always protect us.

ॐ भगवान् प्रजापतिः प्रियताम्

oṁ bhagavān prajāpatiḥ priyatām
May the Supreme Lord, Lord of all beings, be pleased.

आयुष्मते स्वस्तिमते यजमानाय दाशुषे ।
श्रिये दत्ताशिषः सन्तु ऋत्विग्भिर्वेदपारगैः ॥

āyuṣmate svastimate yajamānāya dāśuṣe
śriye dattāśiṣaḥ santu ṛtvigbhirvedapāragaiḥ
May life and eternal blessings be unto those who perform this worship and to those who assist. May respect be given to the priests who impart this wisdom.

ॐ स्वस्तिवाचनसमृद्धिरस्तु

oṁ svastivācanasamṛddhirastu
oṁ May this invocation for eternal blessings find excellent prosperity.

gāyatrī viddhi
system of worship with gāyatrī

ॐ प्रजापतिर्ऋषिर्गायित्रीछन्दोऽग्निर्देवता व्याहृति होमे विनियोगः ।

oṁ prajāptirṛṣirgāyatrī chando-gnirdevatā vyāhṛti home viniyogaḥ
Oṁ The Lord of Creation is the Seer, Gāyatrī is the meter (24 syllables to the verse), Purification is the Divinity, the Proclamations of Delight are applied in offering.

ॐ भूः स्वाहा ॥

oṁ bhūḥ svāhā
Oṁ Gross Perception.

ॐ प्रजापतिर्ऋषिरुष्णिक्छन्दोवायुर्देवता व्याहृति होमे विनियोगः ।

oṁ prajāpatirṛṣiruṣṇik chando vāyurdevatā vyāhṛti home viniyogaḥ
The Lord of Creation is the Seer, Uṣṇik is the meter (28 syllables to the verse), Emancipation is the Divinity, the Proclamations of Delight are applied in offering.

ॐ भुवः स्वाहा ॥

oṁ bhuvaḥ svāhā
Oṁ Subtle Perception.

ॐ प्रजापतिर्ऋषिरनुष्टुपछन्दः सूर्योदेवता व्याहृति होमे विनियोगः ।

oṁ prajāpitirṛṣiranuṣṭup chandaḥ sūryodevatā vyāhṛti home viniyogaḥ
The Lord of Creation is the Seer, Anuṣṭup is the meter (32 syllables to the verse), The Light of Wisdom is the Divinity, the Proclamations of Delight are applied in offering.

ॐ स्वः स्वाहा ॥

oṁ svaḥ svāhā
Oṁ Intuitive Perception.

ॐ प्रजापतिर्ऋषिर्बृहती छन्दः प्रजापतिर्देवता महाव्याहृति होमे विनियोगः ।

oṁ prajāpatirṛṣirbṛhatī chandaḥ prajāpatirdevatā mahāvyāhṛti home viniyogaḥ
The Lord of Creation is the Seer, Bṛhatī is the meter (40 syllables to the verse), The Lord of Creation is the Divinity, the Great (full, complete) Proclamations of Delight are applied in offering.

ॐ भूर्भुवः स्वः स्वाहा ॥

oṁ bhūrbhuvaḥ svaḥ svāhā
Oṁ Gross Perception, oṁ Subtle Perception, oṁ Intuitive Perception.

ॐ गायत्र्या विश्वामित्रऋषिर्गायत्री छन्दः सवितादेवता गायत्री जपे विनियोगः ॥

oṁ gāyatryā viśvāmitraṛṣirgāyatrī chandaḥ savitādevatā gāyatrī jape viniyogaḥ
The Gāyatrī (Mantra), The Friend of the Universe is the Seer, Gāyatrī is the meter (24 syllables to the verse), The Daughter of Light is the Divinity, the Gāyatrī (mantra) is applied in recitation.

Holding tattva mudrā, touch head:

विश्वामित्र ऋषये नमः

viśvāmitra ṛṣaye namaḥ touch head
To the Seer, Friend of the Universe, I bow.

गायत्री छन्दःसे नमः

gāyatrī chandaḥse namaḥ touch mouth
To the Meter, Gāyatrī (24 syllables to the verse), I bow.

सवित्रीदेवतायै नमः

savitrīdevatāyai namaḥ touch heart
To the Divinity, the Daughter of the Light, I bow.

aṅga nyāsa
establishment in the body

ॐ हृदयाय नमः

oṁ hṛdayāya namaḥ touch heart
Oṁ in the heart, I bow.

ॐ भूः शिरसे स्वाहा

oṁ bhūḥ śirase svāhā top of head
Oṁ Gross Perception on the top of the head, I am One with God!

ॐ भुवः शिखायै वषट्

oṁ bhuvaḥ śikhāyai vaṣaṭ back of head
Oṁ Subtle Perception on the back of the head, Purify!

ॐ स्वः कवचाय हुं

oṁ svaḥ kavacāya huṁ cross both arms
Oṁ Intuitive Perception crossing both arms, Cut the Ego!

ॐ भूर्भुवः स्वः नेत्रत्रयाय वौषट्

oṁ bhūrbhuvaḥ svaḥ netratrayāya vauṣaṭ touch three eyes
Oṁ Gross Perception, Subtle Perception, Intuitive Perception in the three eyes, Ultimate Purity!

ॐ भूर्भुवः स्वः करतल कर पृष्ठाभ्यां अस्त्राय फट्

oṁ bhūrbhuvaḥ svaḥ karatal kar pṛṣṭābhyāṁ astrāya phaṭ
Oṁ I bow to Gross Perception, Subtle Perception, Intuitive Perception with the weapon of Virtue.
roll hand over hand front and back and clap

ॐ भूः हृदयाय नमः

oṁ bhūḥ hṛdayāya namaḥ touch heart
Oṁ Gross Perception in the heart, I bow.

ॐ भुवः शिरसे स्वाहा

oṁ bhuvaḥ śirase svāhā top of head
Oṁ Subtle Perception on the top of the head, I am One with God!

ॐ स्वः शिखायै वषट्

oṁ svaḥ śikhāyai vaṣaṭ back of head
Oṁ Intuitive Perception on the back of the head, Purify!

ॐ तत् सवितुर्वरेण्यम् कवचाय हुं

oṁ tat saviturvareṇyam kavacāya huṁ cross both arms
Oṁ That Light of Wisdom that is the Supreme crossing both arms, Cut the Ego!

ॐ भर्गो देवस्य धीमहि नेत्रत्रयाय वौषट्

oṁ bhargo devasya dhīmahi
netratrayāya vauṣaṭ touch three eyes
Oṁ Wealth of the Gods, we meditate in the three eyes, Ultimate Purify!

roll hand over hand front and back and clap saying:

ॐ धियो यो नः प्रचोदयात् ॐ करतल कर पृष्ठाभ्यां अस्त्राय फट्

oṁ dhiyo yo naḥ pracodayāt oṁ karatal kar pṛṣṭābhyāṁ astrāya phaṭ
Oṁ May it grant to us increase in our meditations with the weapon of Virtue.

ॐ तत् सवितुर्हृदयाय नमः

oṁ tat saviturhṛdayāya namaḥ touch heart
Oṁ That Light of Wisdom in the heart, I bow.

ॐ वरेण्यम् शिरसे स्वाहा

oṁ vareṇyam śirase svāhā top of head
Oṁ That is the Supreme on the top of the head, I am One with God!

ॐ भर्गो देवस्य शिखायै वषट्

oṁ bhargo devasya śikhāyai vaṣaṭ back of head
Oṁ Wealth of the Gods on the back of the head, Purify!

ॐ धीमहि कवचाय हुं

oṁ dhīmahi kavacāya huṁ cross both arms
Oṁ We meditate crossing both arms, Cut the Ego!

ॐ धियो योनः नेत्रत्रयाय वौषट्

oṁ dhiyo yo naḥ netratrayāya vauṣaṭ touch three eyes
Oṁ May it grant to us increase in Ultimate Purity in the three eyes

ॐ प्रचोदयात् ॐ करतलकरपृष्ठाभ्यां अस्त्राय फट्

oṁ pracodayāt oṁ karatal kar pṛṣṭhābhyāṁ astrāya phaṭ
Oṁ Increase in our meditations with the weapon of Virtue.
roll hand over hand front and back and clap

ॐ भूर्भुवः स्वः । तत् सवितुर्वरेण्यम् भर्गो देवस्य धीमहि
धियो योनः प्रचोदयात् ॐ ॥

oṁ bhūrbhuvaḥ svaḥ
tat saviturvareṇyam bhargo devasya dhīmahi
dhiyo yo naḥ pracodayāt oṁ
Oṁ the Infinite Beyond Conception, the gross body, the subtle body and the causal body; we meditate on that Light of Wisdom that is the Supreme Wealth of the Gods. May it grant to us increase in our meditations.

महेश-वदनोत्पन्ना विष्णोर्हृदय सम्भवा ।
ब्रह्मणा समनुज्ञाता गच्छ देवि यथेच्छया ॥

maheśa-vadanotpannā viṣṇorhṛdaya sambhavā
brahmaṇā samanujñātā gaccha devi yathecchayā
Arisen from Maheśvara, The Great Seer of All, residing in the heart of the Consciousness that Pervades All, equally in the Wisdom of the Creative Capacity, the Goddess moves according to Her desire.

ātmarakṣa
protection of the soul

ॐ जातवेदस ईत्यस्य काश्यप ऋषिस्त्रिष्टुप् छन्दोऽग्निर्देवता आत्मरक्षायां जपे विनियोगः ।

oṁ jātavedasa ītyasya kāśyapa ṛṣistriṣṭup chando-gnirdevatā ātmarakṣāyāṁ jape viniyogaḥ
Oṁ the mantra beginning, "The Knower of All," etc., Kaśyapa is the Seer, Triṣṭup is the meter (44 syllables to the verse), Agni is the divinity, for the protection of the soul these mantras are applied in recitation.

ॐ जातवेदसे सुनवाम सोममरातीयतोनि दहाति वेदः ।
स नः पर्षदति दुर्गाणि विश्वा नावेव सिन्धुं दुरितात्यग्निः ॥

oṁ jātavedase sunavāma somam
arātīyatoni dahāti vedaḥ
sa naḥ parṣadati Lakṣmīṇi viśvā
nāveva sindhuṁ duritātyagniḥ
Oṁ We worship the Knower of All with the offering of Love and Devotion. May the God of Purity reduce all enmity in the universe to ashes, and as an excellent oarsman, may he steer our ship across the sea of pain and confusion to the shores of Liberation.

ॐ दुर्गे दुर्गे रक्षाणि हुं फट् स्वाहा ॥

oṁ durge durge rakṣāṇi huṁ phaṭ svāhā
Oṁ Reliever of Difficulties, Reliever of Difficulties, Protect us, Cut the Ego! Purify! I am One with God!

ॐ अं हुं फट् स्वाहा ॥

oṁ aṁ huṁ phaṭ svāhā

Oṁ Aṁ (Creation, Beginning) Cut the Ego! Purity! I am One with God!

rudropasthāna

the establishment of the reliever of sufferings

ॐ ऋतमित्यस्य कालाग्निरुद्र ऋषिरनुष्टुप् छन्दोरुद्रो देवता रुद्रोपस्थाने विनियोगः ।

oṁ ṛtamityasya kālāgnirudra ṛṣiranuṣṭup chandorudro devatā rudropasthāne viniyogaḥ

Oṁ "Whose sole form is the Entire Universe," the Reliever of Sufferings, Purifier of Time (or Purifier in Time) is the Seer, Anuṣṭup is the meter (32 syllables to the verse), the establishment of the Reliever of Sufferings is the application.

ॐ ऋतं सत्यं परं ब्रह्मा पुरुषं कृष्णपिङ्गलम् ।

ऊर्द्ध्वरेतं विरूपाक्षं विश्वरूपं नमो नमः ॥

oṁ ṛtaṁ satyaṁ paraṁ brahmā puruṣaṁ kṛṣṇapiṅgalam ūrdvaretaṁ virūpākṣaṁ viśvarūpaṁ namo namaḥ

Oṁ The Supreme Consciousness whose sole form is the Entire Universe, and Infinite Wisdom and Truth, who, for the advancement of Devotion, assumes the form of Consciousness both male and female (Umā, Maheśvara: Consciousness and Nature); whose one half is dark and the other half light, whose semen rises up, and who is the form of the universe, with three eyes, to that Universal Form, again and again we bow down in devotion.

एते गन्धपुष्पे ॐ ब्रह्मणे नमः

ete gandhapuṣpe oṁ brahmaṇe namaḥ

With these scented flowers oṁ we bow to Creative Consciousness.

एते गन्धपुष्पे ॐ ब्राह्मणेभ्यो नमः

ete gandhapuṣpe oṁ brāhmaṇebhyo namaḥ

With these scented flowers oṁ we bow to the Knowers of Divine Wisdom.

एते गन्धपुष्पे ॐ आचार्येभ्यो नमः

ete gandhapuṣpe oṁ ācāryebhyo namaḥ
With these scented flowers oṁ we bow to the Teachers of Divine Wisdom.

एते गन्धपुष्पे ॐ ऋषिभ्यो नमः

ete gandhapuṣpe oṁ ṛṣibhyo namaḥ
With these scented flowers oṁ we bow to the Seers of Divine Wisdom.

एते गन्धपुष्पे ॐ देवेभ्यो नमः

ete gandhapuṣpe oṁ devebhyo namaḥ
With these scented flowers oṁ we bow to the Exemplifiers of Divine Wisdom.

एते गन्धपुष्पे ॐ वेदेभ्यो नमः

ete gandhapuṣpe oṁ vedebhyo namaḥ
With these scented flowers oṁ we bow to the Wisdom of Divine Wisdom.

एते गन्धपुष्पे ॐ वायवे नमः

ete gandhapuṣpe oṁ vāyave namaḥ
With these scented flowers oṁ we bow to Emancipation.

एते गन्धपुष्पे ॐ मृत्यवे नमः

ete gandhapuṣpe oṁ mṛtyave namaḥ
With these scented flowers oṁ we bow to Transformation (moving beyond, death).

एते गन्धपुष्पे ॐ विष्णवे नमः

ete gandhapuṣpe oṁ viṣṇave namaḥ
With these scented flowers oṁ we bow to That which Pervades All.

एते गन्धपुष्पे ॐ वैश्रवणाय नमः
ete gandhapuṣpe oṁ vaiśravaṇāya namaḥ
With these scented flowers oṁ we bow to the Universal Being.

एते गन्धपुष्पे ॐ उपजाय नमः
ete gandhapuṣpe oṁ upajāya namaḥ
With these scented flowers oṁ we bow to The Cause of All.

ॐ भूर्भुवः स्वः । तत् सवितुर्वरेण्यम् भर्गो देवस्य धीमहि ।
धियो यो नः प्रचोदयात् ॐ ॥
oṁ bhūrbhuvaḥ svaḥ tat saviturvareṇyam
bhargo devasya dhīmahi dhiyo yo naḥ pracodayāt oṁ
Oṁ the Infinite Beyond Conception, the gross body, the subtle body and the causal body; we meditate on that Light of Wisdom that is the Supreme Wealth of the Gods. May it grant to us increase in our meditations.

kumārī pūjā
worship of the ever pure one

ॐ कुमारीमृग्वेदयुतां ब्रह्मरूपां विचिन्तायेत् ।
हंसस्थितां कुशहस्तां सूर्यमण्डल संस्थितां ॥
oṁ kumārīmṛgvedayutāṁ brahmarūpāṁ vicintāyet
haṁsasthitāṁ kuśahastāṁ sūryamaṇḍala saṁsthitāṁ
Oṁ We contemplate the Goddess of Purity, embodiment of the Ṛg Veda, the form of Supreme Divinity. Situated upon the swan, with kuśa grass in Her hand, She is situated in the regions of the sun.

ॐ कुमारीं कमलारुढां त्रिनेत्रां चन्द्रशेखराम् ।
तप्तकाञ्चनवर्णाभां नानालङ्कार भूषिताम् ॥
oṁ kumārīṁ kamalāruḍhāṁ
trinetrām candraśekharām
taptakāñcaṇa varnabhāṁ nānālaṅkāra bhūṣitām
Oṁ Kumāri has an orange color with three eyes and the Moon on Her head. Of the color of melted gold, She displays various ornaments.

रक्ताम्बरपरीधानां रक्तमाल्याणुलेपनाम् ।
वामेनाभयदां ध्यायेद्दक्षिणेन वरप्रदाम् ॥

raktāmbāra parīdhanāṁ raktamālyāṇulepanām vāmenābhayadāṁ dhyāyeddakṣiṇena varapradām She wears a red cloth and a red mālā or garland. With Her left hand She gives us freedom from fear, and with Her right hand She grants boons.

ॐ सर्वाभीष्टप्रधे देवि सर्वापद्विनिवारिनि ।
सर्वशान्तिकरे देवि नमस्तेऽस्तु कुमारिके ॥

oṁ sarvabhīṣṭapradhe devi sarvāpadvinivārini
sarvaśānti kare devi namaste-stu kumārike
Oṁ Grant fulfillment of all desires, oh Goddess. Remove all obstacles. Cause all Peace, oh Goddess. We bow to you, to Kumāri.

ब्रह्मी महेश्वरी रौद्री रूप त्रितय धारिणि ।
अभयञ्च वरं देहि नारायणि नमोऽस्तु ते ॥

brahmī maheśvarī raudrī rūpa tritaya dhāriṇi
abhayañca varaṁ dehi nārāyaṇi namo-stu te
Creative Energy, the Energy of the Great Seer of All, the Energy of the Terrible One; She wears three forms. Give freedom from fear and boons; Exposer of Consciousness, we bow to you.

ॐ कौं कौमार्यै नमः

oṁ kauṁ kaumaryai namaḥ
Oṁ kauṁ we bow to the Goddess of Purity.

ॐ सावित्री विष्णुरूपाञ्च तार्क्ष्यस्थां पीतवाससिं ।
युवतीञ्च यजुर्वेद सूर्यमण्डल संस्थितां ॥

oṁ sāvitrī viṣṇurūpāñca tārkṣyasthāṁ pītavāsasiṁ
yuvatīñca yajurveda sūryamaṇḍala saṁsthitāṁ
Oṁ Goddess of Light in the form of Viṣṇu, radiating light of yellow color; appearing in a youthful form as the Yājur Veda, She is situated in the regions of the sun.

ॐ सरस्वती शिवरूपाञ्च वृद्ध वृषभ वहिनीं ।
सूर्यमण्डल मध्यस्थां सामवेद समायुतां ॥

oṁ sarasvatī śivarūpāñca vṛddhā vṛṣabha vahinīṁ
sūryamaṇḍala madhyasthāṁ sāmaveda samāyutāṁ

Oṁ Sarasvati is in the form of Śiva, appearing as an old woman riding upon a bull. Situated in the middle of the regions of the sun, She is united with the Sāma Veda.

gāyatrī saṁpūṭ

gāyatrī with oṁ before and after

ॐ भूर्भुवः स्वः ॐ तत् सवितुर्वरेण्यम् ॐ भर्गो देवस्य
धीमहि ॐ धियो यो नः प्रचोदयात् ॐ ॥

oṁ bhūrbhuvaḥ svaḥ oṁ tat saviturvareṇyam oṁ bhargo
devasya dhīmahi oṁ dhiyo yo naḥ pracodayāt oṁ

Oṁ the Infinite Beyond Conception, the gross body, the subtle body and the causal body; oṁ we meditate on that Light of Wisdom oṁ that is the Supreme Wealth of the Gods. Oṁ may it grant to us increase in our meditations.

ॐ भूर्भुवः स्वः तत् सवितुर्वरेण्यम् ॐ भर्गो देवस्य धीमहि
ॐ धियो यो नः प्रचोदयात् ॐ ॥

oṁ bhūrbhuvaḥ svaḥ tat saviturvareṇyam oṁ bhargo
devasya dhīmahi oṁ dhiyo yo naḥ pracodayāt oṁ

Oṁ the Infinite Beyond Conception, the gross body, the subtle body and the causal body; we meditate on that Light of Wisdom oṁ that is the Supreme Wealth of the Gods. Oṁ may it grant to us increase in our meditations oṁ.

ॐ भूर्भुवः स्वः तत् सवितुर्वरेण्यम् भर्गो देवस्य धीमहि ॐ
धियो यो नः प्रचोदयात् ॐ ॥

oṁ bhūrbhuvaḥ svaḥ tat saviturvareṇyam
bhargo devasya dhīmahi oṁ dhiyo yo naḥ pracodayāt oṁ

Oṁ the Infinite Beyond Conception, the gross body, the subtle body and the causal body; we meditate on that Light of Wisdom that is the Supreme Wealth of the Gods. Oṁ may it grant to us increase in our meditations oṁ.

ॐ भूर्भुवः स्वः तत् सवितुर्वरेण्यम् भर्गो देवस्य धीमहि
धियो यो नः प्रचोदयात् ॐ ॥

oṁ bhūrbhuvaḥ svaḥ
tat saviturvareṇyam bhargo devasya dhīmahi
dhiyo yo naḥ pracodayāt oṁ

Oṁ the Infinite Beyond Conception, the gross body, the subtle body and the causal body; aie meditate upon that Light of Wisdom that is the Supreme Wealth of the Gods. May it grant to us increase in our meditations oṁ.

आगच्छ वरदे देवि जप्ये मे सन्निधा भव ।
गायन्तं त्रायसे यस्माद् गायत्री त्वमतः स्मृता ॥

āgaccha varade devi japye me sannidhā bhava
gāyaṇtaṁ trāyase yasmād gāyatrī tvamataḥ smṛtā

Come, granting boons, oh Goddess, and be situated in me while I continue meditation and prayer. The three forms of wisdom are remembered in you, Gāyatrī.

आयाहि वरदे देवि त्र्यक्षरे ब्रह्मवादिनि ।
गायत्री छन्दसां मातर्ब्रह्मयोनि नमोऽस्तु ते ॥

āyāhi varade devi tryakṣare brahmavādini
gāyatrī chandasāṁ mātarbrahmayoni namo-stu te

Come, granting boons, oh Goddess, the three letters of the word of the Supreme Divinity. Oh Mother, in the rhythm of Gāyatrī (24 syllables to the verse) we bow to you as the womb of creation.

sāmānyārghya

purification of water

Draw the yantra on the plate or space for worship with sandal paste and/or water. Offer rice on the yantra for each of the four mantras.

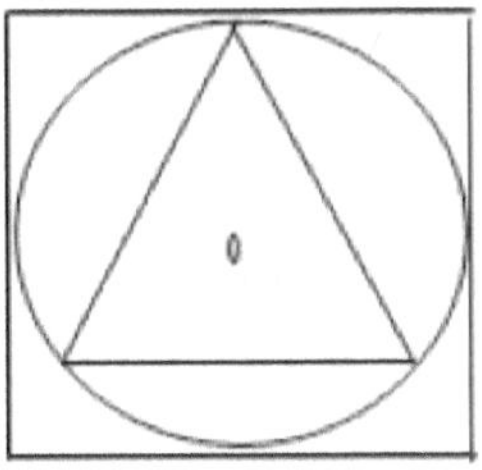

ॐ आधारशक्तये नमः

oṁ ādhāra śaktaye namaḥ
om we bow to the Primal Energy

ॐ कूर्माय नमः

oṁ kūrmāya namaḥ
oṁ we bow to the Support of the Earth

ॐ अनन्ताय नमः

oṁ anantāya namaḥ
oṁ we bow to Infinity

ॐ पृथिव्यै नमः

oṁ pṛthivyai namaḥ
oṁ we bow to the Earth

Place an empty water pot on the bindu in the center of the yantra when saying Phaṭ.

स्थां स्थीं स्थिरो भव फट्

sthāṁ sthīṁ sthiro bhava phaṭ
Be Still in the Gross Body! Be Still in the Subtle Body! Be Still in the Causal Body! Purify!

Fill the pot with water while chanting the mantra.

ॐ गङ्गे च जमुने चैव गोदावरि सरस्वति ।
नर्मदे सिन्धु कावेरि जलऽस्मिन् सन्निधिं कुरु ॥

oṁ gaṅge ca jamune caiva godāvari sarasvati
narmade sindhu kāveri jale-asmin sannidhiṁ kuru
oṁ the Ganges, Jamunā, Godāvarī, Sarasvatī, Narmadā, Sindhu, Kāverī, these waters are mingled together.

The Ganges is the Iḍā, Jamunā is the Piṅgalā, the other five rivers are the five senses. The land of the seven rivers is within the body as well as outside.

Offer Tulasī leaves into water

ॐ ऐं ह्रीं क्लीं श्रीं वृन्दावनवासिन्यै स्वाहा

oṁ aiṁ hrīṁ klīṁ śrīṁ vṛndāvanavāsinyai svāhā

oṁ Wisdom, Māyā, Increase, to She who resides in Vṛndāvana, I am One with God!

Offer 3 flowers into the water pot with the mantras

एते गन्धपुष्पे ॐ अं अर्कमण्डलाय द्वादशकलात्मने नमः

ete gandhapuṣpe oṁ aṁ arkamaṇḍalāya dvādaśakalātmane namaḥ

With these scented flowers oṁ "A" we bow to the twelve aspects of the realm of the sun. Tapinī, Tāpinī, Dhūmrā, Marīci, Jvālinī, Ruci, Sudhūmrā, Bhoga-dā, Viśvā, Bodhinī, Dhārinī, Kṣamā; Containing heat, Emanating heat, Smoky, Ray-producing, Burning, Lustrous, Purple or Smoky-red, Granting enjoyment, Universal, Which makes known, Productive of Consciousness, Which supports, Which forgives.

एते गन्धपुष्पे ॐ उं सोममण्डलाय षोडशकलात्मने नमः

ete gandhapuṣpe oṁ uṁ somamaṇḍalāya ṣoḍaśakalātmane namaḥ

With these scented flowers oṁ "U" we bow to the sixteen aspects of the realm of the moon. Amṛtā, Prāṇadā, Puṣā, Tuṣṭi, Puṣṭi, Rati, Dhṛti, Śaśinī, Candrikā, Kānti, Jyotsnā, Śrī, Prīti, Aṅgadā, Pūrṇā, Pūrṇāmṛtā; Nectar, Which sustains life, Which supports, Satisfying, Nourishing, Playful, Constancy, Unfailing, Producer of Joy, Beauty enhanced by love, Light, Grantor of Prosperity, Affectionate, Purifying the body, Complete, Full of Bliss.

एते गन्धपुष्पे ॐ मं वह्निमण्डलाय दशकलात्मने नमः

ete gandhapuṣpe oṁ maṁ vahnimaṇḍalāya daśakalātmane namaḥ

With these scented flowers oṁ "M" we bow to the ten aspects of the realm of fire: Dhūmrā, Arciḥ, Jvalinī, Śūkṣmā, Jvālinī, Visphuliṅginī, Suśrī, Surūpā, Kapilā, Havya-Kavya-Vahā; Smoky Red, Flaming, Shining, Subtle, Burning, Sparkling, Beautiful, Well-formed, Tawny, The Messenger to Gods and Ancestors.

ॐ श्रीं लक्ष्मयै नमः

oṁ śrīṁ lakṣmyai namaḥ
Oṁ I bow to the Goddess Lakṣmī.

Wave hands in matsyā, dhenu and aṅkuśa mudrās while chanting this mantra.

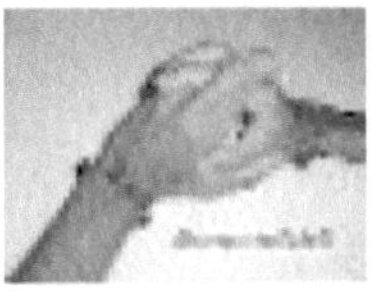

ॐ गङ्गे च जमुने चैव गोदावरि सरस्वति ।
नर्मदे सिन्धु कावेरि जलेऽस्मिन् सन्निधिं कुरु ॥

oṁ gaṅge ca jamune caiva godāvari sarasvati
narmade sindhu kāveri jale-asmin sannidhiṁ kuru
oṁ the Ganges, Jamunā, Godāvarī, Sarasvatī, Narmadā, Sindhu, Kāverī, these waters are mingled together.

ॐ श्रीं लक्ष्मयै नमः

oṁ śrīṁ lakṣmyai namaḥ
Oṁ I bow to the Goddess Lakṣmī.

Sprinkle water over all articles to be offered, then throw some drops of water over your shoulders while repeating the mantra.

अमृताम् कुरु स्वाहा

amṛtām kuru svāhā
Make this immortal nectar! I am One with God!

puṣpa śuddhi

purification of flowers

Wave hands over flowers with prārthanā mudrā while chanting first line, and with dhenu mudrā while chanting second line of this mantra.

ॐ पुष्प पुष्प महापुष्प सुपुष्प पुष्पसम्भवे ।

पुष्पचयावकीर्णे च हुं फट् स्वाहा ॥

oṁ puṣpa puṣpa mahāpuṣpa
supuṣpa puṣpa sambhave
puṣpa cayāvakīrṇe ca huṁ phaṭ svāhā

oṁ Flowers, flowers, Oh Great Flowers, excellent flowers; flowers in heaps and scattered about, cut the ego, purify, I am One with God!

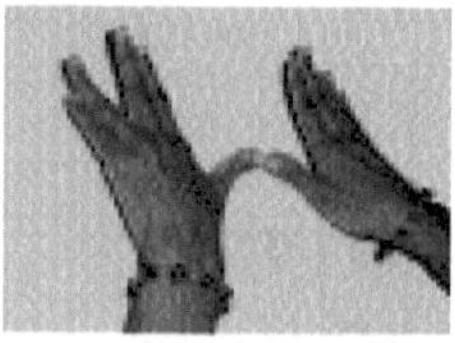

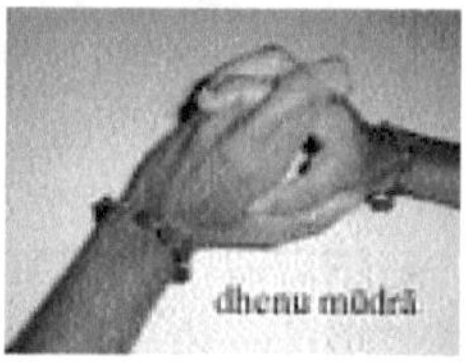

dhenu mūdrā

kara śuddhi

purification of hands

ॐ ऐं रं अस्त्राय फट्

oṁ aiṁ raṁ astrāya phaṭ

oṁ Wisdom, the divine fire, with the weapon, Purify !

kalaśa sthāpan

establishment of the pot

touch earth

ॐ भूरसि भूमिरस्यदितिरसि

विश्वधारा विश्वस्य भुवनस्य धर्त्री ।

पृथिवीं यच्छ पृथिवीं दृंह पृथिवीं मा हिंसीः ॥

oṁ bhūrasi bhūmirasyaditirasi viśvadhārā
viśvasya bhuvanasya dhartrī
pṛthivīṁ yaccha pṛthivīṁ dṛṁha pṛthivīṁ mā hiṁsīḥ

You are the object of sensory perception; you are the Goddess who distributes the forms of the earth. You are the Producer of the Universe, the Support of all existing things in the universe. Control (or sustain) the earth, firmly establish the earth, make the earth efficient in its motion.

give rice

ॐ धान्यमसि धिनुहि देवान् धिनुहि यज्ञं ।

धिनुहि यज्ञपतिं धिनुहि मां यज्ञन्यम् ॥

oṁ dhānyamasi dhinuhi devān dhinuhi yajñaṁ
dhinuhi yajñapatiṁ dhinuhi māṁ yajñanyam

You are the grains which satisfy and gladden the Gods, gladden the sacrifice, gladden the Lord of Sacrifice. Bring satisfaction to us through sacrifice.

place pot

ॐ आजिग्घ्र कलशं मह्या त्वा विशन्त्विन्दवः ।

पुनरूर्जा निवर्त्तस्व सा नः सहस्रं धुक्ष्वोरुधारा पयस्वतीः

पुनर्मा विशताद्रयिः ॥

oṁ ājigghra kalaśaṁ mahyā tvā viśantvindavaḥ
punarūrjā nivarttasva sā naḥ sahasraṁ dhukṣvorudhārā
payasvatīḥ punarmā viśatādrayiḥ

Cause the effulgent fire of perception to enter into your highly honored container for renewed nourishment. Remaining there, let it increase in thousands, so that upon removal, abounding in spotlessly pure strength, it may come flowing into us.

pour water

ॐ वरुणस्योत्तम्भनमसि वरुणस्य स्कम्भसर्जनी स्थो ।
वरुणस्य ऋतसदन्यसि । वरुणस्य ऋतसदनमसि ।
वरुणस्य ऋतसदनमासीद ॥

oṁ varuṇasyottambhanamasi varuṇasya skambhasarjanī stho
varuṇasya ṛtasadanyasi varuṇasya ṛtasadanamasi varuṇasya ṛtasadanamāsīda

You, Waters, are declared the Ultimate of waters established in all creation begotten, abiding in waters as the eternal law of truth; always abiding in waters as the eternal law of truth, and forever abiding in waters as the eternal law of truth.

place wealth

ॐ धन्वना गा धन्वनाजिं जयेम
धन्वना तीव्राः समद्रो जयेम ।
धनुः शत्रोरपकामं कृणोति धन्वना सर्वाः प्रदिशो जयेम ॥

oṁ dhanvanā gā dhanvanājiṁ jayema
dhanvanā tīvrāḥ samadro jayema
dhanuḥ śatrorapakāmaṁ kṛṇoti
dhanvanā sarvāḥ pradiśo jayema

Let wealth, even abundance, be victorious. Let wealth be sufficient as to be victorious over the severe ocean of existence. As a bow to protect us safe from the enemies of desire, let it be victorious to illuminate all.

place fruit

ॐ याः फलिनीर्याऽअफलाऽअपुष्पा याश्च पुष्पिणीः ।
बृहस्पतिप्रसूतास्ता नो मुञ्चन्त्वंहसः ॥

oṁ yāḥ phalinīryā-aphalā-apuṣpā yāśca puṣpiṇīḥ
bṛhaspatiprasūtāstā no muñcantvaṁhasaḥ

That which bears fruit, and that which bears no fruit; that without flowers and that with flowers as well. To we who exist born of the Lord of the Vast, set us FREE! ALL THIS IS GOD!

red powder

ॐ सिन्धोरिव प्राध्वने शूघनासो वातप्रमियः पतयन्ति यह्वाः । घृतस्य धारा अरुषो न वाजी काष्ठा भिन्दन्नूर्मिभिः पिन्वमानः ॥

oṁ sindhoriva prādhvane śūghanāso
vātapramiyaḥ patayanti yahvāḥ
ghṛtasya dhārā aruṣo na vājī kāṣṭhā
bhindannūrmibhiḥ pinvamānaḥ

The pious mark of red vermilion symbolizing the ocean of love placed prominently upon the head above the nose bursting forth, allows the vibrance of youth to fly. As the stream of ghee pours into the flames, those spirited steeds of the Divine Fire consume the logs of wood increasing the will and self-reliance of the worshiper.

ॐ सिन्दूरमरुणाभासं जपाकुसुमसन्निभम् ।
पूजिताऽसि मया देवि प्रसीद परमेश्वरि ॥
ॐ श्रीं लक्ष्मयै नमः सिन्दूरं समर्पयामि

oṁ sindūramaruṇābhāsaṁ japākusumasannibham
pūjitā-si mayā devi prasīda parameśvari
oṁ śrīṁ lakṣmyai namaḥ sindūraṁ samarpayāmi

This red colored powder indicates Love, who drives the chariot of the Light of Wisdom, with which we are worshiping our Lord. Please be pleased, Oh Great Seer of All. With this offering of red colored powder Oṁ I bow to the Goddess Lakṣmī.

kuṅkum

ॐ कुङ्कुमं कान्तिदं दिव्यं कामिनीकामसम्भवम् ।
कुङ्कुमेनाऽर्चिते देवि प्रसीद परमेश्वरि ॥
ॐ श्रीं लक्ष्मयै नमः कुङ्कुमं समर्पयामि

oṁ kuṅkumaṁ kāntidaṁ divyaṁ
kāminī kāmasambhavam
kuṅkumenā-rcite devi prasīda parameśvari
oṁ śrīṁ lakṣmyai namaḥ kuṅkumaṁ samarpayāmi

You are being adorned with this divine red powder, which is made more beautiful by the love we share with you, and is so pleasing. Oh

Lord, when we present this red powder be pleased, Oh Supreme Ruler of All. With this offering of red colored powder Oṁ I bow to the Goddess Lakṣmī.

sandal paste

ॐ श्रीखण्डचन्दनं दिव्यं गन्धाढ्यं सुमनोहरम् ।
विलेपनं च देवेशि चन्दनं प्रतिगृह्यताम् ॥
ॐ श्रीं लक्ष्म्यै नमः चन्दनं समर्पयामि

oṁ śrīkhaṇḍacandanaṁ divyaṁ
gandhāḍhyaṁ sumano haram
vilepanaṁ ca deveśi candanaṁ pratigṛhyatām
oṁ śrīṁ lakṣmyai namaḥ candanaṁ samarpayāmi

You are being adorned with this beautiful divine piece of sandal wood, ground to a paste which is so pleasing. Please accept this offering of sandal paste, Oh Supreme Sovereign of all the Gods. With the offering of sandal paste Oṁ I bow to the Goddess Lakṣmī.

turmeric

ॐ हरिद्रारञ्जिता देवि सुख-सौभाग्यदायिनि ।
तस्मात्त्वं पूजयाम्यत्र दुःखशान्तिं प्रयच्छ मे ॥
ॐ श्रीं लक्ष्म्यै नमः हरिद्रां समर्पयामि

oṁ haridrārañjitā devi sukha saubhāgyadāyini
tasmāttvaṁ pūjayāmyatra duḥkha śāntiṁ prayaccha me
oṁ śrīṁ lakṣmyai namaḥ haridrāṁ samarpayāmi

Oh Lord, you are being gratified by this turmeric, the giver of comfort and beauty. When you are worshiped like this, then you must bestow upon us the greatest peace. With the offering of turmeric Oṁ I bow to the Goddess Lakṣmī.

milk bath

ॐ कामधेनुसमुद्भूतं सर्वेषां जीवनं परम् ।
पावनं यज्ञहेतुश्च स्नानार्थं प्रतिगृह्यताम् ॥
ॐ श्रीं लक्ष्म्यै नमः पयस्नानं समर्पयामि

oṁ kāmadhenu samudbhūtaṁ sarveṣāṁ jīvanaṁ param
pāvanaṁ yajña hetuśca snānārthaṁ pratigṛhyatām
oṁ śrīṁ lakṣmyai namaḥ paya snānaṁ samarpayāmi

Coming from the ocean of being, the Fulfiller of all Desires, Grantor of Supreme Bliss to all souls. For the motive of purifying or sanctifying this holy union, we request you to accept this bath. With this offering of milk for your bath Oṁ I bow to the Goddess Lakṣmī.

yogurt bath

ॐ पयसस्तु समुद्भूतं मधुराम्लं शशिप्रभम् ।
दध्यानितं मया दत्तं स्नानार्थं प्रतिगृह्यताम् ॥
ॐ श्रीं लक्ष्म्यै नमः दधिस्नानं समर्पयामि

oṁ payasastu samudbhūtaṁ madhurāmlaṁ śaśiprabham
dadhyānitaṁ mayā dattaṁ snānārthaṁ pratigṛhyatām
oṁ śrīṁ lakṣmyai namaḥ dadhi snānaṁ samarpayāmi

Derived from milk from the ocean of being, sweet and pleasing like the glow of the moon, let these curds eternally be our ambassador, as we request you to accept this bath. With this offering of yogurt for your bath Oṁ I bow to the Goddess Lakṣmī.

ghee bath

ॐ नवनीतसमुत्पन्नं सर्वसन्तोषकारकम् ।
घृतं तुभ्यं प्रदास्यामि स्नानार्थं प्रतिगृह्यताम् ॥
ॐ श्रीं लक्ष्म्यै नमः घृतस्नानं समर्पयामि

oṁ navanīta samutpannaṁ sarvasantoṣakārakam
ghṛtaṁ tubhyaṁ pradāsyāmi snānārthaṁ pratigṛhyatām
oṁ śrīṁ lakṣmyai namaḥ ghṛta snānaṁ samarpayāmi

Freshly prepared from the ocean of being, causing all fulfillment, we offer this delightful ghee (clarified butter) and request you to accept this bath. With this offering of ghee for your bath Oṁ I bow to the Goddess Lakṣmī.

honey bath

ॐ तरुपुष्पसमुद्भूतं सुस्वादु मधुरं मधु ।
तेजोपुष्टिकरं दिव्यं स्नानार्थं प्रतिगृह्यताम् ॥
ॐ श्रीं लक्ष्म्यै नमः मधुस्नानं समर्पयामि

oṁ tarupuṣpa samudbhūtam susvādu madhuraṁ madhu
tejo puṣṭikaraṁ divyaṁ snānārtham pratigṛhyatām
oṁ śrīṁ lakṣmyai namaḥ madhu snānaṁ samarpayāmi

Prepared from flowers of the ocean of being, enjoyable as the sweetest of the sweet, causing the fire of divine nourishment to burn swiftly, we request you to accept this bath. With this offering of honey for your bath Oṁ I bow to the Goddess Lakṣmī.

sugar bath

ॐ इक्षुसारसमुद्भूता शर्करा पुष्टिकारिका ।
मलापहारिका दिव्या स्नानार्थं प्रतिगृह्यताम् ॥
ॐ श्रीं लक्ष्म्यै नमः शर्करास्नानं समर्पयामि

oṁ ikṣusāra samudbhūtā śarkarā puṣṭikārikā
malāpahārikā divyā snānārthaṁ pratigṛhyatām
oṁ śrīṁ lakṣmyai namaḥ śarkarā snānaṁ samarpayāmi

From the lake of sugar-cane, from the ocean of being, which causes the nourishment of sugar to give divine protection from all impurity, we request you to accept this bath. With this offering of sugar for your bath Oṁ I bow to the Goddess Lakṣmī.

five nectars bath

ॐ पयो दधि घृतं चैव मधु च शर्करायुतम् ।
पञ्चामृतं मयाऽऽनीतं स्नानार्थं प्रतिगृह्यताम् ॥
ॐ श्रीं लक्ष्म्यै नमः पञ्चामृतस्नानं समर्पयामि

oṁ payo dadhi ghṛtaṁ caiva madhu ca śarkarāyutam
pañcāmṛtaṁ mayā--nītaṁ snānārthaṁ pratigṛhyatām
oṁ śrīṁ lakṣmyai namaḥ pañcāmṛta snānaṁ samarpayāmi

Milk, curd, ghee and then honey and sugar mixed together; these five nectars are our ambassador, as we request you to accept this bath. With this offering of five nectars for your bath Oṁ I bow to the Goddess Lakṣmī.

scented oil

ॐ नानासुगन्धिद्रव्यं च चन्दनं रजनीयुतम् ।
उद्वर्तनं मया दत्तं स्नानार्थं प्रतिगृह्यताम् ॥
ॐ श्रीं लक्ष्म्यै नमः उद्वर्तनस्नानं समर्पयामि

oṁ nānāsugandhidravyaṁ ca candanaṁ rajanīyutam
udvartanaṁ mayā dattaṁ snānārthaṁ pratigṛhyatām
oṁ śrīṁ lakṣmyai namaḥ udvartana snānaṁ samarpayāmi

oṁ With various beautifully smelling ingredients, as well as the scent of sandal, we offer you this scented oil, Oh Lord. With this offering of scented oil Oṁ I bow to the Goddess Lakṣmī.

scent bath

गन्धद्वारां दुराधर्षां नित्यपुष्टां करीषिणीम् ।
ईश्वरीं सर्वभूतानां तामिहोपह्वये श्रियम् ॥
ॐ श्रीं लक्ष्म्यै नमः गन्धस्नानं समर्पयामि

gandhadvārāṁ durādharṣāṁ nityapuṣṭāṁ karīṣiṇīm
īśvarīṁ sarvabhūtānāṁ tāmihopahvaye śriyam
oṁ śrīṁ lakṣmyai namaḥ gandha snānaṁ samarpayāmi

She is the cause of the scent which is the door to religious ecstasy, unconquerable (never-failing), continually nurturing for all time. May we never tire from calling that manifestation of the Highest Respect, the Supreme Goddess of all existence. With this offering of scented bath Oṁ I bow to the Goddess Lakṣmī.

water bath

ॐ गङ्गे च जमुने चैव गोदावरि सरस्वति ।
नर्मदे सिन्धु कावेरि स्नानार्थं प्रतिगृह्यताम् ॥
ॐ श्रीं लक्ष्म्यै नमः गङ्गास्नानं समर्पयामि

oṁ gaṅge ca jamune caiva godāvari sarasvati
narmade sindhu kāveri snānārthaṁ pratigṛhyatām
oṁ śrīṁ lakṣmyai namaḥ gaṅgā snānaṁ samarpayāmi

Please accept the waters from the Gaṅges, the Jamunā, Godāvarī, Sarasvatī, Narmadā, Sindhu and Kāverī, which have been provided for your bath. With this offering of Ganges bath waters Oṁ I bow to the Goddess Lakṣmī.

cloth

ॐ शीतवातोष्णसंत्राणं लज्जायै रक्षणं परं ।

देहालंकरणं वस्त्रं अथ शान्तिं प्रयच्छ मे ॥

ॐ श्रीं लक्ष्म्यै नमः वस्त्रं समर्पयामि

oṁ śīta vātoṣṇa saṁ trāṇaṁ lajjāyai rakṣaṇaṁ paraṁ
dehālaṅkaraṇaṁ vastraṁ atha śāntiṁ prayaccha me
oṁ śrīṁ lakṣmyai namaḥ vastraṁ samarpayāmi

To take away the cold and the wind and to fully protect your modesty, we adorn your body with this cloth, and thereby find the greatest Peace. With this offering of wearing apparel Oṁ I bow to the Goddess Lakṣmī.

sacred thread

ॐ यज्ञोपवीतं परमं पवित्रं प्रजापतेर्यत् सहजं पुरस्तात् ।

आयुष्यमग्रं प्रतिमुञ्च शुभ्रं यज्ञोपवीतं बलमस्तु तेजः ॥

oṁ yajñopavītaṁ paramaṁ pavitraṁ
prajāpateryat sahajaṁ purastāt
āyuṣyamagraṁ pratimuñca śubhraṁ
yajñopavītaṁ balamastu tejaḥ

Oṁ the sacred thread of the highest purity is given by Prajāpati, the Lord of Creation, for the greatest facility. You bring life and illuminate the greatness of liberation. Oh sacred thread, let your strength be of radiant light.

शमो दमस्तपः शौचं क्षान्तिरार्जवमेव च ।

ज्ञानं विज्ञानमास्तिक्यं ब्रह्मकर्म स्वभावजम् ॥

śamo damastapaḥ śaucaṁ kṣāntirārjavameva ca
jñānaṁ vijñānamāstikyaṁ brahmakarma svabhāvajam

Peacefulness, self-control, austerity, purity of mind and body, patience and forgiveness, sincerity and honesty, wisdom, knowledge, and self-realization, are the natural activities of a Brahmaṇa.

नवभिस्तन्तुभिर्युक्तं त्रिगुणं देवतामयं ।
उपवीतं मया दत्तं गृहाण त्वं सुरेश्वरि ॥
ॐ श्रीं लक्ष्म्यै नमः यज्ञोपवीतं समर्पयामि

navabhiṣṭantubhiryuktaṁ triguṇaṁ devatā mayaṁ
upavītaṁ mayā dattaṁ gṛhāṇa tvaṁ sureśvari
oṁ śrīṁ lakṣmyai namaḥ yajñopavītaṁ samarpayāmi

With nine desirable threads all united together, exemplifying the three guṇas (or three qualities of harmony of our deity), this sacred thread will be our ambassador. Oh Ruler of the Gods, please accept. With this offering of a sacred thread Oṁ I bow to the Goddess Lakṣmī.

rudrākṣa

त्र्यम्बकं यजामहे सुगन्धिं पुष्टिवर्द्धनम् ।
उर्व्वारुकमिव बन्धनान्मृत्योर्म्मुक्षीयमामृतात् ॥
ॐ श्रीं लक्ष्म्यै नमः रुद्राक्षं समर्पयामि

tryambakaṁ yajāmahe sugandhiṁ puṣṭivarddhanam
urvvārukamiva bandhanānmṛtyormmukṣīyamāmṛtāt
oṁ śrīṁ lakṣmyai namaḥ rudrākṣaṁ samarpayāmi

We adore the Father of the three worlds, of excellent fame, Grantor of Increase. As a cucumber is released from its bondage to the stem, so may we be freed from Death to dwell in immortality. With this offering of rudrākṣa Oṁ I bow to the Goddess Lakṣmī.

mālā

ॐ मां माले महामाये सर्वशक्तिस्वरूपिणि ।
चतुर्वर्गस्त्वयि न्यस्तस्तस्मान्मे सिद्धिदा भव ॥
ॐ श्रीं लक्ष्म्यै नमः मालां समर्पयामि

oṁ māṁ māle mahāmāye sarvaśaktisvarūpiṇi
caturvargastvayi nyastastasmānme siddhidā bhava
oṁ śrīṁ lakṣmyai namaḥ mālāṁ samarpayāmi

Oṁ my rosary, the Great Limitation of Consciousness, containing all energy within as your intrinsic nature, fulfilling the four desires of men, give us the attainment of your perfection. With this offering of a mālā Oṁ I bow to the Goddess Lakṣmī.

rice

अक्षतान् निर्मलान् शुद्धान् मुक्ताफलसमन्वितान् ।
गृहाणेमान् महादेवि देहि मे निर्मलां धियम् ॥
ॐ श्रीं लक्ष्म्यै नमः अक्षतान् समर्पयामि

akṣatān nirmalān śuddhān muktāphalasamanvitān
gṛhāṇemān mahādevi dehi me nirmalāṁ dhiyam
oṁ śrīṁ lakṣmyai namaḥ akṣatān samarpayāmi

Oh Great Lord, please accept these grains of rice, spotlessly clean, bestowing the fruit of liberation, and give us a spotlessly clean mind. With the offering of grains of rice Oṁ I bow to the Goddess Lakṣmī.

flower garland

शङ्ख-पद्मजपुष्पादि शतपत्रैर्विचित्रताम् ।
पुष्पमालां प्रयच्छामि गृहाण त्वं सुरेश्वरि ॥
ॐ श्रीं लक्ष्म्यै नमः पुष्पमालां समर्पयामि

śaṅkha-padma japuṣpādi śatapatrairvicitratām
puṣpamālāṁ prayacchāmi gṛhāṇa tvaṁ sureśvari
oṁ śrīṁ lakṣmyai namaḥ puṣpamālāṁ samarpayāmi

We offer you this garland of flowers with spiraling lotuses, other flowers and leaves. Be pleased to accept it, Oh Ruler of All Gods. With the offering of a garland of flowers Oṁ I bow to the Goddess Lakṣmī.

flower

मल्लिकादि सुगन्धीनि मालित्यादीनि वै प्रभो ।
मयाऽहृतानि पूजार्थं पुष्पाणि प्रतिगृह्यताम् ॥
ॐ श्रीं लक्ष्म्यै नमः पुष्पम् समर्पयामि

mallikādi sugandhīni mālityādīni vai prabho
mayā-hṛtāni pūjārthaṁ puṣpāṇi pratigṛhyatām
oṁ śrīṁ lakṣmyai namaḥ puṣpam samarpayāmi

Various flowers such as mallikā and others of excellent scent, are being offered to you, our Lord. All these flowers have come from the devotion of our hearts for your worship. Be pleased to accept them. With the offering of flowers Oṁ I bow to the Goddess Lakṣmī.

sthirī karaṇa
establishment of stillness

ॐ सर्वतीर्थमयं वारि सर्वदेवसमन्वितम् ।
इमं घटं समागच्छ तिष्ठ देवगणैः सह ॥

oṁ sarvatīrthamayaṁ vāri sarvadevasamanvitam
imaṁ ghaṭaṁ samāgaccha tiṣṭha devagaṇaiḥ saha

All the places of pilgrimage as well as all of the Gods, all are placed within this container. Oh Multitude of Gods, be established within!

lelihānā mudrā
(literally, sticking out or pointing)

स्थां स्थीं स्थिरो भव वीड्वङ्ग आशुर्भव वाज्यर्वन् ।
पृथुर्भव सुषदस्त्वमग्नेः पुरीषवाहनः ॥

sthāṁ sthīṁ sthiro bhava
vīḍvaṅga āśurbhava vājyarvan
pṛthurbhava suṣadastvamagneḥ purīṣavāhanaḥ

Be Still in the Gross Body! Be Still in the Subtle Body! Be Still in the Causal Body! Quickly taking in this energy and shining forth as the Holder of Wealth, oh Divine Fire, becoming abundant, destroy the current of rubbish from the face of this earth.

prāṇa pratiṣṭhā
establishment of life

ॐ अं आं ह्रीं क्रों यं रं लं वं शं षं सं हों हं सः

oṁ aṁ āṁ hrīṁ kroṁ yaṁ raṁ laṁ vaṁ śaṁ ṣaṁ saṁ hoṁ haṁ saḥ

oṁ The Infinite Beyond Conception, Creation (the first letter), Consciousness, Māyā, the cause of the movement of the subtle body to perfection and beyond; the path of fulfillment: control, subtle illumination, one with the earth, emancipation, the soul of peace, the soul of delight, the soul of unity (all this is I), perfection, Infinite Consciousness, this is I.

ॐ श्रीं लक्ष्मयै नमः प्राणा इह प्राणाः

oṁ śrīṁ lakṣmyai namaḥ prāṇā iha prāṇāḥ

Oṁ I bow to the Goddess Lakṣmī. You are the life of this life!

ॐ अं आं ह्रीं क्रों यं रं लं वं शं षं सं हों हं सः

oṁ aṁ āṁ hrīṁ kroṁ yaṁ raṁ laṁ vaṁ śaṁ ṣaṁ saṁ hoṁ haṁ saḥ

oṁ The Infinite Beyond Conception, Creation (the first letter), Consciousness, Māyā, the cause of the movement of the subtle body to perfection and beyond; the path of fulfillment: control, subtle illumination, one with the earth, emancipation, the soul of peace, the soul of delight, the soul of unity (all this is I), perfection, Infinite Consciousness, this is I.

ॐ श्रीं लक्ष्मयै नमः जीव इह स्थितः

oṁ śrīṁ lakṣmyai namaḥ jīva iha sthitaḥ

Oṁ I bow to the Goddess Lakṣmī. You are situated in this life (or individual consciousness).

ॐ अं आं ह्रीं क्रों यं रं लं वं शं षं सं हों हं सः

oṁ aṁ āṁ hrīṁ kroṁ yaṁ raṁ laṁ vaṁ śaṁ ṣaṁ saṁ hoṁ haṁ saḥ

oṁ The Infinite Beyond Conception, Creation (the first letter), Consciousness, Māyā, the cause of the movement of the subtle body to perfection and beyond; the path of fulfillment: control, subtle illumination, one with the earth, emancipation, the soul of peace, the soul of delight, the soul of unity (all this is I), perfection, Infinite Consciousness, this is I.

ॐ श्रीं लक्ष्मयै नमः सर्वेन्द्रियाणि

oṁ śrīṁ lakṣmyai namaḥ sarvendriyāṇi

Oṁ I bow to the Goddess Lakṣmī. You are all these organs (of action and knowledge).

ॐ अं आं ह्रीं क्रों यं रं लं वं शं षं सं हों हं सः

oṁ aṁ āṁ hrīṁ kroṁ yaṁ raṁ laṁ vaṁ śaṁ ṣaṁ saṁ hoṁ haṁ saḥ

oṁ The Infinite Beyond Conception, Creation (the first letter), Consciousness, Māyā, the cause of the movement of the subtle body to perfection and beyond; the path of fulfillment: control, subtle illumination, one with the earth, emancipation, the soul of peace, the soul of delight, the soul of unity (all this is I), perfection, Infinite Consciousness, this is I.

ॐ श्रीं लक्ष्मयै नमः वाग् मनस्त्वक्चक्षुः-श्रोत्र-घ्राण-प्राणा इहागत्य सुखं चिरं तिष्ठन्तु स्वाहा

oṁ śrīṁ lakṣmyai namaḥ vāg manastvakcakṣuḥ śrotra ghrāṇa prāṇā ihāgatya sukhaṁ ciraṁ tiṣṭhantu svāhā

Oṁ I bow to the Goddess Lakṣmī. You are all these vibrations, mind, sound, eyes, ears, tongue, nose and life force. Bring forth infinite peace and establish it forever, I am One with God!

kara nyāsa

establishment in the hands

ॐ श्रां अंगुष्ठाभ्यां नमः

oṁ śrāṁ aṇguṣṭhābhyāṁ namaḥ thumb forefinger

Oṁ śrāṁ in the thumb I bow.

ॐ श्रीं तर्जनीभ्यां स्वाहा

oṁ śrīṁ tarjanībhyāṁ svāhā thumb forefinger

Oṁ śrīṁ in the forefinger, I am One with God!

ॐ श्रूं मध्यमाभ्यां वषट्

oṁ śrūṁ madhyamābhyāṁ vaṣaṭ thumb middlefinger

Oṁ śrūṁ in the middle finger, Purify!

ॐ श्रैं अनामिकाभ्यां हुं

oṁ śraiṁ anāmikābhyāṁ huṁ thumb ring finger

Oṁ śraiṁ in the ring finger, Cut the Ego!

ॐ श्रौं कनिष्ठिकाभ्यां बौषट्

oṁ śrauṁ kaniṣṭhikābhyāṁ vauṣaṭ thumb little finger
Oṁ śrauṁ in the little finger, Ultimate Purity!

Roll hand over hand forwards while reciting karatal kar,
and backwards while chanting pṛṣṭhābhyāṁ,
then clap hands when chanting astrāya phaṭ.

ॐ श्रः करतल कर पृष्ठाभ्यां अस्त्राय फट् ॥

oṁ śraḥ karatal kar pṛṣṭhābhyāṁ astrāya phaṭ
Oṁ śraḥ I bow to the Goddess Lakṣmī, with the weapon of Virtue.

ॐ श्रीं लक्ष्म्यै नमः

oṁ śrīṁ lakṣmyai namaḥ
Oṁ I bow to the Goddess Lakṣmī

aṅga nyāsa
establishment in the body
Holding tattva mudrā, touch heart.

ॐ श्रां हृदयाय नमः

oṁ śrāṁ hṛdayāya namaḥ touch heart
Oṁ śrāṁ in the heart, I bow.

Holding tattva mudrā, touch top of head.

ॐ श्रीं शिरसे स्वाहा

oṁ śrīṁ śirase svāhā top of head
Oṁ śrīṁ on the top of the head, I am One with God!

With thumb extended, touch back of head.

ॐ श्रूं शिखायै वषट्

oṁ śrūṁ śikhāyai vaṣaṭ back of head
Oṁ śrūṁ on the back of the head, Purify!

Holding tattva mudrā, cross both arms.

ॐ श्रैं कवचाय हुं

oṁ śraiṁ kavacāya huṁ cross both arms
Oṁ śraiṁ crossing both arms, Cut the Ego!

Holding tattva mudrā, touch two eyes and in between at once with three middle fingers.

ॐ श्रौं नेत्रत्रयाय वौषट्

oṁ śrauṁ netratrayāya vauṣaṭ touch three eyes
Oṁ śrauṁ in the three eyes, Ultimate Purity!

Roll hand over hand forwards while reciting karatal kar, and backwards while chanting pṛṣṭhābhyāṁ, then clap hands when chanting astrāya phaṭ.

ॐ श्रः करतल कर पृष्ठाभ्यां अस्त्राय फट् ॥

oṁ śraḥ karatal kar pṛṣṭhābhyāṁ astrāya phaṭ
Oṁ śraḥ I bow to the Goddess Lakṣmī with the weapon of Virtue.

ॐ श्रीं लक्ष्म्यै नमः

oṁ śrīṁ lakṣmyai namaḥ
Oṁ I bow to the Goddess Lakṣmī.

japa

prāṇa pratiṣṭhā sūkta

hymn of the establishment of life

ॐ अस्यै प्राणाः प्रतिष्ठन्तु अस्यै प्राणाः क्षरन्तु च ।
अस्यै देवत्वमर्चायै मामहेति कश्चन ॥

oṁ asyai prāṇāḥ pratiṣṭhantu
asyai prāṇāḥ kṣarantu ca
asyai devatvamārcāyai māmaheti kaścana
Thus has the life force been established in you, and thus the life force has flowed into you. Thus to you, God, offering is made, and in this way make us shine.

कलाकला हि देवानां दानवानां कलाकलाः ।
संगृह्य निर्मितो यस्मात् कलशस्तेन कथ्यते ॥

kalākalā hi devānāṁ dānavānāṁ kalākalāḥ
saṁgṛhya nirmito yasmāt kalaśastena kathyate

All the Gods are Fragments of the Cosmic Whole. Also all the asuras are Fragments of the Cosmic Whole. Thus we make a house to contain all these energies.

कलशस्य मुखे विष्णुः कण्ठे रुद्रः समाश्रितः ।
मूले त्वस्य स्थितो ब्रह्मा मध्ये मातृगणाः स्मृताः ॥

kalaśasya mukhe viṣṇuḥ kaṇṭhe rudraḥ samāśritaḥ
mūle tvasya sthito brahmā madhye mātṛgaṇāḥ smṛtāḥ

In the mouth of the pot is Viṣṇu, in the neck resides Rudra. At the base is situated Brahmā, and in the middle we remember the multitude of Mothers.

कुक्षौ तु सागराः सप्त सप्तद्वीपा च मेदिनी ।
अर्जुनी गोमती चैव चन्द्रभागा सरस्वती ॥

kukṣau tu sāgarāḥ sapta saptadvīpā ca medinī
arjunī gomatī caiva candrabhāgā sarasvatī

In the belly are the seven seas and the seven islands of the earth. The rivers Arjunī, Gomatī, Candrabhāgā, Sarasvatī;

कावेरी कृष्णवेणा च गङ्गा चैव महानदी ।
ताप्ती गोदावरी चैव माहेन्द्री नर्मदा तथा ॥

kāverī kṛṣṇaveṇā ca gaṅgā caiva mahānadī
tāptī godāvarī caiva māhendrī narmadā tathā

Kāverī, Kṛṣṇaveṇā and the Gaṅges and other great rivers; the Tāptī, Godāvarī, Māhendrī and Narmadā.

नदाश्च विविधा जाता नद्यः सर्वास्तथापराः ।
पृथिव्यां यानि तीर्थानि कलशस्थानि तानि वै ॥

nadāśca vividhā jātā nadyaḥ sarvāstathāparāḥ
pṛthivyāṁ yāni tīrthāni kalaśasthāni tāni vai

The various rivers and the greatest of beings born, and all the respected places of pilgrimage upon the earth, are established within this pot.

सर्वे समुद्राः सरितस्तीर्थानि जलदा नदाः ।

आयान्तु मम शान्त्यर्थं दुरितक्षयकारकाः ॥

sarve samudrāḥ saritastīrthāni jaladā nadāḥ
āyāntu mama śāntyarthaṁ duritakṣayakārakāḥ

All of the seas, rivers, and waters from all the respected places of pilgrimage have been brought for the peace of that which is bad or wicked.

ऋग्वेदोऽथ यजुर्वेदः सामवेदो ह्यथर्वणः ।

अङ्गैश्च सहिताः सर्वे कलशं तु समाश्रिताः ॥

ṛgvedo-tha yajurvedaḥ sāmavedo hyatharvaṇaḥ
aṅgaiśca sahitāḥ sarve kalaśaṁ tu samāśritāḥ

The Ṛg Veda, the Yajur Veda, Sāma Veda and the Atharva Veda, along with all of their limbs, are assembled together in this pot.

अत्र गायत्री सावित्री शान्तिः पुष्टिकरी तथा ।

आयान्तु मम शान्त्यर्थं दुरितक्षयकारकाः ॥

atra gāyatrī sāvitrī śāntiḥ puṣṭikarī tathā
āyāntu mama śāntyarthaṁ duritakṣayakārakāḥ

Here Gāyatrī, Sāvitrī, Peace and Increase have been brought for the peace of that which is bad or wicked.

देवदानवसंवादे मथ्यमाने महोदधौ ।

उत्पन्नोऽसि तदा कुम्भ विधृतो विष्णुना स्वयम् ॥

deva dānava saṁvāde mathyamāne mahodadhau
utpanno-si tadā kumbha vidhṛto viṣṇunā svayam

The Gods and asuras speaking together are the great givers of churning to the mind. Rise to the top of this pot to separate them from what is actually Viṣṇu, Himself.

त्वत्तोये सर्वतीर्थानि देवाः सर्वे त्वयि स्थिताः ।
त्वयि तिष्ठन्ति भूतानि त्वयि प्राणाः प्रतिष्ठिताः ॥

tvattoye sarvatīrthāni devāḥ sarve tvayi sthitāḥ
tvayi tiṣṭhanti bhūtāni tvayi prāṇāḥ pratiṣṭhitāḥ

Within you are all the pilgrimage places. All the Gods are situated within you. All existence is established within you. All life is established within you.

शिवः स्वयं त्वमेवासि विष्णुस्त्वं च प्रजापतिः ।
आदित्या वसवो रुद्रा विश्वेदेवाः सपैतृकाः ॥

śivaḥ svayaṁ tvamevāsi viṣṇustvaṁ ca prajāpatiḥ
ādityā vasavo rudrā viśvedevāḥ sapaitṛkāḥ

You alone are Śiva; you are Brahmā and Viṣṇu, the sons of Aditi, Finders of the Wealth, Rudra, the Universal Deities and the ancestors.

त्वयि तिष्ठन्ति सर्वेऽपि यतः कामफलप्रदाः ।
त्वत्प्रसादादिमं यज्ञं कर्तुमीहे जलोद्भव ।
सान्निध्यं कुरु मे देव प्रसन्नो भव सर्वदा ॥

tvayi tiṣṭhanti sarve-pi yataḥ kāmaphalapradāḥ
tvatprasādādimaṁ yajñaṁ kartumīhe jalodbhava
sānnidhyaṁ kuru me deva prasanno bhava sarvadā

All and everything has been established in you, from whence you grant the fruits of desires. From you comes the blessed fruit of the sacrifice performed with excellence. May those riches increase. Manifest your presence within us, Lord. Always be pleased.

नमो नमस्ते स्फटिकप्रभाय सुश्वेतहाराय सुमङ्गलाय ।
सुपाशहस्ताय झषासनाय जलाधिनाथाय नमो नमस्ते ॥

namo namaste sphaṭikaprabhāya
suśvetahārāya sumaṅgalāya
supāśahastāya jhaṣāsanāya
jalādhināthāya namo namaste

We bow, we bow to He who shines like crystal, to He who emits excellent clarity and excellent welfare. With the net of unity in his hand, who takes the form of a fish, to the Lord of all waters and that which dwells within, we bow, we bow!

पाशपाणे नमस्तुभ्यं पद्मिनीजीवनायक ।
पुण्याहवाचनं यावत् तावत्त्वं सन्निधौ भव ॥

pāśapāṇe namastubhyaṁ padminījīvanāyaka
puṇyāhavācanaṁ yāvat tāvattvaṁ sannidhau bhava

We bow to He with the net of unity in his hand, Seer of the Life of the Lotus One. With this meritorious invocation, please make your presence manifest.

viśeṣārghya

establishment of the conch shell offering

Draw the yantra on the plate or space for worship with sandal paste and/or water. Offer rice on the yantra for each of the four mantras.

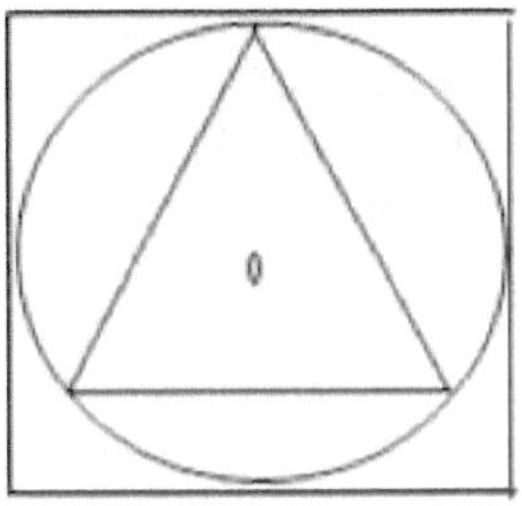

ॐ आधारशक्तये नमः

oṁ ādhāraśaktaye namaḥ

oṁ we bow to the Primal Energy

ॐ कूर्माय नमः

oṁ kūrmāya namaḥ

oṁ we bow to the Support of the Earth

ॐ अनन्ताय नमः

oṁ anantāya namaḥ

oṁ we bow to Infinity

ॐ पृथिव्यै नमः

oṁ pṛthivyai namaḥ

oṁ we bow to the Earth

Place a conch shell on the bindu in the center of the yantra when saying Phaṭ.

स्थां स्थीं स्थिरो भव फट्

sthāṁ sthīṁ sthiro bhava phaṭ

Be Still in the Gross Body! Be Still in the Subtle Body! Be Still in the Causal Body! Purify!

Fill conch shell with water while chanting the mantra.

ॐ गङ्गे च जमुने चैव गोदावरि सरस्वति ।

नर्मदे सिन्धु कावेरि जलेऽस्मिन् सन्निधिं कुरु ॥

oṁ gaṅge ca jamune caiva godāvari sarasvati
narmade sindhu kāveri jale-asmin sannidhiṁ kuru

oṁ the Ganges, Jamunā, Godāvarī, Sarasvatī, Narmadā, Sindhu, Kāverī, these waters are mingled together.

Offer Tulasī leaves into water

ॐ ऐं ह्रीं क्लीं श्रीं वृन्दावनवासिन्यै स्वाहा

oṁ aiṁ hrīṁ klīṁ śrīṁ vṛndāvanavāsinyai svāhā

oṁ Wisdom, Māyā, Increase, to She who resides in Vṛndāvana, I am One with God!

Offer 3 flowers into the water pot with the mantras

एते गन्धपुष्पे ॐ अं अर्कमण्डलाय द्वादशकलात्मने नमः

ete gandhapuṣpe oṁ aṁ arkamaṇḍalāya
dvādaśakalātmane namaḥ

With these scented flowers oṁ "A" we bow to the twelve aspects of the realm of the sun. Tapinī, Tāpinī, Dhūmrā, Marīci, Jvālinī, Ruci, Sudhūmrā, Bhoga-dā, Viśvā, Bodhinī, Dhārinī, Kṣamā; Containing heat, Emanating heat, Smoky, Ray-producing, Burning, Lustrous, Purple or Smoky-red, Granting enjoyment, Universal, Which makes known, Productive of Consciousness, Which supports, Which forgives.

एते गन्धपुष्पे ॐ उं सोममण्डलाय षोडशकलात्मने नमः

ete gandhapuṣpe oṁ uṁ somamaṇḍalāya
ṣoḍaśakalātmane namaḥ

With these scented flowers oṁ "U" we bow to the sixteen aspects of the realm of the moon. Amṛtā, Prāṇadā, Puṣā, Tuṣṭi, Puṣṭi, Rati, Dhṛti, Śaśinī, Caṇḍrikā, Kānti, Jyotsnā, Śrī, Prīti, Aṅgadā, Pūrṇā, Pūrṇāmṛta; Nectar, Which sustains life, Which supports, Satisfying, Nourishing, Playful, Constancy, Unfailing, Producer of Joy, Beauty enhanced by love, Light, Grantor of Prosperity, Affectionate, Purifying the body, Complete, Full of Bliss.

एते गन्धपुष्पे ॐ मं वह्निमण्डलाय दशकलात्मने नमः

ete gandhapuṣpe oṁ maṁ vahnimaṇḍalāya daśakalātmane namaḥ

With these scented flowers oṁ "M" we bow to the ten aspects of the realm of fire: Dhūmrā, Arciḥ, Jvalinī, Śūkṣmā, Jvālinī, Visphūliṅginī, Suśrī, Surūpā, Kapilā, Havya-Kavya-Vahā; Smoky Red, Flaming, Shining, Subtle, Burning, Sparkling, Beautiful, Well-formed, Tawny, The Messenger to Gods and Ancestors.

एते गन्धपुष्पे हुं

ete gandhapuṣpe huṁ

With these scented flowers huṁ

ॐ श्रीं लक्ष्म्यै नमः

oṁ śrīṁ lakṣmyai namaḥ

Oṁ I bow to the Goddess Lakṣmī.

Wave hands in matsyā, dhenu and aṅkuśa mudrās while chanting this mantra.

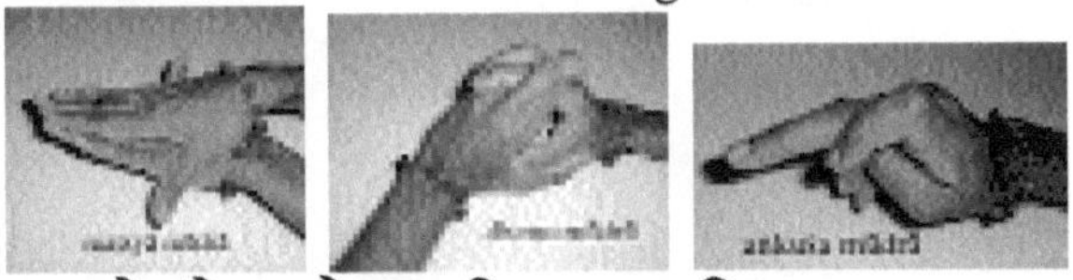

ॐ गङ्गे च जमुने चैव गोदावरि सरस्वति ।
नर्मदे सिन्धु कावेरि जलेऽस्मिन् सन्निधिं कुरु ॥

oṁ gaṅge ca jamune caiva godāvari sarasvati narmade sindhu kāveri jale-asmin sannidhiṁ kuru

oṁ the Ganges, Jamunā, Godāvarī, Sarasvatī, Narmadā, Sindhu, Kāverī, these waters are mingled together.

ॐ श्रीं लक्ष्म्यै नमः

oṁ śrīṁ lakṣmyai namaḥ
Oṁ I bow to the Goddess Lakṣmī.

Sprinkle water over all articles to be offered, then throw some drops of water over your shoulders while repeating the mantra.

अमृतम् कुरु स्वाहा

amṛtam kuru svāhā
Make this immortal nectar! I am One with God!

bhūta śuddhi

purification of the elements

Pronounce each Bījā sixteen times in its proper location:

लं	**Mulādhāra**	(1st Cakra)	**Laṁ**	Indra	Earth
वं	**Swādiṣṭhana**	(2nd Cakra)	**Vaṁ**	Varuṇa	Water
रं	**Maṇipura**	(3rd Cakra)	**Raṁ**	Agni	Fire
यं	**Anahata**	(4th Cakra)	**Yaṁ**	Vāyu	Air
हं	**Viśuddha**	(5th Cakra)	**Haṁ**	Soma	Ether
ॐ	**Āgnyā**	(6th Cakra)	**Oṁ**	Īśvara	The Ultimate

Then move up and down the Suṣumṇa through the cakras, pronouncing each Bījā once, and feeling its presence in its proper location.

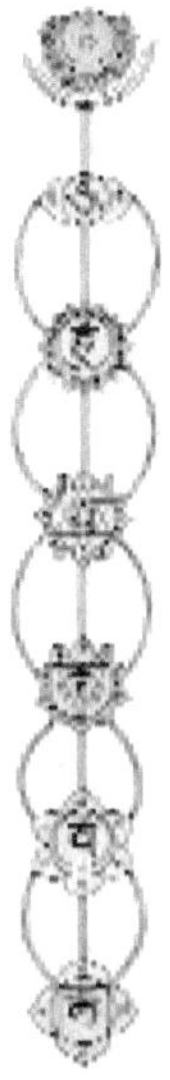

ॐ लं वं रं यं हं ॐ

oṁ laṁ vaṁ raṁ yaṁ haṁ oṁ

oṁ Earth, Water, Fire, Air, Ether, The Ultimate.

ॐ हं यं रं वं लं ॐ

oṁ haṁ yaṁ raṁ vaṁ laṁ oṁ

oṁ The Ultimate, Ether, Air, Fire, Water, Earth.

ॐ मूलशृङ्गाटाच्छिरः सुषुम्नापथेन जीवशिवं परमशिवपदे योजयामि स्वाहा ॥

oṁ mūlaśṛṅgāṭācchiraḥ suṣumnāpathena jīvaśivaṁ paramaśivapade yojayāmi svāhā

Piercing the triangular junction (yantra) situated in the Mulādhāra, the center of energy between the genital and the rectum, I direct the auspicious life force upwards by way of the Suṣumna, the subtle canal which transmits nerve impulses along the spinal column, to unite in Supreme Bliss, I am One with God!

ॐ यं लिङ्गशरीरं शोषय शोषय स्वाहा ॥

oṁ yaṁ liṅgaśarīraṁ śoṣaya śoṣaya svāhā
oṁ Yaṁ (Vāyu, Air, the Spirit of Emancipation) in the subtle body, purify, purify, I am One with God!

ॐ रं सङ्कोचशरीरं दह दह स्वाहा ॥

oṁ raṁ saṅkocaśarīraṁ daha daha svāhā
oṁ Raṁ (Agni, Fire, the Purifying Light of Wisdom) in the limited body, burn, burn, I am One with God!

ॐ परमशिव सुषुम्नापथेन मूलश्रृङ्गाटमुल्लसोल्लस
ज्वल ज्वल प्रज्वल प्रज्वल सोऽहं हंसः स्वाहा ॥

oṁ paramaśiva suṣumnāpathena mūlaśṛṅgāṭa mullasollasa jvala jvala prajvala prajvala so-haṁ haṁsaḥ svāhā
Oh Supreme Bliss, filling the path of the Suṣumna from the triangular junction in the Mulādhāra, dancing brilliantly, shine, shine, radiate, radiate, That is I, I am That, I am One with God!

kara śuddhi

wipe your hands with a flower

ॐ ऐं रं अस्त्राय फट्

oṁ aiṁ raṁ astrāya phaṭ
oṁ Wisdom, the Subtle Body of Light, with this weapon, Purify!

tap ground three times with fist or heel

फट् फट् फट्

phaṭ phaṭ phaṭ
Purify! Purify! Purify!

bhūtāpsāraṇa

dispersion of inimical energies

Bhūta has a number of meanings, which makes the following verses to play on the words, switching meanings even while using the same word. Its noun forms mean variously: a purified being, a good being; created thing, world; uncanny being, spirit, ghost, goblin; past, fact, reality, actual occurence; welfare; elements, especially as applied to the five gross elements of earth, water, fire, air and ether (See Bhūta Śuddhi). Here we are calling upon the friendly or the good Bhūtas to destroy obstacles created by unfriendly or bad Bhūtas.

ॐ अपसर्पन्तु ते भूता ये भूता भुवि संस्थिताः ।
ये भूता विघ्नकर्त्तारस्ते नश्यन्तु शिवज्ञया ॥

oṁ apasarpantu te bhūtā ya bhūtā bhuvi saṁsthitāḥ
ye bhūtā vighnakarttāraste naśyantu śivajñayā

We consign to you friendly spirits, friendly spirits that are situated on this earth plane, the activity of destroying any obstacles placed by unfriendly spirits, by order of the Wisdom of Infinite Goodness.

ॐ भूतप्रेतपिशाचाश्च दानवा राक्षसाश्च ये ।
शान्तिं कुर्वन्तु ते सर्वे ईमं गृह्वतु मद्बलिम् ॥

oṁ bhūtapretapiśācāśca dānavā rākṣasāśca ye
śāntiṁ kurvantu te sarve īmaṁ gṛhvatu madbalim

Hey ghosts, goblins, demons, unfriendly spirits and various forms of negativity projecting egos: you have been made entirely at peace. Please accept this offering from me.

ॐ वेताल्राश्च पिशाचाश्च राक्षसाश्च सरीसुपाः ।
अपसर्पन्तु ते सर्वे नारसिंहेन ताढिताः ॥

oṁ vetālāśca piśācāśca rākṣasāśca sarīsupāḥ
apasarpantu te sarve nārasiṁhena tāḍhitāḥ

Other demons, goblins, various forms of negativity projecting egos, creeping and crawling things: I consign to you completely the striking blows of Nārasiṁha, Viṣṇu in His incarnation of man-lion.

aghamārṣaṇa
internal cleaning

aṅkuśa mudrā

ॐ ऋतमित्यस्य ऋक्त्रयस्याघमर्षण ऋषिरनष्टुप्छन्दोभाववृत्तं देवतामश्वमेधावभृथे विनियोगः ॥

oṁ ṛtamityasya ṛktrayasyāghamarṣaṇa ṛṣiranaṣṭupchandobhāvavṛttaṁ devatāmaśvamedhāvabhṛthe viniyogaḥ

Introducing the three Mantras which begin with "From Truth...", etc., Internal Cleaning is the Seer, Anuṣṭup is the meter (32 syllables to the verse), Who Changes the Intensity of Reality is the divinity, equal in merit to the horse sacrifice, this practice is offered in application.

ॐ ऋतं च सत्यं चाभीद्धात्तपसोऽध्यजायत ।
ततो रत्र्यजायत ततः समुद्रोऽर्णवः ॥

oṁ ṛtaṁ ca satyaṁ cābhīddhāttapaso-dhyajāyata
tato ratryajāyata tataḥ samudro-rṇavaḥ

From truth, from the Imperishable Truth, the Performers of Tapasya, or strict spiritual discipline, have come. Then came forth the night, and then the sea of objects and relationships, with the multitude of its waves.

समुद्रार्णवादधि संवत्सरो अजायत ।
अहोरात्राणिविदधदिश्वस्य भिषतो वशी ॥

samudrārṇavādadhi saṁvatsaro ajāyata
ahorātrāṇividadhadiśvasya bhiṣato vaśī

From the fluctuations of the waves on the sea, the years came forth. The night transformed into day, and the universe took birth.

सूर्या चन्द्रमसौ धाता यथापूर्वमकल्पयत् ।
दिवं च पृथिवीं चान्तरिक्षमथो स्वः ॥

sūryā candramasau dhātā yathāpūrvamakalpayat
divaṁ ca pṛthivīṁ cāntarikṣamatho svaḥ

The Sun and the Moon gave forth their lights in accordance with the command of the Creator. And the earth, the atmosphere and the heavens were His Own.

jāl netī, prāṇāyāma

cleaning of the sinuses, control of breath

Perform Jāl Neti taking water from the Samanyārghya into the left palm. Inhale it through the Iḍa or left nostril, and bring it all the way up into the Āgnyā Cakra, then expel it through the Piṅgalā or right nostril. Blow out the nasal passages so that they are clean.

agni prajvālitaṁ

enkindling the sacred fire

agni gāyatrī

ॐ वैश्वानराय विद्महे लालिलाय धीमहे ।
तन्नो अग्निः प्रचोदयात् ॐ ॥

oṁ vaisvānarāya vidmahe lālilāya dhīmahe
tanno agniḥ pracodayāt oṁ

Oṁ We meditate upon the All-Pervading Being, we contemplate the Luminous One who is the final resting place of all. May that Divine Fire, the Light of Meditation, grant us increase.

upasaṁhara mudrā

ह्वयाम्यग्निं प्रथमं स्वस्तये ।
ह्वयामि मित्रावरुणाविहावसे ।
ह्वयामि रात्रीं जगतो निवेशनीं ।
ह्वयामि देवं सवितारमूतये ॥

hvayāmyagniṁ prathamaṁ svastaye
hvayāmi mitrā varuṇā vihāvase
hvayāmi rātrīṁ jagato niveṣanīṁ
hvayāmi devaṁ savitāramūtaye

I am calling you, Agni, the Divine Fire, the Light of Meditation, first to grant success. I am calling you Friendship and the Continuous Flow of Equilibrium also to receive this offering. I am calling the Night of Duality who covers the universe. I am calling the Light of Wisdom, the Divine Being, to rise up within us.

हिरण्यगर्भः समवर्त्तताग्रे भूतस्य जातः पतिरेक आसीत्।
स दाधार पृथिवीं द्यामुतेमां कस्मै देवाय हविषा विधेम ॥

hiranyagarbhaḥ samavartatāgre
bhūtasya jātaḥ patireka āsīt
sa dādhāra pṛthivīṁ dyāmutemāṁ
kasmai devāya haviṣā vidhema

Oh Golden Womb, You are the One Eternal Existence from which all beings born on the earth have come forth. You always bear the earth and all that rises upon it. (You tell us) to which God shall we offer our knowledge and attention?

यथा विद्वां अरंकरद् विश्वेभ्यो यजतेभ्यः।
अयमग्ने त्वे अपि यं यज्ञं चकृमा वयम् ॥

yathā vidvāṁ araṁkarad viśvebhyoḥ yajatebhyaḥ
ayamagne tve api yaṁ yajñaṁ cakṛmā vayam

Through knowledge of this Eternal Cause, all beings born in the universe have come forth. It is in you, Oh Agni, Oh Light of Meditation, in the flame of sacrifice, that this constant movement will find rest.

त्वमग्ने प्रथमो अङ्गिरा ऋषिर्देवो देवानामभवः शिवः सखा।
तव व्रते कवयो विद्मनापसोऽजायन्त मरुतो भ्राजदृष्टयः ॥

tvamagne prathamo aṅgirā ṛṣirdevo
devānāmabhavaḥ śivaḥ sakhā
tava vrate kavayo vidmanāpaso-
jāyanta maruto bhrājadṛṣṭayaḥ

You, Oh Divine Light of Meditation, are the first among the performers of spiritual discipline, a Seer, a God; your name became one with all the Gods. You are the friend of Śiva, the Consciousness of Infinite Goodness. Through devotion to you, all the inspired poets (Ṛṣis who propound Vedic Knowledge, or Wisdom of Universality) come to Divine Knowledge, as did the Maruts (the 49 Gods of severe penance) did come forth from your worship.

त्वं मुखं सर्वदेवानां सप्तार्चिर्हविरद्मते ।
आगच्छ भगवनग्ने यज्ञेऽस्मिन् सन्निधा भव ॥

tvaṁ mukhaṁ sarvadevānāṁ saptārcirhaviradmate
āgaccha bhagavanagne yajñe-smin sannidhā bhava
You are the mouth of all the Gods, with your seven tongues you accept the offerings. Come here, Oh Lord Divine Fire, and take your seat in the midst of our sacrifice.

ॐ वैश्वानर जातवेद इहावह लोहिताक्ष सर्व कर्माणि
साधय स्वाहा ॥

oṁ vaiśvānara jātaveda ihāvaha lohitākṣa sarva karmāṇi sādhaya svāhā
oṁ Oh Universal Being, Knower of All, come here with your red eyes. All of our Karma burn it! I AM ONE WITH GOD!

ॐ अग्नीमिळे पुरोहितं यज्ञस्य देवमृत्विजम् ।
होतारं रत्न धातमम् ॥

oṁ agnīmiḷe purohitaṁ yajñasya devamṛtvijam
hotāraṁ ratna dhātamam
Oh Agni, Light of Meditation, you are the Priest of Sacrifice, serving the offering of the divine nectar of Immortality. You give jewels to those who offer.

ॐ अग्नि प्रज्वलितं वन्दे जातवेदं हुताशनम् ।
सुवर्णवर्णममलं समिद्धं विश्वतो मुखम्

oṁ agni prajvalitaṁ vande jātavedaṁ hutāśanam
suvarṇavarṇamamalaṁ samiddhaṁ viśvato mukham
We lovingly adore the Divine Fire, Light of Meditation, sparkling, flaming brightly, knower of all, recipient of our offerings. With His excellent golden color, everywhere His omnipresent mouths are devouring oblations.

ॐ अग्नये नमः

oṁ agnaye namaḥ
oṁ We bow to the Divine Fire.

अग्ने त्वं चण्डिकानामसि

agne tvaṁ caṇḍikānāmasi
Oh Divine Fire, we are now calling you by the name Caṇḍi, She who Tears Apart Thoughts.

ॐ वागीश्वरी मृतुस्नातां नीलेन्दीवरलोचनाम् ।
वागीश्वरेण संयुक्तां क्रीडाभाव समन्विताम् ॥

oṁ vāgīśvarī mṛtu-snātāṁ nīlendīvaralocanām
vāgīśvareṇa saṁyuktaṁ krīḍābhāva samanvitam
The Supreme Goddess of Speech, dear Mother Saraswati, has just completed Her bath following Her monthly course of menstruation. With eyes of blue, bestowing boons, She moves into union with Vāgīṣvara, Brahma, the Lord of All Vibrations, and together they create the bhāva or intensity of reality, the attitude which unites all.

एते गन्धपुष्पे ॐ ह्रीं वागीश्वर्यै नमः

ete gandhapuṣpe oṁ hrīṁ vāgīśvaryai namaḥ
With these scented flowers oṁ we bow to the Supreme Goddess of Speech, or all Vibrations.

एते गन्धपुष्पे ॐ ह्रीं वागीश्वराय नमः

ete gandhapuṣpe oṁ hrīṁ vāgīśvarāya namaḥ
With these scented flowers oṁ we bow to the Supreme Lord of Speech, or all Vibrations.

एते गन्धपुष्पे ॐ अग्नेर्हिरण्यादि सप्तजिह्वाभ्यो नमः

ete gandhapuṣpe oṁ agnerhiraṇyādi saptajihvābhyo namaḥ

With these scented flowers oṁ we bow to the seven tongues of the Divine Fire, like golden, etc.

1. Kālī	Black
2. Karālī	Increasing, formidable
3. Mano-javā	Swift as thought
4. Su-Lohitā	Excellent shine
5. Sudhūmra-Varnā	Purple
6. Ugrā or Sphuliṅgīnī	Fearful
7. Pradīptā	Giving light

एते गन्धपुष्पे ॐ सहस्रार्चिषे हृदयाय नमः

ete gandhapuṣpe oṁ sahasrārciṣe hṛdayāya namaḥ

With these scented flowers oṁ we bow to the heart from which emanates a thousand rays.

इत्याद्यग्ने षदङ्गेभ्यो नमः

ityādyagne ṣadaṅgebhyo namaḥ

In this way establish the Divine Fire in the six centers of the body.

एते गन्धपुष्पे ॐ अग्नये जातवेदसे इत्यद्याष्टमूर्त्तिभ्यो नमः

ete gandhapuṣpe oṁ agnaye jātavedase ityadyaṣṭa mūrttibhyo namaḥ

With these scented flowers oṁ we bow to the Divine Fire, the Knower of All, etc, in His eight forms for worship.

1. Jāta-Veda	Knower of All
2. Sapta-Jihva	Seven tongued
3. Vaiśvānara	Universal Being
4. Havyā-Vāhana	Carrier of Oblations
5. Aśwodara-Ja	Fire of Stomach, lower areas
6. Kaumāra Tejaḥ	From which the son of Śiva is born
7. Viśva-Mukha	Which can devour the universe
8. Deva-Mukha	The mouth of the Gods

एते गन्धपुष्पे ॐ ब्राह्म्यद्यष्टशक्तिभ्यो नमः

ete gandhapuṣpe oṁ brāhmyadyaṣṭaśaktibhyo namaḥ

With these scented flowers oṁ we bow to the eight Śaktis or Energies, like Brāhmī, etc.

1. Brāhmī	Creative Energy
2. Nārāyaṇī	Exposer of Consciousness
3. Māheśvarī	Energy of the Seer of All
4. Cāmuṇḍā	Slayer of Passion & Meanness
5. Kaumārī	The Ever Pure One
6. Aparājitā	The Unconquerable
7. Vārāhī	The Boar of Sacrifice
8. Nārasiṁhī	The Man-lion of Courage

एते गन्धपुष्पे ॐ पद्माद्यष्टनिधिभ्यो नमः

ete gandhapuṣpe oṁ padmādyaṣṭa nidhibhyo namaḥ

With these scented flowers oṁ we bow to the eight Treasures of the Lord of Wealth, like Padma, etc.

1. Padma	The lotus of Peace
2. Mahā-Padma	The great lotus of universal Peace
3. Śaṅkha	The conch of all vibrations
4. Makara	The emblem of Love
5. Kacchapa	Tortoise, the emblem of support
6. Mukunda	The Crest gem
7. Nanda	Bliss
8. Nīla	The blue light within like a Sapphire

एते गन्धपुष्पे ॐ इन्द्रादि लोकपालेभ्यो नमः

ete gandhapuṣpe oṁ indrādi lokapālebhyo namaḥ

With these scented flowers oṁ we bow to Indra and the Protectors of the Ten Directions.

1. Indra	East
2. Agni	South-East
3. Yama	South
4. Nairrita	South-West
5. Varuṇa	West
6. Vāyu	North-West
7. Kuvera (Soma)	North
8. Īśāna	North-East
9. Brahmā	Above
10. Viṣṇu (Ananta)	Below

एते गन्धपुष्पे ॐ वज्राद्यस्त्रेभ्यो नमः

ete gandhapuṣpe oṁ vajrādyastrebhyo namaḥ

With these scented flowers oṁ we bow to the Thunderbolt and other weapons.

1. Vajra	Indra's thunderbolt
2. Śakti	Agni's spear, dart, energy
3. Daṇḍa	Yama's staff
4. Khaḍga	Nairrita's sword
5. Pāśa	Varuṇa's net or noose
6. Aṅkuśa	Vāyu's hook
7. Gadā	Kuvera's mace
8. Triśūla	Īśāna's trident
9. Padma or Kamaṇḍelu	Brahma's lotus or begging bowl
10. Cakra	Viṣṇu's discus

एते गन्धपुष्पे ॐ वह्निचैतन्याय नमः

ete gandhapuṣpe oṁ vahni caintanyāya namaḥ

With these scented flowers oṁ we bow to the Consciousness of the Divine Fire.

एते गन्धपुष्पे ॐ अग्नि मूर्त्तये नमः

ete gandhapuṣpe oṁ agni mūrttaye namaḥ

With these scented flowers oṁ we bow to the Image of the Divine Fire, the Light of Meditation.

ॐ अग्नये नमः

oṁ agnaye namaḥ

oṁ we bow to the Divine Fire.

रं रं रं रं रं

raṁ raṁ raṁ raṁ raṁ

R The Subtle Body; a Consciousness ; ṁ Perfection
Raṁ The manifestation of Perfection in the Subtle Body of Consciousness.

japa

mātṛkā pūjā

worship of gaṇeśa and the sixteen mothers

समीपे मातृवर्गस्य सर्वविघ्नहरं सदा ।
त्रैलोक्य वन्दितं देवं गणेशं स्थापयाम्यहम् ॥

samīpe mātṛvargasya sarvavighnaharaṁ sadā
trailokya vanditaṁ devaṁ gaṇeśaṁ sthāpayāmyaham

Situated before the group of Mothers, He always removes all obstacles. He is the God praised by all the Three worlds; I establish Gaṇeśa, the Lord of Wisdom.

ॐ भूर्भुवः स्वः गणपतये नमः । गणपतिमावाहयामि स्थापयामि ॥

oṁ bhūrbhuvaḥ svaḥ gaṇapataye namaḥ
gaṇapatimāvāhayāmi sthāpayāmi

Oṁ the Infinite Beyond Conception, the gross body, the subtle body and the causal body. I bow to Gaṇeśa. I invite Gaṇeśa and establish Him within.

हेमाद्रितनयां देवीं वरदां शङ्करप्रियाम् ।
लम्बोदरस्य जननीं गौरीमावाहयाम्यहम् ॥

hemādritanayāṁ devīṁ varadāṁ śaṅkarapriyām
lambodarasya jananīṁ gaurīmāvāhayāmyaham

The Goddess is the daughter of the snowy mountain, She gives boons and is the beloved of Śiva. With a big stomach, She is the Mother (of existence). I invite Gaurī, She who is Rays of Light.

ॐ भूर्भुवः स्वः गौर्यै नमः । गौरीमावाहयामि स्थापयामि ॥

oṁ bhūrbhuvaḥ svaḥ gauryai namaḥ
gaurīmāvāhayāmi sthāpayāmi

Oṁ the Infinite Beyond Conception, the gross body, the subtle body and the causal body. I bow to Gaurī. I invite Gaurī and establish Her within.

पद्माभां पद्मवदनां पद्मनाभोरुसंस्थिताम् ।
जगत्प्रियां पद्मवासां पद्मामावाहयाम्यहम् ॥

padmābhāṁ padmavadanāṁ padmanābhorusaṁsthitām
jagatpriyāṁ padmavāsāṁ padmāmāvāhayāmyaham
Favorable as a lotus, with a lotus-like mouth, situated in the navel of a lotus. She is beloved of the universe, resident of the lotus. I invite Padma, She who is the Lotus (the wealth of Peace and Love).

ॐ पद्मायै नमः पद्मामावाहयामि स्थापयामि ॥

oṁ padmāyai namaḥ padmāmāvāhayāmi sthāpayāmi
Oṁ I bow to Padma. I invite Padma and establish Her within.

दिव्यरूपां विशालाक्षीं शुचि कुण्डल धारिणीम् ।
रक्तमुक्ताद्यलङ्कारां शचीमावाहयाम्यहम् ॥

divyarūpāṁ viśālākṣīṁ śuci kuṇḍala dhāriṇīm
raktamuktādyalaṅkārāṁ śacīmāvāhayāmyaham
The form of divinity, the goal of the universe, She wears earrings, which shine with purity. Her ornaments are of red pearls. I invite Śacī, the Goddess of Purity.

ॐ शच्ये नमः शचीमावाहयामि स्थापयामि ॥

oṁ śacye namaḥ śacīmāvāhayāmi sthāpayāmi
Oṁ I bow to Śacī. I invite Śacī and establish Her within.

विश्वेऽस्मिन् भूरिवरदां जरां निर्जरसेविताम् ।
बुद्धिप्रबोधिनीं सौम्यां मेधामावाहयाम्यहम् ॥

viśve-smin bhūrivaradāṁ jarāṁ nirjarasevitām
buddhiprabodhinīṁ saumyāṁ medhāmāvāhayāmyaham
She gives boons to the aged of this universe, to the aged She gives the service of freedom from wasting away. To the Intellect She is known as the Beautiful. I invite Medhā, the Intellect of Love.

ॐ मेधायै नमः मेधामावाहयामि स्थापयामि ॥

oṁ medhāyai namaḥ medhāmāvāhayāmi sthāpayāmi
Oṁ I bow to Medhā. I invite Medhā and establish Her within.

जगत्सृष्टिकरीं धात्रीं देवीं प्रणवमातृकाम् ।
वेदगर्भां यज्ञमयीं सावित्रीं स्थापयाम्यहम् ॥

jagatsṛṣṭikarīṁ dhātrīṁ devīṁ praṇavamātṛkām
vedagarbhāṁ yajñamayīṁ sāvitrīṁ sthāpayāmyaham
She is the Goddess who is the Cause, the Giver of Birth to the perceivable universe, the Mother of the Praṇava, oṁ. The Vedas came from Her womb. She is sacrifice incarnate. I establish Sāvitrī, the Goddess of the Light.

ॐ सावित्र्यै नमः सावित्रीमावाहयामि स्थापयामि ॥

oṁ sāvitryai namaḥ sāvitrīmāvāhayāmi sthāpayāmi
Oṁ I bow to Sāvitrī. I invite Sāvitrī and establish Her within.

सर्वास्त्रधारिणीं देवीं सर्वाभरणभूषिताम् ।
सर्वदेवस्तुतां वन्द्यां विजयां स्थापयाम्यहम् ॥

sarvāstradhāriṇīṁ devīṁ sarvābharaṇabhūṣitām
sarvadevastutāṁ vandyāṁ vijayāṁ sthāpayāmyaham
She is the Goddess who holds all weapons, and She shines with all ornaments. All the Gods sing Her praises and hymns. I establish Vijayā, the Goddess of Victory.

ॐ विजयायै नमः विजयामावाहयामि स्थापयामि ॥

oṁ vijayāyai namaḥ vijayāmāvāhayāmi sthāpayāmi
Oṁ I bow to Vijayā. I invite Vijayā and establish Her within.

सुरारिमथिनीं देवीं देवानामभयप्रदाम् ।
त्रैलोक्य वन्दितां शुभ्रां जयामावाहयाम्यहम् ॥

surārimathinīṁ devīṁ devānāmabhayapradām
trailokya vanditāṁ śubhrāṁ jayāmāvāhayāmyaham

She is the Goddess who is the staff of the Gods, whose name removes fear from the Gods. She is the manifestation of excellence who is praised in the three worlds. I invite Jayā, Conquest.

ॐ जयायै नमः जयामावाहयामि स्थापयामि ॥

oṁ jayāyai namaḥ jayāmāvāhayāmi sthāpayāmi
Oṁ I bow to Jayā. I invite Jayā and establish Her within.

मयूरवाहनां देवीं कड्ग-शक्ति-धनुर्धराम् ।
आवाहयेद् देवसेनां तारकासुरमर्दिनीम् ॥

mayūravāhanāṁ devīṁ kaḍga-śakti-dhanurdharām
āvāhayed devasenāṁ tārakāsuramardinīm
She is the Goddess who rides upon a peacock, holding aloft a sword, energy and a bow. I invite the Commander of the forces of the Gods, the Slayer of Tārakāsura, the Illuminator of Duality.

ॐ देवसेनायै नमः देवसेनामावाहयामि स्थापयामि ॥

oṁ devasenāyai namaḥ devasenāmāvāhayāmi sthāpayāmi
Oṁ I bow to the Commander of the forces of the Gods. I invite the commander of the forces of the Gods and establish Her within.

अग्रजा सर्वदेवानां कव्यार्थं या प्रतिष्टिता ।
पितॄणां तृप्तिदां देवीं स्वधामावाहयाम्यहम् ॥

agrajā sarvadevānāṁ kavyārthaṁ yā pratiṣṭitā
pitṝṇāṁ tṛptidāṁ devīṁ svadhāmāvāhayāmyaham
She is the first born of all the Gods, and was established first by the ancient poets. She is the Goddess who gives pleasure to the ancestors. I invite Svadhā, One's own Giving.

ॐ स्वधायै नमः स्वधामावाहयामि स्थापयामि ॥

oṁ svadhāyai namaḥ svadhāmāvāhayāmi sthāpayāmi
Oṁ I bow to Svadhā. I invite Svadhā and establish Her within.

हविर्गृत्वा महादत्ता देवेभ्यो या प्रयच्छति ।
तां दिव्यरूपां वरदां स्वाहामावाहयाम्यहम् ॥

havirgṛtvā mahādattā devebhyo yā prayacchati
tāṁ divyarūpāṁ varadāṁ svāhāmāvāhayāmyaham
The Great Giver of oblations with ghee, which are essential for the Gods. You give blessings in the form of divinity. I invite Svāhā, I am One with God!

ॐ स्वाहायै नमः स्वाहामावाहयामि स्थापयामि ॥

oṁ svāhāyai namaḥ svāhāmāvāhayāmi sthāpayāmi
Oṁ I bow to Svāhā. I invite Svāhā and establish Her within.

आवाहयाम्यहम् मातृः सकलाः लोकपूजिताः ।
सर्वकल्याणरूपिण्यो वरदा दिव्यभूषणाः ॥

āvāhayāmyaham mātṝḥ sakalāḥ lokapūjitāḥ
sarvakalyāṇarūpiṇyo varadā divyabhūṣaṇāḥ
I invite the Mother who is worshipped throughout the three worlds. She is the form of all welfare, and She gives blessings that shine with divinity.

ॐ मातृभ्यो नमः मातृः आवाहयामि स्थापयामि ॥

oṁ mātṛbhyo namaḥ mātṝḥ āvāhayāmi sthāpayāmi
Oṁ I bow to the Mothers. I invite the Mothers and establish them within.

आवाहयेल्लोकमातृर्जयन्तीप्रमुखाः शुभाः ।
नानाऽभीष्टप्रदाः शान्ताः सर्वलोकहितावहाः ॥

āvāhayellokamātṝrjayantīpramukhāḥ śubhāḥ
nānā-bhīṣṭapradāḥ śāntāḥ sarvalokahitāvahāḥ
I invite the Mothers of the Universe, who shine before every Victory! They give various kinds of supremacy and peace, and invite the joy of all the worlds.

ॐ लोकमातृभ्यो नमः लोकमातॄः आवाहयामि
स्थापयामि ॥

oṁ lokamātṛbhyo namaḥ lokamātṝḥ āvāhayāmi sthāpayāmi
Oṁ I bow to the Mothers of the Universe. I invite the Mothers of the Universe and establish them within.

सर्वहर्षकरीं देवीं भाक्तानामभयप्रदाम् ।
हर्षोत्फुल्लास्यकमलां धृतिमावाहयाम्यहम् ॥

sarvaharṣakarīṁ devīṁ bhāktānāmabhayapradām harṣotphullāsyakamalāṁ dhṛtimāvāhayāmyaham
The Goddess is the Cause of all gladness. To devotees who take Her name She grants freedom from fear. She is the blossom of the lotus of Gladness. I invite Dhṛti, Constancy.

ॐ धृत्यै नमः धृतिमावाहयामि स्थापयामि ॥

oṁ dhṛtyai namaḥ dhṛtimāvāhayāmi sthāpayāmi
Oṁ I bow to Dhṛti. I invite Dhṛti and establish Her within.

पोषयन्तीं जगत्सर्वं स्वदेहप्रभवैर्नवैः ।
शाकैः फलैर्जलैरत्नैः पुष्टिमावाहयाम्यहम् ॥

poṣayantīṁ jagatsarvaṁ svadehaprabhavairnavaiḥ śākaiḥ phalairjalairatnaiḥ puṣṭimāvāhayāmyaham
She who gives prosperity (abundance) to the entire universe, bringing forth from Her own body vegetables, fruits, water and gems. I invite Puṣṭi, Increase.

ॐ पुष्ट्यै नमः पुष्टिमावाहयामि स्थापयामि ॥

oṁ puṣṭyai namaḥ puṣṭimāvāhayāmi sthāpayāmi
Oṁ I bow to Puṣṭi. I invite Puṣṭi and establish Her within.

देवैराराधितां देवीं सदा सन्तोषकारिणीम् ।
प्रसादसुमुखीं देवीं तुष्टिमावाहयाम्यहम् ॥

devairārādhitāṁ devīṁ sadā santoṣakāriṇīm
prasādasumukhīṁ devīṁ tuṣṭimāvāhayāmyaham
She is the Goddess who pleases the Gods, always the cause of satisfaction. From the excellent face of the Goddess comes blessings. I invite Tuṣṭi, Satisfaction.

ॐ तुष्ट्यै नमः तुष्टिमावाहयामि स्थापयामि ॥

oṁ tuṣṭyai namaḥ tuṣṭimāvāhayāmi sthāpayāmi
Oṁ I bow to Tuṣṭi. I invite Tuṣṭi and establish Her within.

पत्तने नगरे ग्रामे विपिने पर्वते गृहे ।
नानाजातिकुलेशानीं दुर्गामावाहयाम्यहम् ॥

pattane nagare grāme vipine parvate gṛhe
nānājātikuleśānīṁ durgāmāvāhayāmyaham
In the air, in the city, in the village, in the woods, on the mountains, in a house, She is the Supreme Ruler of the family in various forms of birth. I invite Durgā, the Reliver of Difficulties.

ॐ आत्मनः कुलदेवतायै नमः आत्मनः
कुलदेवतामावाहयामि स्थापयामि ॥

oṁ ātmanaḥ kuladevatāyai namaḥ ātmanaḥ
kuladevatāmāvāhayāmi sthāpayāmi
Oṁ I bow to the soul who is the Goddess of the Family. I invite the soul who is the Goddess of the Family and establish Her within.

ॐ गौरी पद्मा शची मेधा सावित्री विजया जया ।
देवसेना स्वधा स्वाहा मातरो लोकमातरः ॥

oṁ gaurī padmā śacī medhā sāvitrī vijayā jayā
devasenā svadhā svāhā mātaro lokamātaraḥ
Oṁ Gaurī, Padmā, Śacī, Medhā, Sāvitrī, Vijayā, Jayā; Devasenā, Svadhā, Svāhā, Mātaro, Lokamātaraḥ,

धृतिः पुष्टिस्तथा तुष्टिः आत्मनः कुलदेवताः ।
गणेशेनाधिका ह्येता वृद्धौ पूज्यास्तु षौडश ॥

dhṛtiḥ puṣṭistathā tuṣṭiḥ ātmanaḥ kuladevatāḥ
gaṇeśenādhikā hyetā vṛddhau pūjyāstu ṣauḍaśa
Dhṛti, Puṣṭi and then Tuṣṭi, and the soul who is the Goddess of the Family; with Gaṇeśa situated before, we make worship of the sixteen.

आयुरारोग्यमैश्वर्यं ददध्वं मातरो मम ।
निर्विघ्नं सर्वकार्येषु कुरुध्वं सगणाधिपाः ॥

āyurārogyamaiśvaryaṁ dadadhvaṁ mātaro mama
nirvighnaṁ sarvakāryeṣu kurudhvaṁ sagaṇādhipāḥ
Give us life and freedom from disease, imperishable qualities, oh my Mothers. Make all desired effects free from obstacles with your multitudes.

ॐ गणपत्यादि कुलदेवतान्त मातृभ्यो नमः ॥

oṁ gaṇapatyādi kuladevatānta mātṛbhyo namaḥ
Oṁ I bow to Gaṇeśa and the other members of the family of Goddesses and Mothers.

nava durgā pūjā (1)
worship of the nine forms of durgā (1)

ॐ भूर्भुवः स्वः शैलपुत्रि इहा गच्छ इहतिष्ठ शैलपुत्र्यै नमः ।
शैलपुत्रीमावाहयामि स्थापयामि नमः ।
पाध्यादिभिः पूजनम्बिधाय ॥

oṁ bhūrbhuvaḥ svaḥ śailaputri ihā gaccha ihatiṣṭa śailaputryai namaḥ śailputrīmāvāhayāmi sthāpayāmi namaḥ pādhyādibhiḥ pūjanambidhāya

Oṁ the Infinite Beyond Conception, the gross body, the subtle body and the causal body. Goddess of Inspiration, come here, stay here. I bow to the Goddess of Inspiration. I invite the Goddess of Inspiration and establish Her within. You are being worshipped with water for washing your feet.

ॐ जगत्पूज्ये जगद्वन्ध्ये सर्वशक्ति स्वरूपिणि ।
पूजां गृहाण कौमारि जगन्मातर्नमोऽस्तु ते ॥

oṁ jagatpūjye jagadvandhye sarvaśakti svarūpiṇi pūjāṁ gṛhāṇa kaumāri jaganmātarnamo-stu te

Oṁ You are worshipped in the world, praised in the world, as the intrinsic nature of all energy. Oh Ever Pure One, please accept this worship. We bow to you, oh Mother of the universe.

ॐ भूर्भुवः स्वः ब्रह्मचारिणि इहा गच्छ इहतिष्ठ ब्रह्मचारिण्यै नमः । ब्रह्मचारिणीमावाहयामि स्थापयामि नमः ।
पाध्यादिभिः पूजनम्बिधाय ॥

oṁ bhūrbhuvaḥ svaḥ brahmacāriṇi ihā gaccha ihatiṣṭa brahmacāriṇyai namaḥ brahmacāriṇīmāvāhayāmi sthāpayāmi namaḥ pādhyādibhiḥ pūjanambidhāya

Oṁ the Infinite Beyond Conception, the gross body, the subtle body and the causal body. Goddess of Learning, come here, stay here. I bow to the Goddess of Learning. I invite the Goddess of Learning and establish Her within. You are being worshipped with water for washing your feet.

ॐ त्रिपुरां त्रिगुणाधारां मार्गज्ञान स्वरूपिणीम् ।
त्रैलोक्य वन्दितां देवीं त्रिमुर्तिं पूजयाम्यहम् ॥

oṁ tripurāṁ triguṇādhārāṁ mārgajñāna svarūpiṇīm
trailokya vanditāṁ devīṁ trimurtiṁ pūjayāmyaham
Oṁ You are the residence of the three cities, the support of the three guṇas, the intrinsic nature of the road to Wisdom. The Goddess who is praised in the three worlds, oh Image of the Three, I am worshipping you.

ॐ भूर्भुवः स्वः चन्द्रघंटे इहा गच्छ इहतिष्ट चन्द्रघंटायै नमः । चन्द्रघंटामावाहयामि स्थापयामि नमः ।
पाध्यादिभिः पूजनम्बिधाय ॥

oṁ bhūrbhuvaḥ svaḥ caṇdraghaṇṭe ihā gaccha ihatiṣṭa candraghaṇṭāyai namaḥ candraghaṇṭāmāvāhayāmi sthāpayāmi namaḥ pādhyādibhiḥ pūjanambidhāya
Oṁ the Infinite Beyond Conception, the gross body, the subtle body and the causal body. Goddess of Practice, come here, stay here. I bow to the Goddess of Practice. I invite the Goddess of Practice and establish Her within. You are being worshipped with water for washing your feet.

ॐ कालिकां तु कलातीतां कल्याण ह्रिदयां शिवाम् ।
कल्याण जननीं नित्यं कल्याणीं पूजयाम्यहम् ॥

oṁ kālikāṁ tu kalātītāṁ kalyāṇa hridayāṁ śivām
kalyāṇa jananīṁ nityaṁ kalyāṇīṁ pūjayāmyaham
Oṁ You divide Time, but remain beyond division, Welfare in the heart of Lord Śiva. Always grant Welfare, oh Divine Mother, I worship the Goddess of Welfare.

ॐ भूर्भुवः स्वः कुष्माण्ड इहा गच्छ इहतिष्ट कुष्माण्डायै नमः। कुष्माण्डामावाहयामि स्थापयामि नमः। पाध्यादिभिः पूजनम्बिधाय ॥

oṁ bhūrbhuvaḥ svaḥ kuṣmāṇḍa ihā gaccha ihatiṣṭa kuṣmāṇḍāyai namaḥ kuṣmāṇḍāmāvāhayāmi sthāpayāmi namaḥ pādhyādibhiḥ pūjanambidhāya
Oṁ the Infinite Beyond Conception, the gross body, the subtle body and the causal body. Goddess of Refinement, come here, stay here. I bow to the Goddess of Refinement. I invite the Goddess of Refinement and establish Her within. You are being worshipped with water for washing your feet.

ॐ अणिमादि गुणोदारां मकराकार चक्षुसम्।
अनन्त शक्ति भेदां तां कामाक्षीं पूजयाम्यहम् ॥

oṁ aṇimādi guṇodārāṁ makarākāra cakṣusam
ananta śakti bhedāṁ tāṁ kāmākṣīṁ pūjayāmyaham
Oṁ You give rise to the qualities of every atom, the eyes that perceive all form. You distinguish the infinite energy, oh Eyes of Desire, I am worshipping you.

ॐ भूर्भुवः स्वः स्कन्दमातः इहा गच्छ इहतिष्ट स्कन्दमात्रे नमः। स्कन्दमातरमावाहयामि स्थापयामि नमः। पाध्यादिभिः पूजनम्बिधाय ॥

oṁ bhūrbhuvaḥ svaḥ skandamātaḥ ihā gaccha ihatiṣṭa skandamātre namaḥ skandamātaramāvāhayāmi sthāpayāmi namaḥ pādhyādibhiḥ pūjanambidhāya
Oṁ the Infinite Beyond Conception, the gross body, the subtle body and the causal body. Goddess who Nurtures Divinity, come here, stay here. I bow to the Goddess who Nurtures Divinity. I invite the Goddess who Nurtures Divinity and establish Her within. You are being worshipped with water for washing your feet.

ॐ चण्डवीरां चण्डमायां चण्डमुण्ड प्रभञ्जनीम् ।
तां नमामि च देवेशीं चण्डिकां पूजयाम्यहम् ॥

oṁ caṇḍavīrāṁ caṇḍamāyāṁ
caṇḍamuṇḍa prabhañjanīm
tāṁ namāmi ca deveśīṁ caṇḍikāṁ pūjayāmyaham

Oṁ you are the warrior against anger, the limitation of anger, the stupidity of anger you cut asunder. I bow to Her, the Supreme Goddess, I worship She who Tears Apart Thoughts.

ॐ भूर्भुवः स्वः कात्यायनि इहा गच्छ इहतिष्ट कात्यायन्यै नमः । कात्यायनीमावाहयामि स्थापयामि नमः ।
पाध्यादिभिः पूजनम्बिधाय ॥

oṁ bhūrbhuvaḥ svaḥ kātyāyani ihā gaccha ihatiṣṭa
kātyāyanyai namaḥ kātyāyanīmāvāhayāmi sthāpayāmi
namaḥ pādhyādibhiḥ pūjanambidhāya

Oṁ the Infinite Beyond Conception, the gross body, the subtle body and the causal body. Goddess who is Ever Pure, come here, stay here. I bow to the Goddess who is Ever Pure. I invite the Goddess who is Ever Pure and establish Her within. You are being worshipped with water for washing your feet.

ॐ सुखानन्द करीं शान्तां सर्व देवैर्नमस्कृताम् ।
सर्व भूतात्मिकां देवीं शाम्भवीं पूजयाम्यहम् ॥

oṁ sukhānanda karīṁ śāntāṁ
sarva devairnamaskṛtām
sarva bhūtātmikāṁ devīṁ
śāmbhavīṁ pūjayāmyaham

Oṁ the Bliss of happiness, Cause of Peace, all the Gods continually bow to you. You are the soul of all existence, oh Goddess, you who belong to Śiva, I worship you.

ॐ भूर्भुवः स्वः कालरात्रि इहा गच्छ इहतिष्ट कालरात्र्यै नमः । कालरात्रीमावाहयामि स्थापयामि नमः । पाध्यादिभिः पूजनम्बिधाय ॥

oṁ bhūrbhuvaḥ svaḥ kālarātri ihā gaccha ihatiṣṭa kālarātryai namaḥ kālarātrīmāvāhayāmi sthāpayāmi namaḥ pādhyādibhiḥ pūjanambidhāya

Oṁ the Infinite Beyond Conception, the gross body, the subtle body and the causal body. Dark Night (surrendering the ego), come here, stay here. I bow to the Dark Night. I invite the Dark Night and establish Her within. You are being worshipped with water for washing your feet.

ॐ चण्डवीरां चण्डमायां रक्तबीज प्रभञ्जनीम् ।
तां नमामि च देवेशीं गायत्रीं पूजयाम्यहम् ॥

oṁ caṇḍavīrāṁ caṇḍamāyāṁ
raktabīja prabhañjanīm
tāṁ namāmi ca deveśīṁ gāyatrīṁ pūjayāmyaham

Oṁ you are the warrior against anger, the limitation of anger, you cut asunder the Seed of Desire. I bow to Her, the Supreme Goddess. I worship Gāyatrī, the three forms of wisdom.

ॐ भूर्भुवः स्वः महागौरि इहा गच्छ इहतिष्ट महागौर्यै नमः । महागौरीमावाहयामि स्थापयामि नमः । पाध्यादिभिः पूजनम्बिधाय ॥

oṁ bhūrbhuvaḥ svaḥ mahāgauri ihā gaccha ihatiṣṭa mahāgauryai namaḥ mahāgaurīmāvāhayāmi sthāpayāmi namaḥ pādhyādibhiḥ pūjanambidhāya

Oṁ the Infinite Beyond Conception, the gross body, the subtle body and the causal body. The Great Radiant Light, come here, stay here. I bow to the Great Radiant Light. I invite the Great Radiant Light and establish Her within. You are being worshipped with water for washing your feet.

ॐ सुन्दरीं स्वर्णवर्णाङ्गीं सुख सौभाग्यदायिनीम्।
सन्तोष जननीं देवीं सुभद्रां पूजयाम्यहम्॥

oṁ sundarīṁ svarṇavarṇāṅgīṁ
sukha saubhāgyadāyinīm
santoṣa jananīṁ devīṁ subhadrāṁ pūjayāmyaham

Oṁ Beautiful with a golden-colored body, bestower of happiness and beauty. Oh Mother of the Universe, the Goddess of Contentment, I worship the Excellent of excellence.

ॐ भूर्भुवः स्वः सिद्धिदे इहा गच्छ इहतिष्ट सिद्धिदायै नमः।
सिद्धिदामावाहयामि स्थापयामि नमः। पाध्यादिभिः
पूजनम्बिधाय॥

oṁ bhūrbhuvaḥ svaḥ siddhide ihā gaccha ihatiṣṭa
siddhidāyai namaḥ siddhidāmāvāhayāmi sthāpayāmi
namaḥ pādhyādibhiḥ pūjanambidhāya

Oṁ the Infinite Beyond Conception, the gross body, the subtle body and the causal body. The Grantor of Perfection, come here, stay here. I bow to the Grantor of Perfection. I invite the Grantor of Perfection and establish Her within. You are being worshipped with water for washing your feet.

ॐ दुर्गमे दुस्तरेकार्ये भयदुर्ग विनाशिनि।
पूजयामि सदा भक्त्या दुर्गां दुर्गतिनाशिनीम्॥

oṁ durgame dustarekārye bhayadurga vināśini
pūjayāmi sadā bhaktyā durgāṁ durgatināśinīm

Oṁ You are the Destroyer of fear from difficulties for me, from the effects of wickedness. I always worship with devotion the Reliever of Difficulties, who destroys all difficulties.

ॐ प्रथमं शैलपुत्री च द्वितीयं ब्रह्मचारिणी।
तृतीयं चन्द्रघण्टेति कूष्माण्डेति चतुर्थकम्॥

oṁ prathamaṁ śailaputrī ca dvitīyaṁ brahmacāriṇī
tṛtīyaṁ candraghaṇṭeti kūṣmāṇḍeti caturthakam

Oṁ First is the Goddess of Inspiration, and second the Goddess of Learning; third is the Goddess of Practice, the Goddess of Refinement is fourth.

पञ्चमं स्कन्दमातेति षष्ठं कात्यायनीति च ।
सप्तमं कालरात्रीति महागौरीति चाष्टमम् ॥

pañcamaṁ skandamāteti ṣaṣṭhaṁ kātyāyanīti ca
saptamaṁ kālarātrīti mahāgaurīti cāṣṭamam

Fifth is the Goddess who Nurtures Divinity, sixth is the One Who is Ever Pure; seventh is the Goddess of the Dark Night of Surrendering the Ego, the Goddess of the Great Radiant Light is eighth.

नवमं सिद्धिदात्री च नवदुर्गाः प्रकीर्तिताः ।
उक्तान्येतानि नामानि ब्रह्मणैव महात्मना ॥

navamaṁ siddhidātrī ca navadurgāḥ prakīrtitāḥ
uktānyetāni nāmāni brahmaṇaiva mahātmanā

Ninth is the Goddess who Grants Perfection. The nine Durgās, Relievers of Difficulties, have been enumerated, and these names have been revealed by the great soul of the Supreme Himself.

श्री दुर्गायै नमः ॥

śrī durgāyai namaḥ

We bow to the Respected Reliever of Difficulties

nava patrikā pūjā

worship of the nine containers of divinity

ॐ दुर्गे देवि समागच्छ सान्निध्यमिह कल्पय ।
रम्भारूपेण सर्वत्र शान्तिं कुरु नमोऽस्तु ते ॥

oṁ durge devi samāgaccha sānnidhyamiha kalpaya
rambhārūpeṇa sarvatra śāntiṁ kuru namo-stu te

Oṁ Oh Goddess Durgā, come here and reside in my thoughts. In the form of beauty everywhere make peace. I bow to you.

ॐ रम्भाधिष्ठात्र्यै ब्रह्माण्यै नमः

oṁ rambhādhiṣṭhātryai brahmāṇyai namaḥ

Oṁ thus is sung a hymn to Beauty. I bow to the Creative Energy.

महिषासुरयुद्धेषु कच्वीभूतासि सुव्रते ।
मम चानुग्रहार्थाय आगतागि हरप्रिये ॥

mahiṣāsurayuddheṣu kacvībhūtāsi suvrate
mama cānugrahārthāya āgatāgi harapriye

In the battle with the Great Ego, you shined upon all existence, oh One of Excellent Vows. For the purpose of my advancement, come oh Beloved of God.

ॐ कच्व्यधिष्ठात्र्यै कालिकायै नमः

oṁ kacvyadhiṣṭhātryai kālikāyai namaḥ

Oṁ thus is sung a hymn to the Shining One. I bow to She who is Beyond Time.

हरिद्रे वरदे देवि उमारूपासि सुव्रते ।
मम विघ्नविनाशाय प्रसीद त्वं हरप्रिये ॥

haridre varade devi umārūpāsi suvrate
mama vighnavināśāya prasīda tvaṁ harapriye

Oh Goddess covered in tumeric, in the form of Umā you give boons, oh One of Excellent Vows. Destroy all of my obstacles. You be pleased, oh Beloved of God.

ॐ हरिद्राधिष्ठात्र्यै दुर्गायै नमः

oṁ haridrādhiṣṭhātryai durgāyai namaḥ

Oṁ thus is sung a hymn to the Goddess covered in tumeric. I bow to the Reliever of Difficulties.

निशुम्भशुम्भमथने सेन्द्रैर्दैवगणैः सह ।
जयन्ति पूजितासि त्वमस्माकं वरदा भव ॥

niśumbhaśumbhamathane sendrairdaivagaṇaiḥ saha
jayanti pūjitāsi tvamasmākaṁvaradā bhava

You destroy Self-Deprecation and Self-Conceit along with the multitude of the armies of the Gods. You are being worshipped along with those who are victorious. Give us boons.

ॐ जयन्त्याधिष्ठात्र्यै कौमार्यै नमः

oṁ jayantyādhiṣṭhātryai kaumāryai namaḥ

Oṁ thus is sung a hymn to the Goddess of Victory. I bow to the Ever Pure One.

महादेवप्रियकरो वासुदेवप्रियः सदा ।
उमाप्रीतिकरो वृक्षो बिल्वरूप नमोऽस्तु ते ॥

mahādevapriyakaro vāsudevapriyaḥ sadā
umāprītikaro vṛkṣo bilvarūpa namo-stu te

She is the beloved of Mahādeva (Śiva), and She is always beloved of Vāsudeva (Viṣṇu). Umā loves this tree. In the form of Bilva I bow to you.

ॐ बिल्वाधिष्ठात्र्यै शिवायै नमः

bilvādhiṣṭātryai śivāyai namaḥ

Oṁ thus is sung a hymn to the Bilva. I bow to Śivā (Divine Mother).

दाढिमि त्वः पुरा युद्धे रक्तबिजस्य सम्मुखे ।
उमाकार्यं कृतं यस्मात्तस्मात्तं रक्ष मां सदा ॥

dāḍhimi tvaḥ purā yuddhe raktabijasya sammukhe
umākāryaṁ kṛtaṁ yasmāttasmāttaṁ rakṣa māṁ sadā

You fought with the multitudes of Raktabijas facing you. In order to perform the work of Umā, always protect me.

ॐ दाडिम्यधिष्ठात्र्यै रक्तदन्तिकायै नमः

oṁ dāḍhimyadhiṣṭhātryai raktadantikāyai namaḥ
Oṁ thus is sung a hymn to the Multitudes. I bow to She with Red Teeth.

हरप्रीतिकरो वृक्षोह्यशोकः शोकनाशनः ।
दुर्गाप्रीतिकरो यस्मान्मामशोकं सदा कुरु ॥

haraprītikaro vṛkṣohyaśokaḥ śokanāśanaḥ
durgāprītikaro yasmānmāmaśokaṁ sadā kuru
Hara (Śiva) loves this tree, yesterday's grief and all grief it destroys. Durgā especially loves this, so make me eternally free from grief.

ॐ अशोकाधिष्ठात्र्यै शोकरहितायै नमः

oṁ aśokādhiṣṭhātryai śokarahitāyai namaḥ
Oṁ thus is sung a hymn to Freedom from Grief. I bow to She who makes us free from grief.

यस्य पत्रे वसेदेवी मानवृक्षः शचीप्रियः ।
मम चानुग्रहार्थाय पूजां गृह्व प्रसीद मे ॥

yasya patre vasedevī mānavṛkṣaḥ śacīpriyaḥ
mama cānugrahārthāya pūjāṁ gṛhva prasīda me
Upon this leaf from the tree of thought the Goddess sits, the beloved of Sacī (Indra's wife). For the purpose of my progress please accept my worship and be pleased with me.

ॐ मानाधिष्ठात्र्यै चामुण्डायै नमः

oṁ mānādhiṣṭhātryai cāmuṇḍāyai namaḥ
Oṁ thus is sung a hymn to Thoughts. I bow to She who moves in the paradigm of Consciousness.

जगतः प्राणरक्षार्थं ब्रह्मणा निर्मितं पुरा ।
उमाप्रीतिकरं धान्यं तस्मात्त्वं रक्ष मां सदा ॥

jagataḥ prāṇarakṣārthaṁ brahmaṇā nirmitaṁ purā
umāprītikaraṁ dhānyaṁ tasmāttvaṁ rakṣa māṁ sadā
This giving of wealth is beloved by Umā. It protects the life force of the perceivable universe and proves the validity of the Supreme Divinity. Please protect me always.

ॐ धान्याधिष्ठात्र्यै महालक्ष्म्यै नमः

oṁ dhānyādhiṣṭhātryai mahālakṣmyai namaḥ
Oṁ thus is sung a hymn to the Giving of Wealth. I bow to the Great Goddess of True Wealth.

nava durgā pūjā (2)

worship of the nine forms of durgā (2)

चतुर्मुखीं जगद्धात्रीं हंसरूढां वरप्रदाम् ।

सृष्टिरूपां महाभागां ब्रह्माणीं तां नमाम्यहम् ॥

caturmukhīṁ jagaddhātrīṁ haṁsarūḍhāṁ varapradām
sṛṣṭirūpāṁ mahābhāgāṁ brahmāṇīṁ tāṁ namāmyaham

She has four faces, the Progenitress of the Universe who rides upon a swan and grants boons. She is the form of creation, of great parts. We bow to Her, to Brahmāṇī.

ॐ ह्रीं श्रीं ब्रह्माण्यै नमः

oṁ hrīṁ śrīṁ brahmāṇyai namaḥ

Oṁ Māyā, Increase, I bow to the Creative Energy.

वृषारूढां शुभां शुभ्रां त्रिनेत्रां वरदां शिवाम् ।

माहेश्वरीं नमाम्यद्य सृष्टिसंहारकारिणीम् ॥

vṛṣārūḍhāṁ śubhāṁ śubhrāṁ
trinetrāṁ varadāṁ śivām
māheśvarīṁ namāmyadya sṛṣṭisaṁhārakāriṇīm

She rides upon a buffalo, shining radiantly, She is Śivā with three eyes and She grants boons. We bow to Māheśvarī, the Great Seer of All, who is the cause of the dissolution of the creation.

ॐ ह्रीं श्रीं माहेश्वर्यै नमः

oṁ hrīṁ śrīṁ māheśvaryai namaḥ

Oṁ Māyā, Increase, I bow to the Great Seer of All.

कौमारीं पीतवसनां मयूरवरवाहनाम् ।

शक्तिहस्तां महाभागां नमामि वरदां सदा ॥

kaumārīṁ pītavasanāṁ mayūravaravāhanām
śaktihastāṁ mahābhāgāṁ namāmi varadāṁ sadā

Kumārī, the Ever Pure One, is of a yellow color. She rides upon a peacock, with energy in Her hands, of great parts. I bow to She who always grants boons.

ॐ ह्रीं श्रीं कौमार्यै नमः

oṁ hrīṁ śrīṁ kaumāryai namaḥ
Oṁ Māyā, Increase, I bow to the Ever Pure One.

शङ्खचक्रगदापद्मधारिणीं कृष्णरूपिणीम् ।
स्थितिरूपां खगेन्द्रस्थां वैष्णवीं तां नमाम्यहम् ॥

śaṅkhacakragadāpadmadhāriṇīṁ kṛṣṇarūpiṇīm sthitirūpāṁ khagendrasthāṁ vaiṣṇavīṁ tāṁ namāmyaham
She holds the conch shell, discus, club and lotus. As the intrinsic nature of Kṛṣṇa, She is the form of Circumstances. Situated with the king of swords, She is Vaiṣṇavī, the Energy pervading all existence. We bow to Her.

ॐ ह्रीं श्रीं वैष्णव्यै नमः

oṁ hrīṁ śrīṁ vaiṣṇavyai namaḥ
Oṁ Māyā, Increase, I bow to the Energy pervading all existence.

वराहरूपिणीं देवीं दंष्ट्रोद्धृतवसुन्दराम् ।
शुभदां पीतवसनां वाराहीं तां नमाम्यहम् ॥

varāharūpiṇīṁ devīṁ daṁṣṭroddhṛtavasundarām śubhadāṁ pītavasanāṁ vārāhīṁ tāṁ namāmyaham
She is the Goddess who appears as a boar. Her great teeth are beautiful. She is the Giver of Purity, of yellow color. We bow to Her, to Vārāhī, the Boar of Sacrifice.

ॐ ह्रीं श्रीं वाराह्यै नमः

oṁ hrīṁ śrīṁ vārāhyai namaḥ
Oṁ Māyā, Increase, I bow to the Boar of Sacrifice.

नृसिंहरूपिणीं देवीं दैत्यदानवदर्पहाम् ।
शुभां शुभप्रदां शुभ्रां नारसिंहीं नमाम्यहम् ॥

nṛsiṁharūpiṇīṁ devīṁ daityadānavadarpahām
śubhāṁ śubhapradāṁ śubhrāṁ nārasiṁhīṁ namāmyaham

She is the Goddess who appears as the man-lion, the reflection of the forces of duality and animalism. She shines and gives forth the radiance of Her shine. We bow to Nārasiṁhī, the man-lion of courage.

ॐ ह्रीं श्रीं नारसिंह्यै नमः

oṁ hrīṁ śrīṁ nārasiṁhyai namaḥ

Oṁ Māyā, Increase, I bow to Nārasiṁhī, the man-lion of courage.

इन्द्राणीं गजकूम्भस्थां सहस्रानयनोज्ज्वलाम् ।
नमामि वरदां देवीं सर्वदेवनमस्कृताम् ॥

indrāṇīṁ gajakūmbhasthāṁ sahasrānayanojjalām
namāmi varadāṁ devīṁ sarvadevanamaskṛtām

Indrāṇī, the Energy of the Rule of the Pure, sits upon the shoulders of an elephant, with a thousand eyes shining. I bow to the Goddess who gives boons, and to whom all the Gods also bow as well.

ॐ ह्रीं श्रीं इन्द्राण्यै नमः

oṁ hrīṁ śrīṁ indrāṇyai namaḥ

Oṁ Māyā, Increase, I bow to Indrāṇī, the Energy of the Rule of the Pure.

चामुण्डां चण्डमथनीं मुण्डमालोपशोभिताम् ।
अटटहासमूदितां नमाम्यात्मविभूतये ॥

cāmuṇḍāṁ caṇḍamathanīṁ muṇḍamālopaśobhitām
aṭaṭahāsamūditāṁ namāmyātmavibhūtaye

The Slayer of Passion and Meaness, who churns Passion, shines forth with a garland of skulls. She emits a loud laugh. I bow to the soul who manifests in existence.

ॐ ह्रीं श्रीं चामुण्डायै नमः

oṁ hrīṁ śrīṁ cāmuṇḍāyai namaḥ
Oṁ Māyā, Increase, I bow to the Slayer of Passion and Meaness.

कात्यायनीं दशभूजां महिषासुरमर्दिनीम् ।
प्रसन्नवदनां देवीं वरदां तां नमाम्यहम् ॥

kātyāyanīṁ daśabhūjāṁ mahiṣāsuramardinīm
prasannavadanāṁ devīṁ varadāṁ tāṁ namāmyaham
The Ever Pure One has ten arms, the Slayer of the Great Ego. She is the Goddess with the pleased face. We bow to Her, the Giver of Boons.

ॐ ह्रीं श्रीं कात्यायन्यै नमः

oṁ hrīṁ śrīṁ kātyāyanyai namaḥ
Oṁ Māyā, Increase, I bow to the Ever Pure One.

चण्डिके नवदुर्गे त्वं महादेवमनोरमे ।
पूजां समस्तां संगृह्य रक्ष मां त्रिदशेश्वरि ॥

caṇḍike navadurge tvaṁ mahādevamanorame
pūjāṁ samastāṁ saṁgṛhya rakṣa māṁ tridaśeśvari
You Who Tear Apart Thoughts and the other nine Durgās are the beauty of Śiva. Please accept this all-encompassing worship and protect me, oh Supreme among the three qualities.

ॐ ह्रीं श्रीं चण्डिकायै नमः

oṁ hrīṁ śrīṁ caṇḍikāyai namaḥ
Oṁ Māyā, Increase, I bow to She Who Tears Apart Thoughts.

ॐ ह्रीं श्रीं नवदुर्गायै नमः

oṁ hrīṁ śrīṁ navadurgāyai namaḥ
Oṁ Māyā, Increase, I bow to the Nine forms of Durgā.

yantra pūjā

worship of the yantra

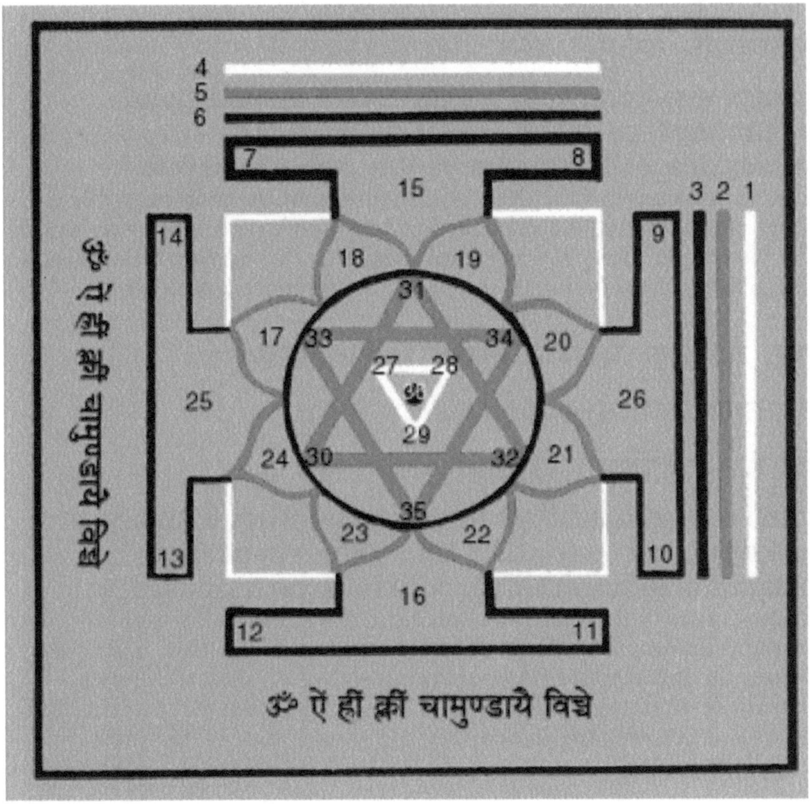

सोभयस्यास्य देवस्य विग्रहो यन्त्र कल्पणा ।
विना यन्त्रेण चेत्पूजा देवता न प्रसीदति ॥

sobhayasyāsya devasya vigraho yantra kalpaṇā
vinā yantreṇa cetpūjā devatā na prasīdati

We contemplate the form of the yantra which depicts the radiance of the Gods. Without using the yantra in the worship of consciousness the Gods are not as pleased.

यन्त्र मन्त्रमयं प्रहुर्देवता मन्त्ररूपिणी ।
यन्त्रेणापूजितो देवः सहसा न प्रसीदति ।
सर्वेषामपि मन्त्रणां यन्त्र पूजा प्रशस्यते ॥

yantra mantramayaṁ prahurdevatā mantrarūpiṇī
yantreṇāpūjito devaḥ sahasā na prasīdati
sarveṣāmapi mantraṇāṁ yantra pūjā praśasyate

The yantra conveys the objective meaning of the mantra, while the deity is the form of the mantra. By worshiping the deity by means of the yantra, the deity is completely satisfied. To attain all the bliss of the mantra, the worship of the yantra is highly recommended.

ततः स्थण्डिलमध्ये तु हसौःगर्भं त्रिकोणकम् ।
षट्कोणं तद्वहिर्वृत्तां ततोऽष्टदलपङ्कजम् ।
भूपुरं तद्वहिर्विद्वान् विलिखेद्यन्त्रमुत्तमम् ॥

tataḥ sthaṇḍilamadhye tu hasauḥgarbhaṁ trikoṇakam
ṣaṭkoṇaṁ tadvahirvṛttāṁ tato-ṣṭadalapaṅkajam
bhūpuraṁ tadvahirvidvān vilikhedhyantramuttamam

In the center of the place of worship is the single point which contains ha and sauḥ, Śiva and Śakti without distinction. Thereafter comes the three cornered equalateral triangle. Then six angles, outside of which is a circle, followed by eight lotus petals. The four doors are outside, and in this way the wise will draw the most excellent yantra.

- 1 -

ॐ मुकुन्दाय नमः

oṁ mukundāya namaḥ

oṁ I bow to the Giver of Liberation.

- 2 -

ॐ ईशनाय नमः

oṁ īśanāya namaḥ

oṁ I bow to the Ruler of All.

- 3 -

ॐ पुरन्दराय नमः

oṁ purandarāya namaḥ

oṁ I bow to the Giver of Completeness.

- 4 -

ॐ ब्रह्मणे नमः

oṁ brahmaṇe namaḥ

oṁ I bow to the Creative Consciousness.

- 5 -

ॐ वैवस्वताय नमः

oṁ vaivasvatāya namaḥ

oṁ I bow to the Universal Radiance.

- 6 -

ॐ इन्दवे नमः

oṁ indave namaḥ

oṁ I bow to the Ruler of Devotion.

- 7 -

ॐ आधारशक्तये नमः

oṁ ādhāraśaktaye namaḥ

oṁ I bow to the primal energy which sustains existence.

- 8 -

ॐ कुर्म्माय नमः

oṁ kurmmāya namaḥ

oṁ I bow to the Tortoise which supports creation.

- 9 -

ॐ अनन्ताय नमः

oṁ anantāya namaḥ
oṁ I bow to Infinity (personified as a thousand hooded snake who stands upon the Tortoise holding aloft the worlds).

- 10 -

ॐ पृथिव्यै नमः

oṁ pṛthivyai namaḥ
oṁ I bow to the Earth.

- 11 -

ॐ क्षीरसमूद्राय नमः

oṁ kṣīrasamūdrāya namaḥ
oṁ I bow to the milk ocean, or ocean of nectar, the infinite expanse of existence from which all manifested.

- 12 -

ॐ श्वेतद्वीपाय नमः

oṁ śvetadvīpāya namaḥ
oṁ I bow to the Island of Purity, which is in the ocean.

- 13 -

ॐ मणिमन्दपाय नमः

oṁ maṇimandapāya namaḥ
oṁ I bow to the Palace of Gems, which is on the island, the home of the Divine Mother.

- 14 -

ॐ कल्पवृक्षाय नमः

oṁ kalpavṛkṣāya namaḥ
oṁ I bow to the Tree of Fulfillment, which satisfies all desires, growing in the palace courtyard.

- 15 -

ॐ मणिवेदिकायै नमः

oṁ maṇivedikāyai namaḥ
oṁ I bow to the altar containing the gems of wisdom.

- 16 -

ॐ रत्नसिंहासनाय नमः

oṁ ratnasiṁhāsanāya namaḥ
oṁ I bow to the throne of the jewel.

- 17 -

ॐ धर्म्माय नमः

oṁ dharmmāya namaḥ
oṁ I bow to the Way of Truth and Harmony.

- 18 -

ॐ ज्ञानाय नमः

oṁ jñānāya namaḥ
oṁ I bow to Wisdom.

- 19 -

ॐ वैराग्याय नमः

oṁ vairāgyāya namaḥ
oṁ I bow to Detachment.

- 20 -

ॐ ऐश्वर्याय नमः

oṁ aiśvaryāya namaḥ
oṁ I bow to the Imperishable Qualities.

- 21 -

ॐ अधर्म्माय नमः

oṁ adharmmāya namaḥ
oṁ I bow to Disharmony.

- 22 -

ॐ अज्ञानाय नमः

oṁ ajñānāya namaḥ
oṁ I bow to Ignorance.

- 23 -

ॐ अवैराग्याय नमः

oṁ avairāgyāya namaḥ
oṁ I bow to Attachment.

- 24 -

ॐ अनैश्वर्याय नमः

oṁ anaiśvaryāya namaḥ
oṁ I bow to the Transient.

- 25 -

ॐ अनन्ताय नमः

oṁ anantāya namaḥ
oṁ I bow to the Infinite.

- 26 -

ॐ पद्माय नमः

oṁ padmāya namaḥ
oṁ I bow to the Lotus.

- 27 -

अं अर्कमण्डलाय द्वादशकलात्मने नमः

aṁ arkamaṇḍalāya dvādaśakalātmane namaḥ
"A" we bow to the twelve aspects of the realm of the sun. Tapinī, Tāpinī, Dhūmrā, Marīci, Jvālinī, Ruci, Sudhūmrā, Bhoga-dā, Viśvā, Bodhinī, Dhārinī, Kṣamā; Containing heat, Emanating heat, Smoky, Ray-producing, Burning, Lustrous, Purple or Smoky-red, Granting enjoyment, Universal, Which makes known, Productive of Consciousness, Which supports, Which forgives.

- 28 -

उं सोममण्डलाय षोडशकलात्मने नमः

uṁ somamaṇḍalāya ṣoḍaśakalātmane namaḥ
"U" we bow to the sixteen aspects of the realm of the moon. Amṛtā, Prāṇadā, Puṣā, Tuṣṭi, Puṣṭi, Rati, Dhṛti, Śaśinī, Candrikā, Kānti, Jyotsnā, Śrī, Prīti, Aṅgadā, Pūrṇā, Pūrṇāmṛtā; Nectar, Which sustains life, Which supports, Satisfying, Nourishing, Playful, Constancy, Unfailing, Producer of Joy, Beauty enhanced by love, Light, Grantor of Prosperity, Affectionate, Purifying the body, Complete, Full of Bliss.

- 29 -

मं वह्निमण्डलाय दशकलात्मने नमः

maṁ vahnimaṇḍalāya daśakalātmane namaḥ
"M" we bow to the ten aspects of the realm of fire: Dhūmrā, Arciḥ, Jvalinī, Śūkṣmā, Jvālinī, Visphuliṅginī, Suśrī, Surūpā, Kapilā, Havya-Kavya-Vahā; Smoky Red, Flaming, Shining, Subtle,

Burning, Sparkling, Beautiful, Well-formed, Tawny, The Messenger to Gods and Ancestors.

- 30 -

ॐ सं सत्त्वाय नमः

oṁ saṁ sattvāya namaḥ
oṁ I bow to activity, execution, light, knowledge, being.

- 31 -

ॐ रं रजसे नमः

oṁ raṁ rajase namaḥ
oṁ I bow to desire, inspiration, becoming.

- 32 -

ॐ तं तमसे नमः

oṁ taṁ tamase namaḥ
oṁ I bow to wisdom, to the darkness which exposes light, to rest.

- 33 -

ॐ आं आत्मने नमः

oṁ āṁ ātmane namaḥ
oṁ I bow to the Soul.

- 34 -

ॐ अं अन्तरात्मने नमः

oṁ aṁ antarātmane namaḥ
oṁ I bow to the Innermost Soul.

- 35 -

ॐ पं परमात्मने नमः

oṁ paṁ paramātmane namaḥ
oṁ I bow to the Universal Soul, or the Consciousness which exceeds manifestation.

- 36 -

ॐ ह्रीं ज्ञानात्मने नमः

oṁ hrīṁ jñānātmane namaḥ
oṁ I bow to the Soul of Infinite Wisdom.

Place yantra on altar.

ॐ श्रीं लक्ष्म्यै नमः फट्

oṁ śrīṁ lakṣmyai namaḥ phaṭ
Oṁ I bow to the Goddess Lakṣmī, Purify!

ॐ यन्त्रराजाय विद्महे महायन्त्राय धीमहे ।
तन्नो यन्त्रः प्रचोदयात् ॥

oṁ yantrarājāya vidmahe mahāyantrāya dhīmahe
tanno yantraḥ pracodayāt
oṁ we meditate upon the King of Yantras, contemplate the greatest yantra. May that yantra grant us increase.

ॐ श्रीं लक्ष्म्यै नमः सिन्दूरं समर्पयामि

oṁ śrīṁ lakṣmyai namaḥ sindūraṁ samarpayāmi
With this offering of red colored powder Oṁ I bow to the Goddess Lakṣmī.

ॐ यन्त्रराजाय विद्महे महायन्त्राय धीमहे ।
तन्नो यन्त्रः प्रचोदयात् ॥

oṁ yantrarājāya vidmahe mahāyantrāya dhīmahe
tanno yantraḥ pracodayāt
oṁ we meditate upon the King of Yantras, contemplate the greatest yantra. May that yantra grant us increase.

ॐ श्रीं लक्ष्म्यै नमः चन्दनं समर्पयामि

oṁ śrīṁ lakṣmyai namaḥ candanaṁ samarpayāmi
With this offering of red colored powder Oṁ I bow to the Goddess Lakṣmī.

ॐ परमेश्वराय विद्महे परातत्त्वाय धीमहे ।
तन्नो ब्रह्माः प्रचोदयात् ॥

oṁ parameśvarāya vidmahe parātattvāya dhīmahe
tanno brahmāḥ pracodayāt

oṁ we meditate upon the Highest Supreme Divinity, contemplate the Highest Principle. May that Supreme Divinity grant us increase.

ॐ श्रीं लक्ष्म्यै नमः अक्षतान् समर्पयामि

oṁ śrīṁ lakṣmyai namaḥ akṣatān samarpayāmi

With the offering of grains of rice Oṁ I bow to the Goddess Lakṣmī.

सर्वतो भद्रमण्डल देवता स्थापनम

sarvato bhadramaṇḍala devatā sthāpanam

Establishment of the Excellent Circle of Deities

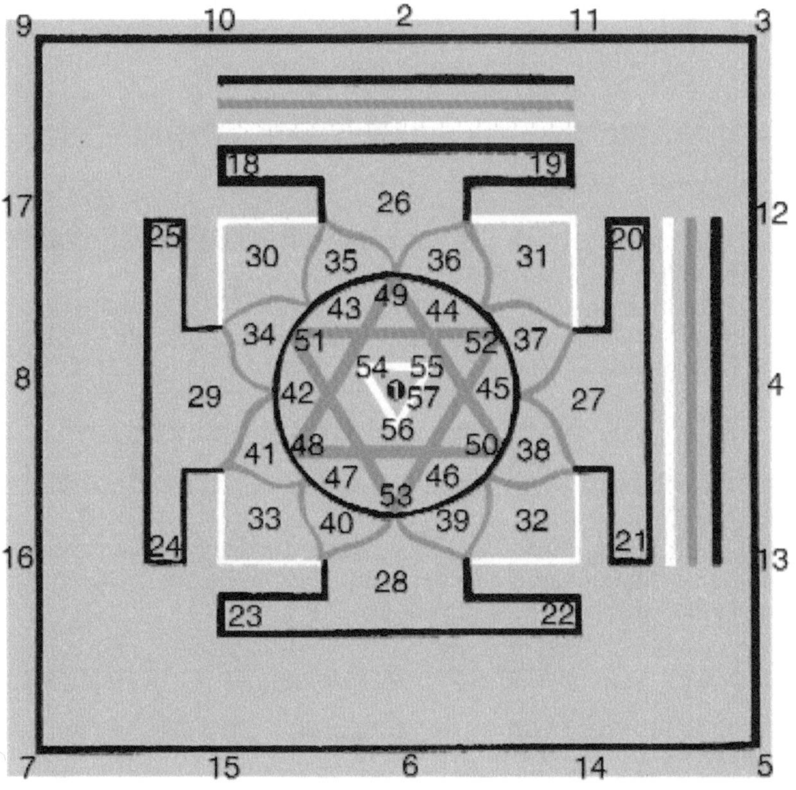

- 1 -

ॐ भूर्भुवः स्वः ब्रह्मणे नमः ब्रह्मणमावाहयामि स्थापयामि

oṁ bhūrbhuvaḥ svaḥ brahmaṇe namaḥ brahmaṇamāvāhayāmi sthāpayāmi

oṁ the Infinite Beyond Conception, the gross body, the subtle body and the causal body, we bow to the Creative Consciousness (Center). We invoke you, invite you and establish your presence.

- 2 -

ॐ भूर्भुवः स्वः सोमाय नमः सोममावाहयामि स्थापयामि

oṁ bhūrbhuvaḥ svaḥ somāya namaḥ somamāvāhayāmi sthāpayāmi

oṁ the Infinite Beyond Conception, the gross body, the subtle body and the causal body, we bow to the Lord of Devotion (N). We invoke you, invite you and establish your presence.

- 3 -

ॐ भूर्भुवः स्वः ईशानाय नमः ईशानमावाहयामि स्थापयामि

oṁ bhūrbhuvaḥ svaḥ īśānāya namaḥ īśānamāvāhayāmi sthāpayāmi

oṁ the Infinite Beyond Conception, the gross body, the subtle body and the causal body, we bow to the Ruler of All (NE). We invoke you, invite you and establish your presence.

- 4 -

ॐ भूर्भुवः स्वः इन्द्राय नमः इन्द्रमावाहयामि स्थापयामि

oṁ bhūrbhuvaḥ svaḥ indrāya namaḥ indramāvāhayāmi sthāpayāmi

oṁ the Infinite Beyond Conception, the gross body, the subtle body and the causal body, we bow to the Rule of the Pure (E). We invoke you, invite you and establish your presence.

- 5 -

ॐ भूर्भुवः स्वः अग्नये नमः अग्निमावाहयामि स्थापयामि

oṁ bhūrbhuvaḥ svaḥ agnaye namaḥ agnimāvāhayāmi sthāpayāmi

oṁ the Infinite Beyond Conception, the gross body, the subtle body and the causal body, we bow to the Divine Fire (SE). We invoke you, invite you and establish your presence.

- 6 -

ॐ भूर्भुवः स्वः यमाय नमः यममावाहयामि स्थापयामि

oṁ bhūrbhuvaḥ svaḥ yamāya namaḥ yamamāvāhayāmi sthāpayāmi

oṁ the Infinite Beyond Conception, the gross body, the subtle body and the causal body, we bow to the Supreme Controller (S). We invoke you, invite you and establish your presence.

- 7 -

ॐ भूर्भुवः स्वः निर्ऋतये नमः निर्ऋतिमावाहयामि स्थापयामि

oṁ bhūrbhuvaḥ svaḥ nirṛtaye namaḥ nirṛtimāvāhayāmi sthāpayāmi

oṁ the Infinite Beyond Conception, the gross body, the subtle body and the causal body, we bow to the Destroyer (SW). We invoke you, invite you and establish your presence.

- 8 -

ॐ भूर्भुवः स्वः वरुणाय नमः वरुणमावाहयामि स्थापयामि

oṁ bhūrbhuvaḥ svaḥ varuṇāya namaḥ varuṇamāvāhayāmi sthāpayāmi

oṁ the Infinite Beyond Conception, the gross body, the subtle body and the causal body, we bow to the Lord of Equilibrium (W). We invoke you, invite you and establish your presence.

- 9 -

ॐ भूर्भुवः स्वः वायवे नमः वायुमावाहयामि स्थापयामि

oṁ bhūrbhuvaḥ svaḥ vāyave namaḥ vāyumāvāhayāmi sthāpayāmi

oṁ the Infinite Beyond Conception, the gross body, the subtle body and the causal body, we bow to the Lord of Liberation (NW). We invoke you, invite you and establish your presence.

- 10 -

ॐ भूर्भुवः स्वः अष्टवसुभ्यो नमः अष्टवसुन्

आवाहयामि स्थापयामि

oṁ bhūrbhuvaḥ svaḥ aṣṭavasubhyo namaḥ aṣṭavasun āvāhayāmi sthāpayāmi

oṁ the Infinite Beyond Conception, the gross body, the subtle body and the causal body, we bow to the Eight Lords of Benificence. We invoke you, invite you and establish your presence.

- 11 -

ॐ भूर्भुवः स्वः एकादशरुद्रेभ्यो नमः

एकादशरुद्रानावाहयामि स्थापयामि

oṁ bhūrbhuvaḥ svaḥ ekādaśarudrebhyo namaḥ ekādaśarudrānāvāhayāmi sthāpayāmi

oṁ the Infinite Beyond Conception, the gross body, the subtle body and the causal body, we bow to the Eleven Relievers from Sufferings. We invoke you, invite you and establish your presence.

- 12 -

ॐ भूर्भुवः स्वः द्वादशादित्येभ्यो नमः

द्वादशादित्यानावाहयामि स्थापयामि

oṁ bhūrbhuvaḥ svaḥ dvādaśādityebhyo namaḥ dvādaśādityānāvāhayāmi sthāpayāmi

oṁ the Infinite Beyond Conception, the gross body, the subtle body and the causal body, we bow to the Twelve Sons of Light. We invoke you, invite you and establish your presence.

- 13 -

ॐ भूर्भुवः स्वः अश्विभ्यां नमः अश्विनौ आवाहयामि

स्थापयामि

oṁ bhūrbhuvaḥ svaḥ aśvibhyāṁ namaḥ aśvinau āvāhayāmi sthāpayāmi

oṁ the Infinite Beyond Conception, the gross body, the subtle body and the causal body, we bow to the Two Horses of Pure Desire. We invoke you, invite you and establish your presence.

- 14 -

ॐ भूर्भुवः स्वः सपैतृकविश्वेभ्यो देवेभ्यो नमः सपैतृकविश्वान् देवानावाहयामि स्थापयामि

oṁ bhūrbhuvaḥ svaḥ sapaitṛkaviśvebhyo devebhyo namaḥ sapaitṛkaviśvān devānāvāhayāmi sthāpayāmi

oṁ the Infinite Beyond Conception, the gross body, the subtle body and the causal body, we bow to the Ancestors along with the Shining Ones of the Universe. We invoke you, invite you and establish your presence.

- 15 -

ॐ भूर्भुवः स्वः सप्तयक्षेभ्यो नमः सप्तयक्षानावाहयामि स्थापयामि

oṁ bhūrbhuvaḥ svaḥ saptayakṣebhyo namaḥ saptayakṣānāvāhayāmi sthāpayāmi

oṁ the Infinite Beyond Conception, the gross body, the subtle body and the causal body, we bow to the Energy which brings the good and bad of wealth. We invoke you, invite you and establish your presence.

- 16 -

ॐ भूर्भुवः स्वः अष्टकुलनागेभ्यो नमः अष्टकुलनागानावाहयामि स्थापयामि

oṁ bhūrbhuvaḥ svaḥ aṣṭakulanāgebhyo namaḥ aṣṭakulanāgānāvāhayāmi sthāpayāmi

oṁ the Infinite Beyond Conception, the gross body, the subtle body and the causal body, we bow to the Family of eight snakes. We invoke you, invite you and establish your presence.

- 17 -

ॐ भूर्भुवः स्वः गन्धर्वाऽप्सरोभ्यो नमः गन्धर्वाऽप्सरसः आवाहयामि स्थापयामि

oṁ bhūrbhuvaḥ svaḥ gandharvā-psarobhyo namaḥ gandharvā-psarasaḥ āvāhayāmi sthāpayāmi

oṁ the Infinite Beyond Conception, the gross body, the subtle body and the causal body, we bow to the celestial musicians and heavenly maidens. We invoke you, invite you and establish your presence.

- 18 -

ॐ भूर्भुवः स्वः स्कन्दाय नमः स्कन्दमावाहयामि स्थापयामि

oṁ bhūrbhuvaḥ svaḥ skandāya namaḥ skandamāvāhayāmi sthāpayāmi

oṁ the Infinite Beyond Conception, the gross body, the subtle body and the causal body, we bow to the God of War. We invoke you, invite you and establish your presence.

- 19 -

ॐ भूर्भुवः स्वः वृषभाय नमः वृषभमावाहयामि स्थापयामि

oṁ bhūrbhuvaḥ svaḥ vṛṣabhāya namaḥ vṛṣabhamāvāhayāmi sthāpayāmi

oṁ the Infinite Beyond Conception, the gross body, the subtle body and the causal body, we bow to the Bull of Discipline, Conveyance of Śiva - Nandi. We invoke you, invite you and establish your presence.

- 20 -

ॐ भूर्भुवः स्वः शूलाय नमः शूलमावाहयामि स्थापयामि

oṁ bhūrbhuvaḥ svaḥ śūlāya namaḥ śūlamāvāhayāmi sthāpayāmi

oṁ the Infinite Beyond Conception, the gross body, the subtle body and the causal body, we bow to the Spear of Concentration. We invoke you, invite you and establish your presence.

- 21 -

ॐ भूर्भुवः स्वः महाकालाय नमः महाकालमावाहयामि स्थापयामि

oṁ bhūrbhuvaḥ svaḥ mahākālāya namaḥ mahākālamāvāhayāmi sthāpayāmi

oṁ the Infinite Beyond Conception, the gross body, the subtle body and the causal body, we bow to the Great Time. We invoke you, invite you and establish your presence.

- 22 -

ॐ भूर्भुवः स्वः दक्षादि सप्तगणेभ्यो नमः दक्षादि सप्तगणानावाहयामि स्थापयामि

oṁ bhūrbhuvaḥ svaḥ dakṣādi saptagaṇebhyo namaḥ dakṣādi saptagaṇānāvāhayāmi sthāpayāmi

oṁ the Infinite Beyond Conception, the gross body, the subtle body and the causal body, we bow to Ability and the other seven qualities. We invoke you, invite you and establish your presence.

- 23 -

ॐ भूर्भुवः स्वः दुर्गायै नमः दुर्गामावाहयामि स्थापयामि

oṁ bhūrbhuvaḥ svaḥ durgāyai namaḥ durgāmāvāhayāmi sthāpayāmi

oṁ the Infinite Beyond Conception, the gross body, the subtle body and the causal body, we bow to the Reliever of Difficulties. We invoke you, invite you and establish your presence.

- 24 -

ॐ भूर्भुवः स्वः विष्णवे नमः विष्णुमावाहयामि स्थापयामि

oṁ bhūrbhuvaḥ svaḥ viṣṇave namaḥ viṣṇumāvāhayāmi sthāpayāmi

oṁ the Infinite Beyond Conception, the gross body, the subtle body and the causal body, we bow to the All-Pervading Consciousness. We invoke you, invite you and establish your presence.

- 25 -

ॐ भूर्भुवः स्वः स्वधायै नमः स्वधामावाहयामि स्थापयामि

oṁ bhūrbhuvaḥ svaḥ svadhāyai namaḥ svadhāmāvāhayāmi sthāpayāmi

oṁ the Infinite Beyond Conception, the gross body, the subtle body and the causal body, we bow to the Ancestors. We invoke you, invite you and establish your presence.

- 26 -

ॐ भूर्भुवः स्वः मृत्युरोगेभ्यो नमः मृत्युरोगानावाहयामि स्थापयामि

oṁ bhūrbhuvaḥ svaḥ mṛtyurogebhyo namaḥ mṛtyurogānāvāhayāmi sthāpayāmi

oṁ the Infinite Beyond Conception, the gross body, the subtle body and the causal body, we bow to the Spirit of deadly illnesses. We invoke you, invite you and establish your presence.

- 27 -

ॐ भूर्भुवः स्वः गणपतये नमः गणपतिमावाहयामि स्थापयामि

oṁ bhūrbhuvaḥ svaḥ gaṇapataye namaḥ gaṇapatimāvāhayāmi sthāpayāmi

oṁ the Infinite Beyond Conception, the gross body, the subtle body and the causal body, we bow to the Lord of the Multitudes. We invoke you, invite you and establish your presence.

- 28 -

ॐ भूर्भुवः स्वः अद्भ्यो नमः अपः आवाहयामि स्थापयामि

oṁ bhūrbhuvaḥ svaḥ adbhyo namaḥ apaḥ āvāhayāmi sthāpayāmi

oṁ the Infinite Beyond Conception, the gross body, the subtle body and the causal body, we bow to Acts of Sacrifice. We invoke you, invite you and establish your presence.

- 29 -

ॐ भूर्भुवः स्वः मरुद्भ्यो नमः मरुतः आवाहयामि स्थापयामि

oṁ bhūrbhuvaḥ svaḥ marudbhyo namaḥ marutaḥ āvāhayāmi sthāpayāmi

oṁ the Infinite Beyond Conception, the gross body, the subtle body and the causal body, we bow to the Shining Ones. We invoke you, invite you and establish your presence.

- 30 -

ॐ भूर्भुवः स्वः पृथिव्यै नमः पृथ्वीमावाहयामि स्थापयामि

oṁ bhūrbhuvaḥ svaḥ pṛthivyai namaḥ pṛthvīmāvāhayāmi sthāpayāmi

oṁ the Infinite Beyond Conception, the gross body, the subtle body and the causal body, we bow to the Earth. We invoke you, invite you and establish your presence.

- 31 -

ॐ भूर्भुवः स्वः गङ्गादिनदीभ्यो नमः गङ्गादिनदीः आवाहयामि स्थापयामि

oṁ bhūrbhuvaḥ svaḥ gaṅgādinadībhyo namaḥ gaṅgādinadīḥ āvāhayāmi sthāpayāmi

oṁ the Infinite Beyond Conception, the gross body, the subtle body and the causal body, we bow to the Ganges and other rivers. We invoke you, invite you and establish your presence.

- 32 -

ॐ भूर्भुवः स्वः सप्तसागरेभ्यो नमः सप्तसागरानावाहयामि स्थापयामि

oṁ bhūrbhuvaḥ svaḥ saptasāgarebhyo namaḥ saptasāgarānāvāhayāmi sthāpayāmi

oṁ the Infinite Beyond Conception, the gross body, the subtle body and the causal body, we bow to the Seven Seas. We invoke you, invite you and establish your presence.

- 33 -

ॐ भूर्भुवः स्वः मेरवे नमः मेरुमावाहयामि स्थापयामि

oṁ bhūrbhuvaḥ svaḥ merave namaḥ merumāvāhayāmi sthāpayāmi

oṁ the Infinite Beyond Conception, the gross body, the subtle body and the causal body, we bow to Mount Meru. We invoke you, invite you and establish your presence.

- 34 -

ॐ भूर्भुवः स्वः गदाय नमः गदामावाहयामि स्थापयामि

oṁ bhūrbhuvaḥ svaḥ gadāya namaḥ gadāmāvāhayāmi sthāpayāmi

oṁ the Infinite Beyond Conception, the gross body, the subtle body and the causal body, we bow to the Club. We invoke you, invite you and establish your presence.

- 35 -

ॐ भूर्भुवः स्वः त्रिशूलाय नमः त्रिशूलमावाहयामि स्थापयामि

oṁ bhūrbhuvaḥ svaḥ triśūlāya namaḥ triśūlamāvāhayāmi sthāpayāmi

oṁ the Infinite Beyond Conception, the gross body, the subtle body and the causal body, we bow to the Trident. We invoke you, invite you and establish your presence.

- 36 -

ॐ भूर्भुवः स्वः वज्राय नमः वज्रमावाहयामि स्थापयामि

oṁ bhūrbhuvaḥ svaḥ vajrāya namaḥ vajramāvāhayāmi sthāpayāmi

oṁ the Infinite Beyond Conception, the gross body, the subtle body and the causal body, we bow to the Thunderbolt. We invoke you, invite you and establish your presence.

- 37 -

ॐ भूर्भुवः स्वः शक्तये नमः शक्तिमावाहयामि स्थापयामि

oṁ bhūrbhuvaḥ svaḥ śaktaye namaḥ śaktimāvāhayāmi sthāpayāmi

oṁ the Infinite Beyond Conception, the gross body, the subtle body and the causal body, we bow to Energy. We invoke you, invite you and establish your presence.

- 38 -

ॐ भूर्भुवः स्वः दण्डाय नमः दण्डमावाहयामि स्थापयामि

oṁ bhūrbhuvaḥ svaḥ daṇḍāya namaḥ daṇḍamāvāhayāmi sthāpayāmi

oṁ the Infinite Beyond Conception, the gross body, the subtle body and the causal body, we bow to the Staff. We invoke you, invite you and establish your presence.

- 39 -

ॐ भूर्भुवः स्वः खड्गाय नमः खड्गमावाहयामि स्थापयामि

oṁ bhūrbhuvaḥ svaḥ khaḍgāya namaḥ khaḍgamāvāhayāmi sthāpayāmi

oṁ the Infinite Beyond Conception, the gross body, the subtle body and the causal body, we bow to the Sword. We invoke you, invite you and establish your presence.

- 40 -

ॐ भूर्भुवः स्वः पाशाय नमः पाशमावाहयामि स्थापयामि

oṁ bhūrbhuvaḥ svaḥ pāśāya namaḥ pāśamāvāhayāmi sthāpayāmi

oṁ the Infinite Beyond Conception, the gross body, the subtle body and the causal body, we bow to the Net. We invoke you, invite you and establish your presence.

- 41 -

ॐ भूर्भुवः स्वः अङ्कुशाय नमः अङ्कुशमावाहयामि स्थापयामि

oṁ bhūrbhuvaḥ svaḥ aṅkuśāya namaḥ aṅkuśamāvāhayāmi sthāpayāmi

oṁ the Infinite Beyond Conception, the gross body, the subtle body and the causal body, we bow to the Goad. We invoke you, invite you and establish your presence.

- 42 -

ॐ भूर्भुवः स्वः गौतमाय नमः गौतममावाहयामि स्थापयामि

oṁ bhūrbhuvaḥ svaḥ gautamāya namaḥ gautamamāvāhayāmi sthāpayāmi

oṁ the Infinite Beyond Conception, the gross body, the subtle body and the causal body, we bow to Ṛṣi Gautam. We invoke you, invite you and establish your presence.

- 43 -

ॐ भूर्भुवः स्वः भरद्वाजाय नमः भरद्वाजमावाहयामि स्थापयामि

oṁ bhūrbhuvaḥ svaḥ bharadvājāya namaḥ bharadvājamāvāhayāmi sthāpayāmi

oṁ the Infinite Beyond Conception, the gross body, the subtle body and the causal body, we bow to Ṛṣi Bharadvāj. We invoke you, invite you and establish your presence.

- 44 -

ॐ भूर्भुवः स्वः विश्वामित्राय नमः विश्वामित्रमावाहयामि स्थापयामि

oṁ bhūrbhuvaḥ svaḥ viśvāmitrāya namaḥ viśvāmitramāvāhayāmi sthāpayāmi

oṁ the Infinite Beyond Conception, the gross body, the subtle body and the causal body, we bow to Ṛṣi Viśvāmitra we invoke you, invite you and establish your presence.

- 45 -

ॐ भूर्भुवः स्वः कश्यपाय नमः कश्यपमावाहयामि स्थापयामि

oṁ bhūrbhuvaḥ svaḥ kaśyapāya namaḥ kaśyapamāvāhayāmi sthāpayāmi

oṁ the Infinite Beyond Conception, the gross body, the subtle body and the causal body, we bow to Ṛṣi Kaśyapa.
We invoke you, invite you and establish your presence.

- 46 -

ॐ भूर्भुवः स्वः जमदग्नये नमः जमदग्निमावाहयामि स्थापयामि

oṁ bhūrbhuvaḥ svaḥ jamadagnaye namaḥ jamadagnimāvāhayāmi sthāpayāmi

oṁ the Infinite Beyond Conception, the gross body, the subtle body and the causal body, we bow to Ṛṣi Jamadagni. We invoke you, invite you and establish your presence.

- 47 -

ॐ भूर्भुवः स्वः वसिष्ठाय नमः वसिष्ठमावाहयामि स्थापयामि

oṁ bhūrbhuvaḥ svaḥ vasiṣṭhāya namaḥ vasiṣṭhamāvāhayāmi sthāpayāmi

oṁ the Infinite Beyond Conception, the gross body, the subtle body and the causal body, we bow to Ṛṣi Vaṣiṣṭha. We invoke you, invite you and establish your presence.

- 48 -

ॐ भूर्भुवः स्वः अत्रये नमः अत्रिमावाहयामि स्थापयामि

oṁ bhūrbhuvaḥ svaḥ atraye namaḥ atrimāvāhayāmi sthāpayāmi

oṁ the Infinite Beyond Conception, the gross body, the subtle body and the causal body, we bow to Ṛṣi Atri. We invoke you, invite you and establish your presence.

- 49 -

ॐ भूर्भुवः स्वः अरुन्धत्यै नमः अरुन्धतीमावाहयामि स्थापयामि

oṁ bhūrbhuvaḥ svaḥ arundhatyai namaḥ arundhatīmāvāhayāmi sthāpayāmi

oṁ the Infinite Beyond Conception, the gross body, the subtle body and the causal body, we bow to Devi Arundati, wife of Vaṣiṣṭha, example of purity. We invoke you, invite you and establish your presence.

- 50 -

ॐ भूर्भुवः स्वः ऐन्द्र्यै नमः ऐन्द्रीमावाहयामि स्थापयामि

oṁ bhūrbhuvaḥ svaḥ aindryai namaḥ aindrīmāvāhayāmi sthāpayāmi

oṁ the Infinite Beyond Conception, the gross body, the subtle body and the causal body, we bow to Aindri, the energy of the Rule of the Pure. We invoke you, invite you and establish your presence.

- 51 -

ॐ भूर्भुवः स्वः कौमार्य्यै नमः कौमारीमावाहयामि स्थापयामि

oṁ bhūrbhuvaḥ svaḥ kaumāryyai namaḥ kaumārīmāvāhayāmi sthāpayāmi

oṁ the Infinite Beyond Conception, the gross body, the subtle body and the causal body, we bow to Kumari, the energy of the ever pure one. We invoke you, invite you and establish your presence.

- 52 -

ॐ भूर्भुवः स्वः ब्राह्मयै नमः ब्राह्मीमावाहयामि स्थापयामि

oṁ bhūrbhuvaḥ svaḥ brāhmyai namaḥ brāhmīmāvāhayāmi sthāpayāmi

oṁ the Infinite Beyond Conception, the gross body, the subtle body and the causal body, we bow to Brahmi, the energy of Creative Consciousness. We invoke you, invite you and establish your presence.

- 53 -

ॐ भूर्भुवः स्वः वाराह्यै नमः वाराहीमावाहयामि स्थापयामि

oṁ bhūrbhuvaḥ svaḥ vārāhyai namaḥ vārāhīmāvāhayāmi sthāpayāmi

oṁ the Infinite Beyond Conception, the gross body, the subtle body and the causal body, we bow to Varāhi, the energy of the Boar of Sacrifice. We invoke you, invite you and establish your presence.

- 54 -

ॐ भूर्भुवः स्वः चामुण्डायै नमः चामुण्डामावाहयामि स्थापयामि

oṁ bhūrbhuvaḥ svaḥ cāmuṇḍāyai namaḥ cāmuṇḍāmāvāhayāmi sthāpayāmi

oṁ the Infinite Beyond Conception, the gross body, the subtle body and the causal body, we bow to Camuṇḍa, the Conquerer of Passion and Meaness. We invoke you, invite you and establish your presence.

- 55 -

ॐ भूर्भुवः स्वः वैष्णव्यै नमः वैष्णवीमावाहयामि स्थापयामि

oṁ bhūrbhuvaḥ svaḥ vaiṣṇavyai namaḥ vaiṣṇavīmāvāhayāmi sthāpayāmi

oṁ the Infinite Beyond Conception, the gross body, the subtle body and the causal body, we bow to Vaiṣṇāvi, the energy of All-Pervading Consciousness. We invoke you, invite you and establish your presence.

- 56 -

ॐ भूर्भुवः स्वः माहेश्वर्यै नमः माहेश्वरीमावाहयामि स्थापयामि

oṁ bhūrbhuvaḥ svaḥ māheśvaryai namaḥ māheśvarīmāvāhayāmi sthāpayāmi

oṁ the Infinite Beyond Conception, the gross body, the subtle body and the causal body, we bow to Maheśvarī, the energy of the Supreme Sovereign. We invoke you, invite you and establish your presence.

- 57 -

ॐ भूर्भुवः स्वः वैनायक्यै नमः वैनायकीमावाहयामि स्थापयामि

oṁ bhūrbhuvaḥ svaḥ vaināyakyai namaḥ vaināyakīmāvāhayāmi sthāpayāmi

oṁ the Infinite Beyond Conception, the gross body, the subtle body and the causal body, we bow to Vaināki, the energy of excellent conduct. We invoke you, invite you and establish your presence.

aṣṭāśakti pūjā

worship of the eight forms of passion

ऊग्रचण्डा तु वरदा मध्याह्नार्कसमप्रभा ।
सा मे सदास्तु वरदा तस्यै नित्यं नमो नमः ॥

ūgracaṇḍā tu varadā madhyāhnārkasamaprabhā
sā me sadāstu varadā tasyai nityaṁ namo namaḥ

The Terrible Slayer of Passion, Giver of Boons, who shines within the middle of the Sun. May He always give to me boons. Therefore, I always bow and bow.

ॐ ह्रीं श्रीं ऊग्रचण्डायै नमः

oṁ hrīṁ śrīṁ ūgracaṇḍāyai namaḥ

Oṁ Māyā, Increase, I bow to the Terrible Slayer of Passion.

प्रचण्डे पुत्रदे नित्यं प्रचण्डगणसंस्थिते ।
सर्वानन्दकरे देवि तुभ्यं नित्यं नमो नमः ॥

pracaṇḍe putrade nityaṁ pracaṇḍagaṇasaṁsthite
sarvānandakare devi tubhyaṁ nityaṁ namo namaḥ

Whose Nature Removes Passion, always give children. Situated with the multitude of what preceds Passion, oh Goddess, cause all bliss. I always bow to you and bow to you.

ॐ ह्रीं श्रीं प्रचण्डायै नमः

oṁ hrīṁ śrīṁ pracaṇḍāyai namaḥ

Oṁ Māyā, Increase, I bow to She Whose Nature Removes Passion.

लक्ष्मीस्त्वं सर्वभूतानां सर्वभूताभयप्रदा ।
देवि त्वं सर्वकार्येषु वरदा भव सर्वदा ॥

lakṣmīstvaṁ sarvabhūtānāṁ sarvabhūtābhayapradā
devi tvaṁ sarvakāryeṣu varadā bhava sarvadā

You are Lakṣmī, all existence; you grant freedom from fear to all existence. Oh Goddess, you reside within all effects. Always give boons.

ॐ ह्रीं श्रीं चण्डोग्रायै नमः

oṁ hrīṁ śrīṁ caṇḍogrāyai namaḥ
Oṁ Māyā, Increase, I bow to She Who Slays Passion.

या सिद्धिरिति नाम्ना च देवेशवरदायिनी ।
कलिकल्मषनाशाय नमामि चण्डनायिकाम् ॥

yā siddhiriti nāmnā ca deveśavaradāyinī
kalikalmaṣanāśāya namāmi caṇḍanāyikām
Her name brings perfection, and She is the Supreme among the Gods who grants boons. I bow down to She who destroys the iniquities of darkness, the Leader of Passion.

ॐ ह्रीं श्रीं चण्डनायिकायै नमः

oṁ hrīṁ śrīṁ caṇḍanāyikāyai namaḥ
Oṁ Māyā, Increase, I bow to the Leader of Passion.

देवि चण्डात्मिके चण्डि चण्डारिविजयप्रदे ।
धर्मार्थमोक्षदे दुर्गे नित्यं मे वरदा भव ॥

devi caṇḍātmike caṇḍi caṇḍārivijayaprade
dharmārthamokṣade durge nityaṁ me varadā bhava
Oh Goddess, to the soul of She Who Tears Apart Passion, She Who Tears Apart Thought, and She Who Conquers over Passion; hey Durgā, give me the boons of the Ideal of Perfection, the necessities for physical sustenance and Liberation.

ॐ ह्रीं श्रीं चण्डायै नमः

oṁ hrīṁ śrīṁ caṇḍāyai namaḥ
Oṁ Māyā, Increase, I bow to She who Conquers over Passion.

या सृष्टिस्थितिसंहारगुणत्रयसमन्विता ।
या परा परमा शक्तिश्चण्डवत्यै नमो नमः ॥

yā sṛṣṭisthitisaṁhāraguṇatrayasamanvitā
yā parā paramā śaktiścaṇḍavatyai namo namaḥ

Hers are creation, preservation and dissolution; the three qualities are equally present. To She who is Higher than the Highest Energy, to the Spirit of Passion I bow, I bow.

ॐ ह्रीं श्रीं चण्डवत्यै नमः

oṁ hrīṁ śrīṁ caṇḍavatyai namaḥ
Oṁ Māyā, Increase, I bow to the Spirit of Passion.

चण्डरूपात्मिका चण्डा चण्डनायकनायिका ।

सर्वसिद्धिप्रदा देवी तस्यै नित्यं नमो नमः ॥

caṇḍarūpātmikā caṇḍā caṇḍanāyakanāyikā
sarvasiddhipradā devī tasyai nityaṁ namo namaḥ
The form of the soul of Passion, She who Conquers over Passion, the Leader of the Leaders of Passion, oh Goddess, give all attainments of perfection. Therefore, always I bow, I bow.

ॐ ह्रीं श्रीं चण्डरूपायै नमः

oṁ hrīṁ śrīṁ caṇḍarūpāyai namaḥ
Oṁ Māyā, Increase, I bow to the Form of Passion.

बालार्कारुणनयना सर्वदा भक्तवत्सला ।

चण्डासुरस्य मथनी वरदा त्वतिचण्डिका ॥

bālārkāruṇanayanā sarvadā bhaktavatsalā
caṇḍāsurasya mathanī varadā tvaticaṇḍikā
You have the Strength of the Sun and are always compassionate to devotees. The Warrior of Passion has a churning rod.
Give boons, oh you who Tear Apart Extreme Passion.

ॐ ह्रीं श्रीं अतिचण्डिकायै नमः

oṁ hrīṁ śrīṁ aticaṇḍikāyai namaḥ
Oṁ Māyā, Increase, I bow to You who Tears Apart Extreme Passion.

उग्रचण्डा प्रचण्डा च चण्डोग्रा चण्डनायिका ।
चण्डा चण्डवती चैव चण्डरूपातिचण्डिका ॥

ūgracaṇḍā pracaṇḍā ca caṇḍogrā caṇḍanāyikā
caṇḍā caṇḍavatī caiva caṇḍarūpāticaṇḍikā
The Terrible Slayer of Passion, Whose Nature Removes Passion, She Who Slays Passion, the Leader of Passion, She Who Conquers Over Passion, the Spirit of Passion, the Form of Passion and She who Tears Apart Extreme Passion.

ॐ ह्रीं श्रीं अष्टाशक्तिभ्यो नमः

oṁ hrīṁ śrīṁ aṣṭāśaktibhyo namaḥ
Oṁ I bow to the eight forms of energy

नव ग्रहण पूजा
nava grahaṇa pūjā
worship of the nine planets

ॐ जबाकुसुम सङ्काशं काश्यपेयं महाद्युतिम् ।
तमोऽरिं सर्वपापघ्नं प्रनतोऽस्मि दिवाकरम् ॥
ॐ ह्रीं ह्रीं सूर्याय नमः

oṁ jabākusuma saṅkāśaṁ
kāśyapayaṁ mahādyutim
tamo-riṁ sarvapāpaghnaṁ
pranato-smi divākaram
oṁ hrīṁ hrīṁ sūryāya namaḥ

Oṁ Crimson red like a hybiscus flower, the Great Light shines onto the earth, removing all the darkness and eradicating sin. We bow down with devotion to that Shining Light. Oṁ we bow to the Sun, Light of Wisdom, Dispeller of Ignorance.

दधि मुख तुषाराभं क्षीरोदार्णसम्भवम् ।
नमामि शशिनम् सोमम् शम्भोर्मुकुट भुषनम् ॥
ॐ ऐं क्लीं सोमाय नमः

dadhi mukha tuṣārābhaṁ
kṣīrodārṇasambhavam
namāmi śaśinam somam
śambhormukuṭa bhuṣanam
oṁ aiṁ klīṁ somāya namaḥ

Creamy white like a container of curds and most pleasing, the Moon is born from the churning of the milk ocean. We bow down to the effulgent emblem of devotion, which is an ornament on the crown of Lord Śiva. Oṁ we bow to the Moon, emblem of devotion.

धरणीगर्भसम्भुतम् विद्युत्कान्ति समप्रभम् ।
कुमारं शक्तिहस्तं च तं मङ्गलम् प्रनमाम्यहम् ॥
ॐ हुं श्रीं मङ्गलाय नमः

dharaṇīgarbhasambhutam
vidyutkānti samaprabham
kumāraṁ śaktihastaṁ ca
taṁ maṅgalam pranamāmyaham
oṁ huṁ śrīṁ maṅgalāya namaḥ

Supporting the womb of all existence, Mars shines forth with the radiance of beauty enhanced by love, the son wielding energy in his hand. We bow down to Mars, Bearer of Welfare. Oṁ we bow down to Mars, Bearer of Welfare.

प्रियङ्गुकलिकश्यामम् रूपेणाऽप्रतिमं बुधम् ।
सौम्यं सौम्यगुणोपेतं तं बुधम् प्रनमाम्यहम् ॥
ॐ ऐं स्त्रीं श्रीं बुद्धाय नमः

priyaṅgukalikaśyāmam
rūpeṇā-pratimaṁ budham
saumyaṁ saumyaguṇopetaṁ
taṁ budham pranamāmyaham
oṁ aiṁ strīṁ śrīṁ budhāya namaḥ

Whose beloved body is dark like darkness, whose image is like the form of Intelligence, whose qualities are most beautiful, to that Mercury, emblem of Intelligence, we bow down in devotion. Oṁ we bow down to Mercury, the emblem of Intelligence.

देवानां च ऋषिनां च गुरुं काञ्चनसन्निभम् ।
बुद्धि भुतं त्रिलोकेशम् तं नमामि बृहास्पतिम् ॥
ॐ ह्रीं क्लीं हुं बृहस्पतये नमः

devānāṁ ca ṛṣināṁ ca
guruṁ kāñcana sannibham
buddhi bhutaṁ trilokeśam
taṁ namāmi bṛhāspatim
oṁ hrīṁ klīṁ huṁ bṛhaspataye namaḥ

The Guru of the Gods and also the ṛṣis, who is like the highest wealth, who is the most intelligent of all beings, to that Jupiter, Guru of the Gods, we bow down in devotion. Oṁ we bow down to the Guru of the Gods.

हिम कुन्द मृणालाभं दैत्यानां परमं गुरुम् ।
सर्वशास्त्रप्रवक्तारं भार्गवम् प्रनमाम्यहम् ॥
ॐ ह्रीं श्रीं शुक्राय नमः

hima kunda mṛṇālābhaṁ
daityānāṁ paramaṁ gurum
sarvaśāstrapravaktāraṁ
bhārgavam pranamāmyaham
oṁ hrīṁ śrīṁ śukrāya namaḥ

Like sandal and jasmine that have been crushed, the foremost Guru of the forces of duality, who expounds all the scriptures; to that descendant of Bṛgu we bow down in devotion. Oṁ we bow down to Venus, the emblem of love and attachment.

नीलाम्बुजसमाभासं रविपुत्रं यमाग्रजम् ।
छायामार्तण्डसम्भूतं तं नमामि शनैश्चरम् ॥
ॐ ऐं ह्रीं श्रीं शनैश्चराय नमः

nīlāmbujasamābhāsaṁ
raviputraṁ yamāgrajam
chāyāmārtaṇḍasambhūtaṁ
taṁ namāmi śanaiścaram
oṁ aiṁ hrīṁ śrīṁ śanaiścarāya namaḥ

Looking like a blue cloud, the son of the Sun, he is foremost of those who control. He can even put his shadow over the glorious sun. To that Saturn, emblem of control, we bow down in devotion. Oṁ we bow down to Saturn, the emblem of control.

अर्द्धकायं महावीर्यं चन्द्रादित्यविमर्दनम् ।
सिंहिकागर्भ सम्भूतं तं राहु प्रनमाम्यहम् ॥
ॐ ऐं ह्रीं राहवे नमः

arddhakāyaṁ mahāvīryaṁ candrādityavimardanam
siṁhikāgarbha sambhūtaṁ taṁ rāhu pranamāmyaham
oṁ aiṁ hrīṁ rāhave namaḥ

The great warrior divides even the sun and moon in half. He is born from the womb of Siṁhikā, and we bow down in devotion to the North Node, who commands direction. Oṁ we bow down to the North Node, who commands direction.

पालाशपुष्प सङ्काशं तारकाग्रहमस्तकम् ।
रौद्रं रौद्रात्मकं घोरं तं केतु प्रनमाम्यहम् ॥
ॐ ह्रीं ऐं केतवे नमः

pālāśapuṣpa saṅkāśaṁ tārakāgrahamastakam
raudraṁ raudrātmakaṁ ghoraṁ
taṁ ketu pranamāmyaham
oṁ hrīṁ aiṁ ketave namaḥ

Red like a pālāśa flower, who makes the starry-eyed constellation to set; he is terrible and awsome to see, and we bow down in devotion to the South Node, who presents obstacles. Oṁ we bow down to the South Node, who presents obstacles.

ब्रह्मा मुरारिस्त्रिपुरान्तकारी भानुः शशी भूमिसुतो बुधश्च ।
गुरुश्च शुक्रः शनि राहु केतवः सर्वे ग्रहा शान्तिकरा भवन्तु ॥

brahmā murāristripurāntakārī
bhānuḥ śaśī bhūmisuto budhaśca
guruśca śukraḥ śani rāhu ketavaḥ
sarve grahā śāntikarā bhavantu

Brahmā, Viṣṇu and Śiva always contemplate the Sun, Moon, Earth, Mercury, Jupiter, Venus, Saturn, the North and South Nodes. May all the constellations remain in Peace.

ॐ नव ग्रहेभ्योः नमः

oṁ nava grahebhyoḥ namaḥ

Oṁ we bow to the nine planets.

yoginī pūjā

worship of the sixty-four yoginīs

1. ॐ ह्रीं श्रीं ब्रह्माण्यै नमः

oṁ hrīṁ śrīṁ brahmāṇyai namaḥ
Oṁ Māyā, Increase, I bow to Creative Energy.

2. ॐ ह्रीं श्रीं चण्डिकायै नमः

oṁ hrīṁ śrīṁ caṇḍikāyai namaḥ
Oṁ Māyā, Increase, I bow to She who Tears Apart Thoughts.

3. ॐ ह्रीं श्रीं रौद्र्यै नमः

oṁ hrīṁ śrīṁ raudryai namaḥ
Oṁ Māyā, Increase, I bow to Fearful One.

4. ॐ ह्रीं श्रीं गौर्य्यै नमः

oṁ hrīṁ śrīṁ gauryai namaḥ
Oṁ Māyā, Increase, I bow to She who is Rays of Light.

5. ॐ ह्रीं श्रीं इन्द्राण्यै नमः

oṁ hrīṁ śrīṁ indrāṇyai namaḥ
Oṁ Māyā, Increase, I bow to the Energy of the Rule of the Pure.

6. ॐ ह्रीं श्रीं कौमार्य्यै नमः

oṁ hrīṁ śrīṁ kaumāryyai namaḥ
Oṁ Māyā, Increase, I bow to the Ever Pure One.

7. ॐ ह्रीं श्रीं भैरव्यै नमः

oṁ hrīṁ śrīṁ bhairavyai namaḥ
Oṁ Māyā, Increase, I bow to the Fearless One.

8. ॐ ह्रीं श्रीं दुर्गायै नमः

oṁ hrīṁ śrīṁ durgāyai namaḥ
Oṁ Māyā, Increase, I bow to the Reliever of Difficulties

9. ॐ ह्रीं श्रीं नरसिंह्यै नमः

oṁ hrīṁ śrīṁ narasiṁhyai namaḥ
Oṁ Māyā, Increase, I bow to the Man-Lion of Courage.

10. ॐ ह्रीं श्रीं कालिकायै नमः

oṁ hrīṁ śrīṁ kālikāyai namaḥ
Oṁ Māyā, Increase, I bow to She Who is Beyond Time.

11. ॐ ह्रीं श्रीं चामुण्डायै नमः

oṁ hrīṁ śrīṁ cāmuṇḍāyai namaḥ
Oṁ Māyā, Increase, I bow to She Who Conquers Over Passion and Meanness.

12. ॐ ह्रीं श्रीं शिवदूत्यै नमः

oṁ hrīṁ śrīṁ śivadūtyai namaḥ
Oṁ Māyā, Increase, I bow to She Who Sends Śiva as an ambassador.

13. ॐ ह्रीं श्रीं वाराह्यै नमः

oṁ hrīṁ śrīṁ vārāhyai namaḥ
Oṁ Māyā, Increase, I bow to the Boar of Sacrifice.

14. ॐ ह्रीं श्रीं कौशिक्यै नमः

oṁ hrīṁ śrīṁ kauśikyai namaḥ
Oṁ Māyā, Increase, I bow to She Who Manifests from Within.

15. ॐ ह्रीं श्रीं माहेश्वर्य्यै नमः

oṁ hrīṁ śrīṁ māheśvaryyai namaḥ
Oṁ Māyā, Increase, I bow to the Great Seer of All.

16. ॐ ह्रीं श्रीं शाङ्कर्य्यै नमः

oṁ hrīṁ śrīṁ śāṅkaryyai namaḥ
Oṁ Māyā, Increase, I bow to the Cause of Peace

17. ॐ ह्रीं श्रीं जयन्त्यै नमः
oṁ hrīṁ śrīṁ jayantyai namaḥ
Oṁ Māyā, Increase, I bow to Victory.

18. ॐ ह्रीं श्रीं सर्वमङ्गलायै नमः
oṁ hrīṁ śrīṁ sarvamaṅgalāyai namaḥ
Oṁ Māyā, Increase, I bow to She Who is All Welfare.

19. ॐ ह्रीं श्रीं काल्यै नमः
oṁ hrīṁ śrīṁ kālyai namaḥ
Oṁ Māyā, Increase, I bow to She Who is Beyond Time.

20. ॐ ह्रीं श्रीं करालिन्यै नमः
oṁ hrīṁ śrīṁ karālinyai namaḥ
Oṁ Māyā, Increase, I bow to She with the Gaping Mouth.

21. ॐ ह्रीं श्रीं मेधायै नमः
oṁ hrīṁ śrīṁ medhāyai namaḥ
Oṁ Māyā, Increase, I bow to the Intellect of Love.

22. ॐ ह्रीं श्रीं शिवायै नमः
oṁ hrīṁ śrīṁ śivāyai namaḥ
Oṁ Māyā, Increase, I bow to the Energy of Śiva.

23. ॐ ह्रीं श्रीं साकम्भर्य्यै नमः
oṁ hrīṁ śrīṁ sākambharyyai namaḥ
Oṁ Māyā, Increase, I bow to She Who Nourishes with Vegetables.

24. ॐ ह्रीं श्रीं भीमायै नमः
oṁ hrīṁ śrīṁ bhīmāyai namaḥ
Oṁ Māyā, Increase, I bow to She Who is Fearless.

25. ॐ ह्रीं श्रीं शान्तायै नमः

oṁ hrīṁ śrīṁ śāntāyai namaḥ
Oṁ Māyā, Increase, I bow to Peace.

26. ॐ ह्रीं श्रीं भ्रामर्य्यै नमः

oṁ hrīṁ śrīṁ bhrāmaryyai namaḥ
Oṁ Māyā, Increase, I bow to She Who is like a Bee.

27. ॐ ह्रीं श्रीं रुद्राण्यै नमः

oṁ hrīṁ śrīṁ rudrāṇyai namaḥ
Oṁ Māyā, Increase, I bow to She Who Relieves the Sufferings of all.

28. ॐ ह्रीं श्रीं अम्बिकायै नमः

oṁ hrīṁ śrīṁ ambikāyai namaḥ
Oṁ Māyā, Increase, I bow to the Divine Mother.

29. ॐ ह्रीं श्रीं क्षमायै नमः

oṁ hrīṁ śrīṁ kṣamāyai namaḥ
Oṁ Māyā, Increase, I bow to Patient Forgiveness.

30. ॐ ह्रीं श्रीं धात्र्यै नमः

oṁ hrīṁ śrīṁ dhātryai namaḥ
Oṁ Māyā, Increase, I bow to the Creatress.

31. ॐ ह्रीं श्रीं स्वाहायै नमः

oṁ hrīṁ śrīṁ svāhāyai namaḥ
Oṁ Māyā, Increase, I bow to the oblation 'I Am One with God!'

32. ॐ ह्रीं श्रीं स्वधायै नमः

oṁ hrīṁ śrīṁ svadhāyai namaḥ
Oṁ Māyā, Increase, I bow to the Oblations to the Ancestors.

33. ॐ ह्रीं श्रीं अपर्णायै नमः
oṁ hrīṁ śrīṁ aparṇāyai namaḥ
Oṁ Māyā, Increase, I bow to She Who is Indivisible.

34. ॐ ह्रीं श्रीं महोदर्य्यै नमः
oṁ hrīṁ śrīṁ mahodaryyai namaḥ
Oṁ Māyā, Increase, I bow to She with the Big Belly.

35. ॐ ह्रीं श्रीं घोररूपायै नमः
oṁ hrīṁ śrīṁ ghorarūpāyai namaḥ
Oṁ Māyā, Increase, I bow to the Form of Whiteness.

36. ॐ ह्रीं श्रीं महाकाल्यै नमः
oṁ hrīṁ śrīṁ mahākālyai namaḥ
Oṁ Māyā, Increase, I bow to the Great She Who is Beyond Time.

37. ॐ ह्रीं श्रीं भद्रकाल्यै नमः
oṁ hrīṁ śrīṁ bhadrakālyai namaḥ
Oṁ Māyā, Increase, I bow to the Excellent One Who is Beyond Time.

38. ॐ ह्रीं श्रीं कपालिन्यै नमः
oṁ hrīṁ śrīṁ kapālinyai namaḥ
Oṁ Māyā, Increase, I bow to She Who Wears Skulls.

39. ॐ ह्रीं श्रीं क्षेमङ्कर्य्यै नमः
oṁ hrīṁ śrīṁ kṣemaṅkaryyai namaḥ
Oṁ Māyā, Increase, I bow to She Who Destroys.

40. ॐ ह्रीं श्रीं उग्रचण्डायै नमः
oṁ hrīṁ śrīṁ ūgracaṇḍāyai namaḥ
Oṁ Māyā, Increase, I bow to the Terrible Slayer of Passion.

41. ॐ ह्रीं श्रीं चण्डोग्रायै नमः

oṁ hrīṁ śrīṁ caṇḍogrāyai namaḥ
Oṁ Māyā, Increase, I bow to She Who Slays Passion.

42. ॐ ह्रीं श्रीं चण्डनायिकायै नमः

oṁ hrīṁ śrīṁ caṇḍanāyikāyai namaḥ
Oṁ Māyā, Increase, I bow to the Leader of Passion.

43. ॐ ह्रीं श्रीं चण्डायै नमः

oṁ hrīṁ śrīṁ caṇḍāyai namaḥ
Oṁ Māyā, Increase, I bow to She Who Slays Passion.

44. ॐ ह्रीं श्रीं चण्डवत्यै नमः

oṁ hrīṁ śrīṁ caṇḍavatyai namaḥ
Oṁ Māyā, Increase, I bow to the Spirit of Passion.

45. ॐ ह्रीं श्रीं चण्ड्यै नमः

oṁ hrīṁ śrīṁ caṇḍyai namaḥ
Oṁ Māyā, Increase, I bow to She Who Tears Apart Extreme Passion.

46. ॐ ह्रीं श्रीं महामोहायै नमः

oṁ hrīṁ śrīṁ mahāmohāyai namaḥ
Oṁ Māyā, Increase, I bow to She Who Covers the World with Ignorance.

47. ॐ ह्रीं श्रीं महामायायै नमः

oṁ hrīṁ śrīṁ mahāmāyāyai namaḥ
Oṁ Māyā, Increase, I bow to She Who is the Great Māyā.

48. ॐ ह्रीं श्रीं प्रियङ्कर्य्यै नमः

oṁ hrīṁ śrīṁ priyaṅkaryyai namaḥ
Oṁ Māyā, Increase, I bow to She Who Causes Love.

49. ॐ ह्रीं श्रीं बलविकरण्यै नमः

oṁ hrīṁ śrīṁ balavikaraṇyai namaḥ
Oṁ Māyā, Increase, I bow to She Who is Extremely Powerful.

50. ॐ ह्रीं श्रीं बलप्रमथन्यै नमः

oṁ hrīṁ śrīṁ balapramathanyai namaḥ
Oṁ Māyā, Increase, I bow to She Who is the Strength of Disembodied Spirits.

51. ॐ ह्रीं श्रीं मदनोन्मथन्यै नमः

oṁ hrīṁ śrīṁ madanonmathanyai namaḥ
Oṁ Māyā, Increase, I bow to She Who Churns with Love.

52. ॐ ह्रीं श्रीं सर्वभूतदमन्यै नमः

oṁ hrīṁ śrīṁ sarvabhūtadamanyai namaḥ
Oṁ Māyā, Increase, I bow to She Who Controls All Existence.

53. ॐ ह्रीं श्रीं उमायै नमः

oṁ hrīṁ śrīṁ umāyai namaḥ
Oṁ Māyā, Increase, I bow to the Mother of Protection.

54. ॐ ह्रीं श्रीं तारायै नमः

oṁ hrīṁ śrīṁ tārāyai namaḥ
Oṁ Māyā, Increase, I bow to She Who Shines like a Star.

55. ॐ ह्रीं श्रीं महानिद्रायै नमः

oṁ hrīṁ śrīṁ mahānidrāyai namaḥ
Oṁ Māyā, Increase, I bow to She Who is the Great Sleep.

56. ॐ ह्रीं श्रीं विजायायै नमः

oṁ hrīṁ śrīṁ vijāyāyai namaḥ
Oṁ Māyā, Increase, I bow to Victory.

57. ॐ ह्रीं श्रीं जयायै नमः
oṁ hrīṁ śrīṁ jayāyai namaḥ
Oṁ Māyā, Increase, I bow to Conquest.

58. ॐ ह्रीं श्रीं शैलपुत्र्यै नमः
oṁ hrīṁ śrīṁ śailaputryai namaḥ
Oṁ Māyā, Increase, I bow to the Goddess of Inspiration.

59. ॐ ह्रीं श्रीं ब्रह्मचारिण्यै नमः
oṁ hrīṁ śrīṁ brahmacāriṇyai namaḥ
Oṁ Māyā, Increase, I bow to the Goddess of Learning.

60. ॐ ह्रीं श्रीं चण्डघण्टायै नमः
oṁ hrīṁ śrīṁ caṇḍaghaṇṭāyai namaḥ
Oṁ Māyā, Increase, I bow to the Goddess of Practice.

61. ॐ ह्रीं श्रीं कूष्माण्डायै नमः
oṁ hrīṁ śrīṁ kūṣmāṇḍāyai namaḥ
Oṁ Māyā, Increase, I bow to the Goddess of Refinement.

62. ॐ ह्रीं श्रीं स्कन्दमात्र्यै नमः
oṁ hrīṁ śrīṁ skandamātryai namaḥ
Oṁ Māyā, Increase, I bow to the Goddess Who Nurtures Divinity.

63. ॐ ह्रीं श्रीं कात्यायन्यै नमः
oṁ hrīṁ śrīṁ kātyāyanyai namaḥ
Oṁ Māyā, Increase, I bow to the Goddess Who is Ever Pure.

64. ॐ ह्रीं श्रीं कालरात्र्यै नमः
oṁ hrīṁ śrīṁ kālarātryai namaḥ
Oṁ Māyā, Increase, I bow to the Goddess of the Great Night of Surrendering the Ego.

ॐ ह्रीं श्रीं महागौर्य्यै नमः

oṁ hrīṁ śrīṁ mahāgauryyai namaḥ
Oṁ Māyā, Increase, I bow to the Goddess of the Great Radiant Light.

ॐ ह्रीं श्रीं कोटियोगिनीभ्यो नमः

oṁ hrīṁ śrīṁ koṭiyoginībhyo namaḥ
Oṁ Māyā, Increase, I bow to the tens of millions of Goddesses.

astra pūjā

worship of the weapons of war

ॐ सर्वायुधानां प्रथमो निमितस्त्वं पिनाकिना ।
शूलात् सारं समाकृष्य कृत्वा मुष्ठि ग्रहं शुभम् ॥

oṁ sarvāyudhānāṁ prathamo nimitastvaṁ pinākinā
śūlāt sāraṁ samākṛṣya kṛtvā muṣṭi grahaṁ śubham
Oṁ First among all the implements of war is the trident. From the trident the ocean of existence comes together. Make a fist and accept the radiance.

ॐ त्रिशूलाय नमः

oṁ triśūlāya namaḥ
Oṁ I bow to the trident.

असिर्विशसनः खड्गस्तीक्ष्नधारो दुरासदः ।
श्रीगर्भो विजयश्चैव धर्मपाल नमोऽस्तु ते ॥

asirviśasanaḥ khaṅgastīkṣnadhāro durāsadaḥ
śrīgarbho vijayaścaiva dharmapāla namo-stu te
The sword that protects the universe, you hold aloft the sharp blade against iniquity. In the respected womb of Victory, only to protect dharma, I bow down to you.

ॐ खड्गाय नमः

oṁ khaḍgāya namaḥ
Oṁ I bow to the sword.

चक्र त्वं विष्णुरूपोऽसि विष्णुपानौ सदा स्थितः ।
देवीहस्तस्थितो नित्यं शुदर्शन नमोऽस्तु ते ॥

cakra tvaṁ viṣṇurūpo-si viṣṇupānau sadā sthitaḥ
devīhastasthito nityaṁ śudarśana namo-stu te
Oh Discus, you are of the form of Viṣṇu, and you always reside in Viṣṇu's hands. Always stay in the hands of the Goddess. Excellent Intuitive Vision, I bow to you.

ॐ चक्राय नमः

oṁ cakrāya namaḥ
Oṁ I bow to the discus.

सर्वायुधानां श्रेष्ठोऽसि दैत्यसेनानिसूदनः ।
भयेभ्यः सर्वतो रक्ष तीक्ष्नबाण नमोऽस्तु ते ॥

sarvāyudhānāṁ śreṣṭo-si daityasenānisūdanaḥ
bhayebhyaḥ sarvato rakṣa tīkṣnabāṇa namo-stu te
You are the ultimate of all implements of war, eradicating the armies of duality. Always protect from all fear. I bow to the arrows.

ॐ तीक्ष्नबाणाय नमः

oṁ tīkṣnabāṇāya namaḥ
Oṁ I bow to the sharp arrows.

शक्तिस्त्वं सर्वदेवानां गुहस्य च विशेषतः ।
शक्तिरूपेण सर्वत्र रक्षां कुरु नमोऽस्तु ते ॥

śaktistvaṁ sarvadevānāṁ guhasya ca viśeṣataḥ
śaktirūpeṇa sarvatra rakṣāṁ kuru namo-stu te
You are the energy of all the Gods, especially hidden. By means of this energy always protect me. I bow to you.

ॐ शक्तये नमः

oṁ śaktaye namaḥ
Oṁ I bow to Energy.

षष्ठिरूपेण खेट त्वं वैरिसंहारकारकः ।
देवीहस्तस्थितो नित्यं मम रक्षां कुरुष्व च ॥

ṣaṣṭirūpeṇa kheṭa tvaṁ vairisaṁhārakārakaḥ
devīhastasthito nityaṁ mama rakṣāṁ kuruṣva ca

With the form of six points you are the shield, the cause of dissolution of adversity. Always stay in the hand of the Goddess, and protect me.

ॐ खेटकाय नमः

oṁ kheṭakāya namaḥ

Oṁ I bow to the Shield.

सर्वायुध महामात्र सर्वदेवारिसुदन ।
चाप मां सर्वतो रक्ष साकं सायकसत्तमैः ॥

sarvāyudha mahāmātra sarvadevārisudana
cāpa māṁ sarvato rakṣa sākaṁ sāyakasattamaiḥ

The great measurement of all warriors makes all the Gods victorious. Always protect me with the bow, with arrows ready to be hurled.

ॐ पूर्णचापाय नमः

oṁ pūrṇacāpāya namaḥ

Oṁ I bow to the bow.

पाश त्वं नागरूपोऽसि विषपूर्णो विषोदरः ।
शत्रुणां दुःसहो नित्यं नागपाश नमोऽस्तु ते ॥

pāśa tvaṁ nāgarūpo-si viṣapūrṇo viṣodaraḥ
śatruṇāṁ duḥsaho nityaṁ nāgapāśa namo-stu te

You are the bond in the form of a snake full of venom ready to strike. You always cause pain to enemies. Snake-bond, I bow to you.

ॐ नागपाशाय नमः

oṁ nāgapāśāya namaḥ

Oṁ I bow to the Snake-bond.

अङ्कुशोऽसि नमस्तुभ्यं गजानां नियमः सदा ।
लोकानां सर्वरक्षार्थं विधृतः पार्वतीकरे ॥

aṅkuśo-si namastubhyaṁ gajānāṁ niyamaḥ sadā
lokānāṁ sarvarakṣārthaṁ vidhṛtaḥ pārvatīkare

Curved Sword or prod, we bow to you. Always you discipline elephants. In order to protect the worlds, remain in Pārvatī's hands.

ॐ अङ्कुशाय नमः

oṁ aṅkuśāya namaḥ

Oṁ I bow to the Curved Sword.

हिनस्ति दैत्यतेजांसि स्वनेनापूर्य या जगत् ।
सा घण्टा पातु नो देवि पापेभ्योऽनः सुतानिव ॥

hinasti daitya tejāṁsi svanenāpūrya yā jagat
sā ghaṇṭā pātu no devi pāpebhyo-naḥ sutāniva

Oh Goddess, may the sound of your bell, which fills the perceivable world, destroying the prowess of all thoughts, protect us from evil as a Mother protects Her children.

ॐ घण्टाय नमः

oṁ ghaṇṭāya namaḥ

Oṁ I bow to the Bell.

परशो त्वं महातीक्ष्न सर्वदेवारिसूदनः ।
देवीहास्तस्थितो नित्यं शत्रुक्षय नमोऽस्तु ते ॥

paraśo tvaṁ mahātīkṣna sarvadevārisūdanaḥ
devīhāstasthito nityaṁ śatrukṣaya namo-stu te

Oh Battle Axe, you are very sharp as you defend all the Gods. Always stay in the hands of the Goddess. Destroyer of enemies, we bow to you.

ॐ परशवे नमः

oṁ paraśave namaḥ

Oṁ I bow to the Battle Axe.

ॐ ह्रीं श्रीं सर्वायुधधारिण्यै दुर्गायै नमः

oṁ hrīṁ śrīṁ sarvāyudhadhāriṇyai durgāyai namaḥ
Oṁ Māyā, Increase, I bow to Durgā, who holds all the weapons of war.

सर्वायुधानां श्रेष्ठानि यानि यानि त्रिपिष्ठपे ।
तानि तानि दधत्यै ते चण्डिकायै नमो नमः ॥

sarvāyudhānāṁ śreṣṭāni yāni yāni tripiṣṭape
tāni tāni dadhatyai te caṇḍikāyai namo namaḥ
She is the most excellent of all warriors, wherever, wherever in the three worlds. Where there exist forces of duality, we bow to You, to She Who Tears Apart Thought, we bow.

ॐ ह्रीं श्रीं सर्वायुधधारिण्यै चण्डिकायै नमः

oṁ hrīṁ śrīṁ sarvāyudhadhāriṇyai caṇḍikāyai namaḥ
Oṁ Māyā, Increase, I bow to Caṇḍikā who holds all the weapons of war.

bāhya mātrikā nyāsa

establishment of the letters in the external body

Every object in creation has a name to correspond to its form. There is a name which is agreed upon by the customs of language, what we may call an object; and there is a natural sound which is being emitted as a consequence of the vibrations which are taking place in the object itself, the movement of protons, nutrons, electrons, etc. Every manifested object of creation has a vibration, whether perceivable or not, and every vibration emits a sound whether audible to the physical organ of hearing or not. Every sound is expressible by a letter which symbolizes the sound that most closely approximates the vibration indicated, so that all the letters of the alphabets symbolize the total possibility of all vibrations which can be evolved or can be expressed the totality of creation.

This natural name is called a Bījā Mantra, often translated as Seed Mantra. These Bījās are another name for the Mātṛkās, the letters of the Saṁskṛta alphabet. In Saṁskṛta Philosophy, the microcosm is an exact replica of the macrocosm. Hence every physical body contains all the vibrations possible in the cosmos. Bāhya Mātṛkā Nyāsa means the establishment of the letters of the Saṁskṛta Alphabet within the "Outside" or the gross body of the worshiper. Bāhya Mātṛkā Nyāsa ascribes a position in each of the centers of activity for each of the letters, so that the worshiper can understand and experience the totality of creation as existing within the physical body. By using the different Mudrās described, the worshiper begins by placing the sixteen vowels in their respective positions.

Thumb 1 Pointer 2 Middle 3 Ring 4 Pinky 5

ॐ अं नमः

oṁ aṁ namaḥ R.1.4 base top of head

ॐ आं नमः

oṁ āṁ namaḥ R.1.4 base mouth

ॐ इं नमः

oṁ iṁ namaḥ R. 4 R. eye

ॐ ईं नमः

oṁ īṁ namaḥ L. 4 L. eye

ॐ उं नमः
oṁ uṁ namaḥ R. 1 R. ear

ॐ ऊं नमः
oṁ ūṁ namaḥ L. 1 L. ear

ॐ ऋं नमः
oṁ ṛṁ namaḥ R. 1.5 R. nostril

ॐ ॠं नमः
oṁ ṝṁ namaḥ L. 1.5 L. nostril

ॐ ऌं नमः
oṁ ḷṛṁ namaḥ R. 2.3.4 R. cheek

ॐ ॡं नमः
oṁ ḷṝṁ namaḥ L. 2.3.4 L. cheek

ॐ एं नमः
oṁ eṁ namaḥ R. 3 upper lip

ॐ ऐं नमः
oṁ aiṁ namaḥ R. 3 lower lip

ॐ ओं नमः
oṁ oṁ namaḥ R. 4 upper teeth

ॐ औं नमः
oṁ auṁ namaḥ R. 4 lower teeth

ॐ अं नमः
oṁ aṁ namaḥ R. 3.4 crown of head

ॐ अः नमः
oṁ aḥ namaḥ R. 3.4 mouth

ॐ कं नमः
oṁ kaṁ namaḥ L. 1.3.5 R. shoulder

ॐ खं नमः
oṁ khaṁ namaḥ L. 1.3.5 R. crook of elbow

ॐ गं नमः
oṁ gaṁ namaḥ L. 1.3.5 R. wrist

ॐ घं नमः
oṁ ghaṁ namaḥ L. 1.3.5 R. joint of hand

ॐ ङं नमः
oṁ ṅaṁ namaḥ L. 1.3.5 R. finger tips

ॐ चं नमः
oṁ caṁ namaḥ R. 1.3.5 L. shoulder

ॐ छं नमः
oṁ chaṁ namaḥ R. 1.3.5 L. crook of elbow

ॐ जं नमः
oṁ jaṁ namaḥ R. 1.3.5 L. wrist

ॐ झं नमः
oṁ jhaṁ namaḥ R. 1.3.5 L. joint of hand

ॐ ञं नमः

oṁ ñaṁ namaḥ R. 1.3.5 L. finger tips

ॐ टं नमः

oṁ ṭaṁ namaḥ L. 1.3.5 R. hip

ॐ ठं नमः

oṁ ṭhaṁ namaḥ L. 1.3.5 R. knees

ॐ डं नमः

oṁ ḍaṁ namaḥ L. 1.3.5 R. ankle

ॐ ढं नमः

oṁ ḍhaṁ namaḥ L. 1.3.5 R. joint of toes

ॐ णं नमः

oṁ ṇaṁ namaḥ L. 1.3.5 R. tip of toes

ॐ तं नमः

oṁ taṁ namaḥ R. 1.3.5 L. hip

ॐ थं नमः

oṁ thaṁ namaḥ R. 1.3.5 L. knees

ॐ दं नमः

oṁ daṁ namaḥ R. 1.3.5 L. ankle

ॐ धं नमः

oṁ dhaṁ namaḥ R. 1.3.5 L. joint of toes

ॐ नं नमः

oṁ naṁ namaḥ R. 1.3.5 L. tip of toes

ॐ पं नमः
oṁ paṁ namaḥ L. 1.4 base R. side

ॐ फं नमः
oṁ phaṁ namaḥ R. 1.4 base L. side

ॐ बं नमः
oṁ baṁ namaḥ R. 1.4 base Belly

ॐ भं नमः
oṁ bhaṁ namaḥ L. 1.4 base Back

ॐ मं नमः
oṁ maṁ namaḥ R. 1.2.3.4.5. flat Navel

ॐ यं नमः
oṁ yaṁ namaḥ R. 1.4 base Heart

ॐ रं नमः
oṁ raṁ namaḥ L. 1.4 base R. shoulder

ॐ लं नमः
oṁ laṁ namaḥ R. 1.4 base back of neck

ॐ वं नमः
oṁ vaṁ namaḥ R. 1.4 base L. shoulder

ॐ शं नमः
oṁ śaṁ namaḥ R. 1.4 L. shoulder to hand full

ॐ षं नमः
oṁ ṣaṁ namaḥ L. 1.4 R. shoulder to hand full

ॐ सं नमः
oṁ saṁ namaḥ L. 1.4 R. hip to leg full

ॐ हं नमः
oṁ haṁ namaḥ R. 1.4 L. hip to leg full

ॐ ळं नमः
oṁ ḷaṁ namaḥ L. 1.4 sternum to navel

ॐ क्षं नमः
oṁ kṣaṁ namaḥ R. 1.4 sternum to throat

ॐ श्रीं लक्ष्मयै नमः
oṁ śrīṁ lakṣmyai namaḥ
Oṁ I bow to the Goddess Lakṣmī.

mātṛkā nyāsa

establishment of the letters in the cakras

Following Pāṇinī's Grammar, which is the most authoritative on the subject, in the Bāhya Mātṛkā Nyāsa there are thirty-five consonants. Actually the number of letters varies according to different enumerations regarding differing functions, and in the Mātṛkā Nyāsa which follows, only fifty letters are to be placed. Saṁskṛt is commonly taught with fifty letters, sixteen vowels and thirty-four consonants. Occasionally it is taught with fifty-two letters, with the addition of oṁ and hrīṁ. For the purpose of these Nyāsas, we will follow the two formats presented, as the best authorities for their accuracy agree from all the versions consulted. The explanation as to why they differ in the number of letters contained, will not be addressed here. Mātṛkā Nyāsa places the Bījās or natural names inside the Cakras, which are the energy centers within the body. In this meditation we conceive that not only is all existence moving in My every movement, as in the former Nyāsa, but also that all the vibrations of the universe comprise the very essence of my being. Haṁ stands for the Prāṇātman, the second ḷaṁ, for the Jīvātman, and kṣaṁ for Paramātman. In this way, Jīva puts on, so to speak, or wears the universe as a gown. All the vibrations of existence make up the cloak which covers the ever more subtle essence of consciousness, which is the Silent Witness to the Dance of Creation.

Viśuddha (5th Cakra) 16 petals

ॐ अं नमः
oṁ aṁ namaḥ

ॐ आं नमः
oṁ āṁ namaḥ

ॐ इं नमः
oṁ iṁ namaḥ

ॐ ईं नमः
oṁ īṁ namaḥ

ॐ उं नमः
oṁ uṁ namaḥ

ॐ ऊं नमः
oṁ ūṁ namaḥ

ॐ ऋं नमः
oṁ ṛṁ namaḥ

ॐ ॠं नमः
oṁ ṝṁ namaḥ

ॐ ऌं नमः
oṁ lṛṁ namaḥ

ॐ ॡं नमः
oṁ lṝṁ namaḥ

ॐ एं नमः
oṁ eṁ namaḥ

ॐ ऐं नमः
oṁ aiṁ namaḥ

ॐ ओं नमः
oṁ oṁ namaḥ

ॐ औं नमः
oṁ auṁ namaḥ

ॐ अं नमः
oṁ aṁ namaḥ

ॐ अः नमः
oṁ aḥ namaḥ

Anahāta (4th Cakra) 12 petals

ॐ कं नमः
oṁ kaṁ namaḥ

ॐ खं नमः
oṁ khaṁ namaḥ

ॐ गं नमः
oṁ gaṁ namaḥ

ॐ घं नमः
oṁ ghaṁ namaḥ

ॐ ङं नमः
oṁ ṅaṁ namaḥ

ॐ चं नमः
oṁ caṁ namaḥ

ॐ छं नमः
oṁ chaṁ namaḥ

ॐ जं नमः
oṁ jaṁ namaḥ

ॐ झं नमः
oṁ jhaṁ namaḥ

ॐ ञं नमः
oṁ ñaṁ namaḥ

ॐ टं नमः
oṁ ṭaṁ namaḥ

ॐ ठं नमः
oṁ ṭhaṁ namaḥ

Maṇipura (3rd Cakra) 10 petals

ॐ डं नमः
oṁ ḍaṁ namaḥ

ॐ ढं नमः
oṁ ḍhaṁ namaḥ

ॐ णं नमः
oṁ ṇaṁ namaḥ

ॐ तं नमः
oṁ taṁ namaḥ

ॐ थं नमः
oṁ thaṁ namaḥ

ॐ दं नमः
oṁ daṁ namaḥ

ॐ धं नमः
oṁ dhaṁ namaḥ

ॐ नं नमः
oṁ naṁ namaḥ

ॐ पं नमः
oṁ paṁ namaḥ

ॐ फं नमः
oṁ phaṁ namaḥ

Swādiṣṭhana (2nd Cakra) 6 petals

ॐ बं नमः
oṁ baṁ namaḥ

ॐ भं नमः
oṁ bhaṁ namaḥ

ॐ मं नमः
oṁ maṁ namaḥ

ॐ यं नमः
oṁ yaṁ namaḥ

ॐ रं नमः
oṁ raṁ namaḥ

ॐ लं नमः
oṁ laṁ namaḥ

Mulādhāra (1st Cakra) 4 petals

ॐ वं नमः
oṁ vaṁ namaḥ

ॐ शं नमः
oṁ śaṁ namaḥ

ॐ षं नमः
oṁ ṣaṁ namaḥ

ॐ सं नमः
oṁ saṁ namaḥ

Āgnyā (6th Cakra) 2 petals

ॐ हं नमः
oṁ haṁ namaḥ

ॐ क्षं नमः
oṁ kṣaṁ namaḥ

ॐ श्रीं लक्ष्म्यै नमः

oṁ śrīṁ lakṣmyai namaḥ
Oṁ I bow to the Goddess Lakṣmī.

Then perform Saṁhara Mātṛkā Nyāsa and Bāhya Mātṛkā Nyāsa by repeating the processes in reverse order from the end to the beginning.

aṅga pūjā

worship of the Divine Mother's body
Using Tattva Mudrā on both hands touch:

ॐ दुर्गायै नमः पादौ पूजयामि

oṁ durgāyai namaḥ pādau pūjayāmi feet
I bow to the Reliever of Difficulties and worship Her feet.

ॐ गिरिजायै नमः गुल्फौ पूजयामि

oṁ girijāyai namaḥ gulphau pūjayāmi ankles
I bow to the Unconquerable One from the Mountains and worship Her ankles.

ॐ अपर्णायै नमः जानुनी पूजयामि

oṁ aparṇāyai namaḥ jānunī pūjayāmi knees
I bow to the Unseverable Energy and worship Her knees.

ॐ हरिप्रियायै नमः ऊरू पूजयामि

oṁ haripriyāyai namaḥ ūrū pūjayāmi thighs
I bow to the Beloved of Consciousness and worship Her thighs.

ॐ पार्वत्यै नमः कटिं पूजयामि

oṁ pārvatyai namaḥ kaṭiṁ pūjayāmi hips
I bow to the Daughter of the Mountains and worship Her hips.

ॐ आर्यायै नमः नाभिं पूजयामि

oṁ āryāyai namaḥ nābhiṁ pūjayāmi navel
I bow to the One Purified by Knowledge and worship Her navel.

ॐ जगन्मात्रे नमः उदरं पूजयामि

oṁ jaganmātre namaḥ udaraṁ pūjayāmi stomach

I bow to the Mother of the Perceivable Universe and worship Her stomach.

ॐ मंगलायै नमः कुक्षिं पूजयामि

oṁ maṁgalāyai namaḥ kukṣiṁ pūjayāmi sternum

I bow to the Energy of Welfare and worship Her sternum.

ॐ शिवायै नमः हृदयं पूजयामि

oṁ śivāyai namaḥ hṛdayaṁ pūjayāmi heart

I bow to the Energy of Infinite Goodness and worship Her heart.

ॐ महेश्वर्यै नमः कण्ठं पूजयामि

oṁ maheśvaryai namaḥ kaṇṭhaṁ pūjayāmi throat

I bow to the Energy of the Great Seer of All and worship Her throat.

ॐ विश्ववन्द्यायै नमः स्कन्धौ पूजयामि

oṁ viśvavandyāyai namaḥ skandhau pūjayāmi shoulders

I bow to She who is Praised by the Universe and worship Her shoulders.

ॐ काल्यै नमः बाहू पूजयामि

oṁ kālyai namaḥ bāhū pūjayāmi arms

I bow to She who Takes Away Darkness and worship Her arms.

ॐ आद्यायै नमः हस्तौ पूजयामि

oṁ ādyāyai namaḥ hastau pūjayāmi hands

I bow to She who is Sacred Study and worship Her hands.

ॐ वरदायै नमः मुखं पूजयामि

oṁ varadāyai namaḥ mukhaṁ pūjayāmi mouth

I bow to She who Grants Boons and worship Her mouth.

ॐ सुवाण्यै नमः नासिकां पूजयामि

oṁ suvāṇyai namaḥ nāsikāṁ pūjayāmi nose

I bow to She of Excellent Music and worship Her nose.

ॐ कमलाक्ष्म्यै नमः नेत्रे पूजयामि

oṁ kamalākṣmyai namaḥ netre pūjayāmi three eyes

I bow to the Lotus-eyed and worship Her eyes.

ॐ अम्बिकायै नमः शिरः पूजयामि

oṁ ambikāyai namaḥ śiraḥ pūjayāmi top of head

I bow to the Mother of All and worship Her head.

ॐ देव्यै नमः सर्वाङ्ग पूजयामि

oṁ devyai namaḥ sarvāṅga pūjayāmi entire body

I bow to the Goddess and worship Her entire body.

हं रं ईं ह्रीं

haṁ raṁ īṁ hrīṁ

ॐ हकारः स्थूलदेहः स्याद्रकार सूक्ष्मदेहकः ।
ईकारः कारणात्मासौ ह्रीङ्कारोऽहं तुरीयकम् ॥

oṁ hakāraḥ sthūladehaḥ syād
rakāra sūkṣmadehakaḥ
īkāraḥ kāraṇātmāsau hrīṅkāro-haṁ turīyakam

The letter Ha indicates the Gross Body; the letter Ra is the Subtle Body. The letter Ī is the Causal Body; and as the entire letter Hrīṁ, I am beyond manifestation.

pītha nyāsa

establishment of the place of internal worship
With Tattva Mudrā place on the yantra on your chest:

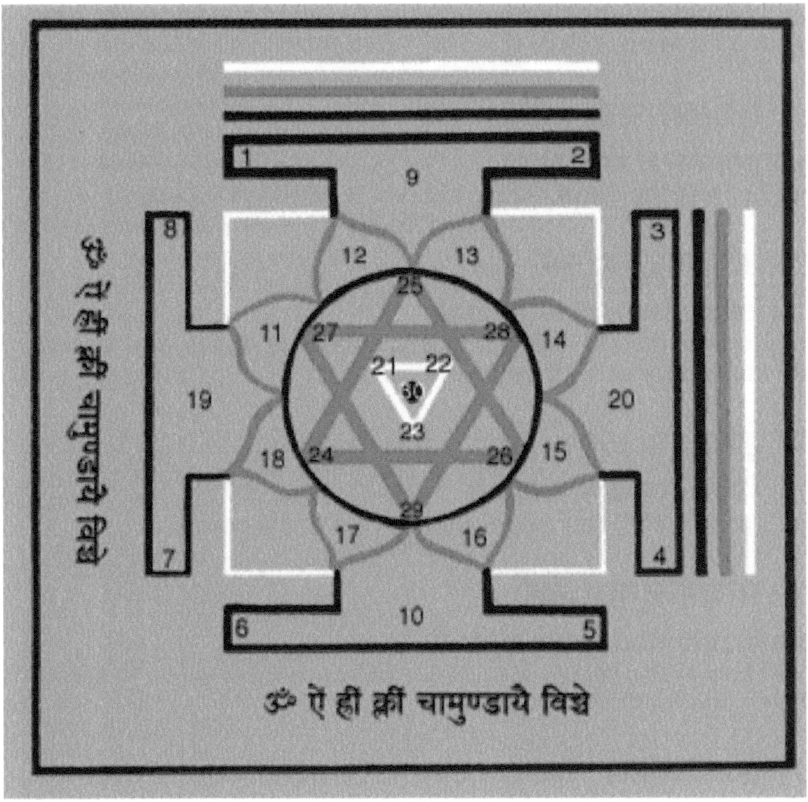

- 1 -

ॐ आधारशक्तये नमः

oṁ ādhāraśaktaye namaḥ
oṁ I bow to the primal energy which sustains existence.

- 2 -

ॐ कूर्माय नमः

oṁ kūrmāya namaḥ
oṁ I bow to the Tortoise which supports creation.

- 3 -

ॐ अनन्ताय नमः

oṁ anantāya namaḥ
oṁ I bow to Infinity (personified as a thousand hooded snake who holds aloft the worlds).

- 4 -

ॐ पृथिव्यै नमः

oṁ pṛthivyai namaḥ
oṁ I bow to the Earth.

- 5 -

ॐ क्षीरसमूद्राय नमः

oṁ kṣīrasamūdrāya namaḥ
oṁ I bow to the milk ocean, or ocean of nectar, the infinite expanse of existence from which all manifested.

- 6 -

ॐ श्वेतद्वीपाय नमः

oṁ śvetadvīpāya namaḥ
oṁ I bow to the Island of Purity, which is in the ocean.

- 7 -

ॐ मणिमन्दपाय नमः

oṁ maṇimandapāya namaḥ
oṁ I bow to the Palace of Gems, which is on the island, the home of the Divine Mother.

- 8 -

ॐ कल्पवृक्षाय नमः

oṁ kalpavṛkṣāya namaḥ
oṁ I bow to the Tree of Fulfillment, which satisfies all desires, growing in the palace courtyard.

- 9 -

ॐ मणिवेदिकायै नमः

oṁ maṇivedikāyai namaḥ
oṁ I bow to the altar containing the gems of wisdom.

- 10 -

ॐ रत्नसिंहासनाय नमः

oṁ ratnasiṁhāsanāya namaḥ
oṁ I bow to the throne of the jewel.

- 11 -

ॐ धर्माय नमः

oṁ dharmāya namaḥ
oṁ I bow to the Way of Truth and Harmony.

- 12 -

ॐ ज्ञानाय नमः

oṁ jñānāya namaḥ
oṁ I bow to Wisdom.

- 13 -

ॐ वैराग्याय नमः

oṁ vairāgyāya namaḥ
oṁ I bow to Detachment.

- 14 -

ॐ ऐश्वर्याय नमः

oṁ aiśvaryāya namaḥ
oṁ I bow to the Imperishable Qualities.

- 15 -

ॐ अधर्माय नमः

oṁ adharmāya namaḥ
oṁ I bow to Disharmony.

- 16 -

ॐ अज्ञानाय नमः

oṁ ajñānāya namaḥ
oṁ I bow to Ignorance.

- 17 -

ॐ अवैराग्याय नमः

oṁ avairāgyāya namaḥ
oṁ I bow to Attachment.

- 18 -

ॐ अनैश्वर्याय नमः

oṁ anīśvaryāya namaḥ
oṁ I bow to the Transient.

- 19 -

ॐ अनन्ताय नमः

oṁ anantāya namaḥ
oṁ I bow to the Infinite.

- 20 -

ॐ पद्माय नमः

oṁ padmāya namaḥ
oṁ I bow to the Lotus.

- 21 -

अं अर्कमण्डलाय द्वादशकलात्मने नमः

aṁ arkamaṇḍalāya dvādaśakalātmane namaḥ
"A" we bow to the twelve aspects of the realm of the sun. Tapinī, Tāpinī, Dhūmrā, Marīci, Jvālinī, Ruci, Sudhūmrā, Bhoga-dā, Viśvā, Bodhinī, Dhāriṇī, Kṣamā; Containing heat, Emanating heat, Smoky, Ray-producing, Burning, Lustrous, Purple or Smoky-red, Granting enjoyment, Universal, Which makes known, Productive of Consciousness, Which supports, Which forgives.

- 22 -

उं सोममण्डलाय षोडशकलात्मने नमः

uṁ somamaṇḍalāya ṣoḍaśakalātmane namaḥ
"U" I bow to the sixteen aspects of the realm of the moon. Amṛta, Prāṇada, Puṣā, Tuṣṭi, Puṣṭi, Rati, Dhṛti, Śaśinī, Candrikā, Kānti, Jyotsnā, Śrī, Prīti, Angadā, Pūrṇā, Pūrnāmṛta; Nectar, Which sustains life, Which supports, Satisfying, Nourishing, Playful, Constancy, Unfailing, Producer of Joy, Beauty enhanced by love, Light, Grantor of Prosperity, Affectionate, Purifying the body, Complete, Full of Bliss.

- 23 -

मं वह्निमण्डलाय दशकलात्मने नमः

maṁ vahnimaṇḍalāya daśakalātmane namaḥ
"M" we bow to the ten aspects of the realm of fire: Dhūmrā, Arciḥ, Jvalinī, Śūkṣmā, Jvālinī, Visphuliṅginī, Suśrī, Surūpā, Kapilā, Havya-Kavya-Vahā; Smoky Red, Flaming, Shining, Subtle,

Burning, Sparkling, Beautiful, Well-formed, Tawny, The Messenger to Gods and Ancestors.

- 24 -

ॐ सं सत्त्वाय नमः

oṁ saṁ sattvāya namaḥ
oṁ I bow to activity, execution, light, knowledge, being.

- 25 -

ॐ रं रजसे नमः

oṁ raṁ rajase namaḥ
oṁ I bow to desire, inspiration, becoming.

- 26 -

ॐ तं तमसे नमः

oṁ taṁ tamase namaḥ
oṁ I bow to wisdom, to the darkness which exposes light, to rest.

- 27 -

ॐ आं आत्मने नमः

oṁ āṁ ātmane namaḥ
oṁ I bow to the Soul.

- 28 -

ॐ अं अन्तरात्मने नमः

oṁ aṁ antarātmane namaḥ
oṁ I bow to the Innermost Soul.

- 29 -

ॐ पं परमात्मने नमः

oṁ paṁ paramātmane namaḥ
oṁ I bow to the Universal Soul, or the Consciousness which exceeds manifestation.

- 30 -

ॐ ह्रीं ज्ञानात्मने नमः

oṁ hrīṁ jñānātmane namaḥ
oṁ I bow to the Soul of Infinite Wisdom.

āvāhaṇa

invitation

अनेकरत्न संयुक्तं नानामणि गणान्वितम् ।

कार्तस्वरमयं दिव्यमासनं प्रतिगृह्यताम् ॥

ॐ श्रीं लक्ष्म्यै नमः आसनं समर्पयामि

anekaratna saṁyuktaṁ nānāmaṇi gaṇānvitam
kārtasvaramayaṁ divyamāsanaṁ pratigṛhyatām
oṁ śrīṁ lakṣmyai namaḥ āsanaṁ samarpayāmi

United with many gems and a multitude of various jewels, voluntarily accept my offering of a divine seat. With the offering of a seat Oṁ I bow to the Goddess Lakṣmī.

establishment within

āvāhaṇi mudrā (I invite you, please come.)

ॐ श्रीं लक्ष्म्यै नमः इहागच्छ

oṁ śrīṁ lakṣmyai namaḥ ihāgaccha

Oṁ I bow to the Goddess Lakṣmī,
I invite you, please come.

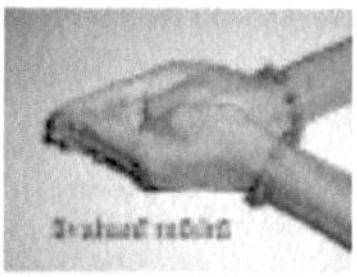

sthāpanī mudrā (I establish you within.)

इह तिष्ठ

iha tiṣṭha

I establish you within.

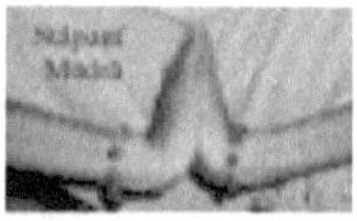

sannidhāpanī mudrā (I know you have many devotees who are requesting your attention, but I request that you pay special attention to me.)

इह सन्निरुध्यस्व

iha sannirudhyasva

I am binding you to remain here.

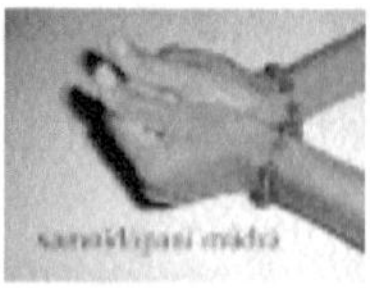

saṁrodhanī mudrā (I am sorry for any inconvenience caused.)

इह सनिहित भव

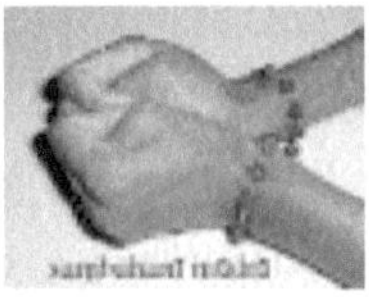

iha sanihita bhava
You bestow abundant wealth.

atmā samarpaṇa mudrā (I surrender my soul to you.)

अत्राधिष्ठानं कुरु

atrādhiṣṭhānaṁ kuru
I am depending upon you to forgive me in this matter.

prakṣan (I bow to you with devotion.)

देवि मम पूजां गृहाण
देवेशि भक्तशूल्वे परित्राण करायिते ।
यावत् त्वं पूजयिष्यामि तावत् त्वं सुस्थिरा भव ॥

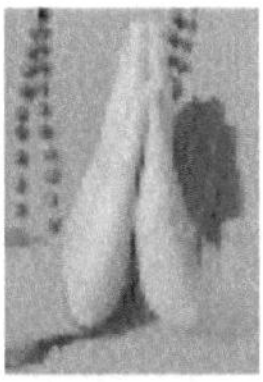

devi mama pūjāṁ gṛhāṇa
deveśi bhaktaśūlave paritrāṇa karāyite
yāvat tvaṁ pūjayiṣyāmi tāvat tvaṁ susthirā bhava
Oh Goddess, please accept my worship. Oh Goddess, remove all pain from your devotees. For so long as I worship you, please remain sitting still.

prāṇa pratiṣṭhā
establishment of life

ॐ अं आं ह्रीं क्रों यं रं लं वं शं षं सं हों हं सः

oṁ aṁ āṁ hrīṁ kroṁ yaṁ raṁ laṁ vaṁ śaṁ ṣaṁ saṁ hoṁ haṁ saḥ

oṁ The Infinite Beyond Conception, Creation (the first letter), Consciousness, Māyā, the cause of the movement of the subtle body to perfection and beyond; the path of fulfillment: control, subtle illumination, one with the earth, emancipation, the soul of peace, the soul of delight, the soul of unity (all this is I), perfection, Infinite Consciousness, this is I.

ॐ श्रीं लक्ष्मयै नमः प्राणा इह प्राणाः

oṁ śrīṁ lakṣmyai namaḥ prāṇā iha prāṇāḥ

Oṁ I bow to the Goddess Lakṣmī. You are the life of this life!

ॐ अं आं ह्रीं क्रों यं रं लं वं शं षं सं हों हं सः

oṁ aṁ āṁ hrīṁ kroṁ yaṁ raṁ laṁ vaṁ śaṁ ṣaṁ saṁ hoṁ haṁ saḥ

oṁ The Infinite Beyond Conception, Creation (the first letter), Consciousness, Māyā, the cause of the movement of the subtle body to perfection and beyond; the path of fulfillment: control, subtle illumination, one with the earth, emancipation, the soul of peace, the soul of delight, the soul of unity (all this is I), perfection, Infinite Consciousness, this is I.

ॐ श्रीं लक्ष्मयै नमः जीव इह स्थितः

oṁ śrīṁ lakṣmyai namaḥ jīva iha sthitaḥ

Oṁ I bow to the Goddess Lakṣmī. You are situated in this life (or individual consciousness).

ॐ अं आं ह्रीं क्रों यं रं लं वं शं षं सं हों हं सः

oṁ aṁ āṁ hrīṁ kroṁ yaṁ raṁ laṁ vaṁ śaṁ ṣaṁ saṁ hoṁ haṁ saḥ

oṁ The Infinite Beyond Conception, Creation (the first letter), Consciousness, Māyā, the cause of the movement of the subtle body to perfection and beyond; the path of fulfillment: control, subtle illumination, one with the earth, emancipation, the soul of peace, the soul of delight, the soul of unity (all this is I), perfection, Infinite Consciousness, this is I.

ॐ श्रीं लक्ष्म्यै नमः सर्वेन्द्रियाणि

oṁ śrīṁ lakṣmyai namaḥ sarvendriyāṇi
Oṁ I bow to the Goddess Lakṣmī. You are all these organs (of action and knowledge).

ॐ अं आं ह्रीं क्रों यं रं लं वं शं षं सं होंं हं सः

oṁ aṁ āṁ hrīṁ kroṁ yaṁ raṁ laṁ vaṁ śaṁ ṣaṁ saṁ hoṁ haṁ saḥ
oṁ The Infinite Beyond Conception, Creation (the first letter), Consciousness, Māyā, the cause of the movement of the subtle body to perfection and beyond; the path of fulfillment: control, subtle illumination, one with the earth, emancipation, the soul of peace, the soul of delight, the soul of unity (all this is I), perfection, Infinite Consciousness, this is I.

ॐ श्रीं लक्ष्म्यै नमः वाग् मनस्त्वक्चक्षुः-श्रोत्र-घ्राण-प्राणा इहागत्य सुखं चिरं तिष्ठन्तु स्वाहा

oṁ śrīṁ lakṣmyai namaḥ vāg manastvakcakṣuḥ śrotra ghrāṇa prāṇā ihāgatya sukhaṁ ciraṁ tiṣṭhantu svāhā
Oṁ I bow to the Goddess Lakṣmī. You are all these vibrations, mind, sound, eyes, ears, tongue, nose and life force. Bring forth infinite peace and establish it forever, I am One with God!

kara nyāsa
establishment in the hands

ॐ श्रां अंगुष्ठाभ्यां नमः

oṁ śrāṁ aṅguṣṭhābhyāṁ namaḥ thumb forefinger
Oṁ śrāṁ in the thumb I bow.

ॐ श्रीं तर्जनीभ्यां स्वाहा

oṁ śrīṁ tarjanībhyāṁ svāhā thumb forefinger
Oṁ śrīṁ in the forefinger, I am One with God!

ॐ श्रूं मध्यमाभ्यां वषट्

oṁ śrūṁ madhyamābhyāṁ vaṣaṭ thumb middlefinger
Oṁ śrūṁ in the middle finger, Purify!

ॐ श्रैं अनामिकाभ्यां हुं

oṁ śraiṁ anāmikābhyāṁ huṁ thumb ring finger
Oṁ śraiṁ in the ring finger, Cut the Ego!

ॐ श्रौं कनिष्ठिकाभ्यां बौषट्

oṁ śrauṁ kaniṣṭhikābhyāṁ vauṣaṭ thumb little finger
Oṁ śrauṁ in the little finger, Ultimate Purity!

Roll hand over hand forwards while reciting karatal kar,
and backwards while chanting pṛṣṭhābhyāṁ,
then clap hands when chanting astrāya phaṭ.

ॐ श्रः करतल कर पृष्ठाभ्यां अस्त्राय फट् ॥

oṁ śraḥ karatal kar pṛṣṭhābhyāṁ astrāya phaṭ
Oṁ śraḥ I bow to the Goddess Lakṣmī, with the weapon of Virtue.

ॐ श्रीं लक्ष्मयै नमः

oṁ śrīṁ lakṣmyai namaḥ
Oṁ I bow to the Goddess Lakṣmī

aṅga nyāsa

establishment in the body
Holding tattva mudrā, touch heart.

ॐ श्रां हृदयाय नमः

oṁ śrāṁ hṛdayāya namaḥ touch heart
Oṁ śrāṁ in the heart, I bow.

Holding tattva mudrā, touch top of head.

ॐ श्रीं शिरसे स्वाहा

oṁ śrīṁ śirase svāhā top of head
Oṁ śrīṁ on the top of the head, I am One with God!

With thumb extended, touch back of head.

ॐ श्रूं शिखायै वषट्

oṁ śrūṁ śikhāyai vaṣaṭ back of head
Oṁ śrūṁ on the back of the head, Purify!

Holding tattva mudrā, cross both arms.

ॐ श्रैं कवचाय हुं

oṁ śraiṁ kavacāya huṁ cross both arms
Oṁ śraiṁ crossing both arms, Cut the Ego!

Holding tattva mudrā, touch two eyes and in between at once with three middle fingers.

ॐ श्रौं नेत्रत्रयाय वौषट्

oṁ śrauṁ netratrayāya vauṣaṭ touch three eyes
Oṁ śrauṁ in the three eyes, Ultimate Purity!

Roll hand over hand forwards while reciting karatal kar,
and backwards while chanting pṛṣṭhābhyāṁ,
then clap hands when chanting astrāya phaṭ.

ॐ श्रः करतल कर पृष्ठाभ्यां अस्त्राय फट् ॥

oṁ śraḥ karatal kar pṛṣṭhābhyāṁ astrāya phaṭ
Oṁ śraḥ I bow to the Goddess Lakṣmī with the weapon of Virtue.

ॐ श्रीं लक्ष्म्यै नमः

oṁ śrīṁ lakṣmyai namaḥ
Oṁ I bow to the Goddess Lakṣmī.

japa

stapana

establishment upon the altar

hold flower to your heart

ॐ अम्बे ऽअम्बिकेऽम्बालिके न मा नयति कश्चन ।
ससस्त्यश्वकः सुभद्रिकां कापीलोवासिनीम् ॥

oṁ ambe-ambike-mbālike na mā nayati kaścana
sasastyaśvakaḥ subhadrikāṁ kāpīlovāsinīm
Mother of the Perceivable Universe, Mother of the Conceivable Universe, Mother of the Universe of Intuitive Vision, lead me to that True Existence. As excellent crops (or grains) are harvested, so may I be taken to reside with the Infinite Consciousness.

place flower on yantra

ॐ जयन्ती मङ्गला काली भद्रकाली कपालिनी ।
दुर्गा क्षमा शिवा धात्री स्वाहा स्वधा नमोऽस्तु ते ॥

oṁ jayantī maṅgalā kālī bhadra kālī kapālinī
durgā kṣamā śivā dhātrī svāhā svadhā namo-stu te
Oṁ. She Who Conquers Over All, All-Auspicious, She Who is Beyond Time, the Excellent One Beyond Time, the Bearer of the Skulls of Impure Thought, the Reliever of Difficulties, Loving Forgiveness, Supporter of the Universe, Oblations of I am One with God, Oblations of Ancestral Praise, to You, we bow.

upasaṁhara sthāpana mudrā

दुर्गां शिवां शान्तिकरीं ब्रह्माणीं ब्रह्मणः प्रियाम् ।
सर्वलोक प्रणेत्रीञ्च प्रणमामि सदा शिवाम् ॥

durgāṁ śivāṁ śāntikarīṁ brahmāṇīṁ brahmaṇaḥ priyām
sarvaloka praṇetrīñca praṇamāmi sadā śivām

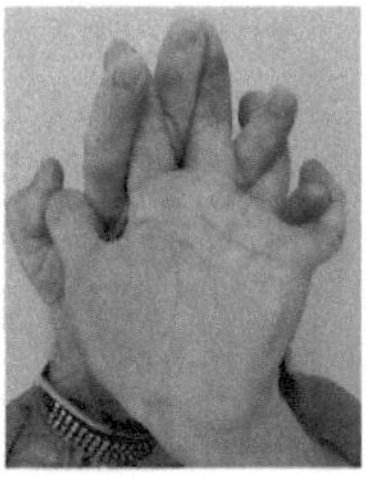

The Reliever of Difficulties, Exposer of Goodness, Cause of Peace, Infinite Consciousness, Beloved by Knowers of Consciousness; all the inhabitants of all the worlds always bow to Her, and I am bowing to Goodness Herself.

मङ्गलां शोभनां शुद्धां निष्कलां परमां कलाम् ।
विश्वेश्वरीं विश्वमातां चण्डिकां प्रणमाम्यहम् ॥

maṅgalāṁ śobhanāṁ śuddhāṁ niṣkalāṁ paramāṁ kalām
viśveśvarīṁ viśvamātāṁ caṇḍikāṁ praṇamāmyaham

Welfare, Radiant Beauty, Completely Pure, Without Limitations, the Ultimate Limitation, the Lord of the Universe, the Mother of the Universe, to you Caṇḍi, to the Energy that Tears Apart Thought, I bow in submission.

ॐ महालक्ष्मयै च विद्महे सर्वशक्त्यै च धीमहे ।
तन्नो देवी प्रचोदयात् ॥

oṁ mahālakṣmyai ca vidmahe sarvaśaktyai ca dhīmahe
tanno devī pracodayāt

Oṁ We meditate upon the Great Goddess of True Wealth, we contemplate She Who Embodies all Energy. May that Goddess grant us increase.

āvāhaṇi mudrā (I invite you, please come.)

ॐ श्रीं लक्ष्मयै नमः इहागच्छ

oṁ śrīṁ lakṣmyai namaḥ ihāgaccha

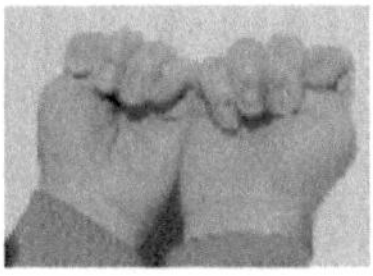

Oṁ I bow to the Goddess Lakṣmī,
I invite you, please come.

sthāpanī mudrā (I establish you within.)

इह तिष्ठ

iha tiṣṭha

I establish you within.

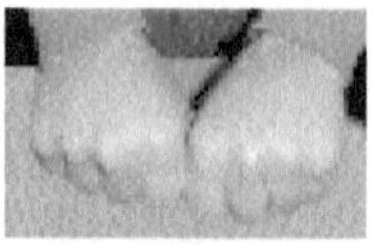

sannidhāpanī mudrā (I know you have many devotees who are requesting your attention, but I request that you pay special attention to me.)

इह सन्निदेहि

iha sannidehi

I am binding you to remain here.

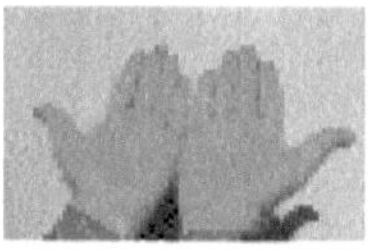

saṁrodhanī mudrā (I am sorry for any inconvenience caused.)

इह सनिहित भव

iha sanihita bhava

You bestow abundant wealth.

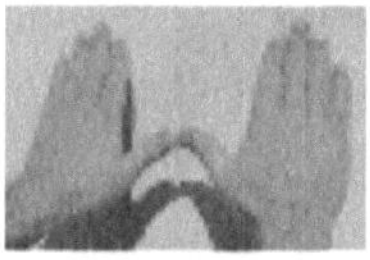

atmā samarpaṇa mudrā (I surrender my soul to you.)

अत्राधिष्ठानं कुरु

atrādhiṣṭhānaṁ kuru

I am depending upon you to forgive me in this matter.

prakṣan (I bow to you with devotion.)

देवि मम पूजां गृहाण

देवेशि भक्तशूलवे परित्राण करायिते ।

यावत् त्वं पूजयिष्यामि तावत् त्वं सुस्थिरा भव ॥

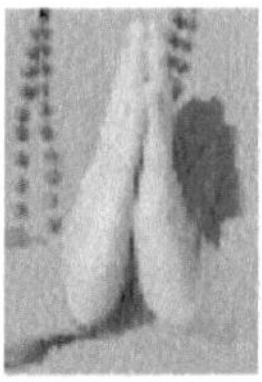

devi mama pūjāṁ gṛhāṇa
deveśi bhaktaśūlave paritrāṇa karāyite
yāvat tvaṁ pūjayiṣyāmi tāvat tvaṁ susthirā bhava

Oh Goddess, please accept my worship. Oh Goddess, remove all pain from your devotees. For so long as I worship you, please remain sitting still.

pūjā naivedya
offerings of worship
invitation

आगच्छेह महादेवि ! सर्वसम्पत्प्रदायिनि ।
यावद् व्रतं समाप्येत तावत्त्वं सन्निधौ भव ॥
ॐ श्रीं लक्ष्मयै नमः आवाहनं समर्पयामि

āgaccheha mahādevi ! sarvasampatpradāyini
yāvad vrataṁ samāpyeta tāvattvaṁ sannidhau bhava
oṁ śrīṁ lakṣmyai namaḥ āvāhanaṁ samarpayāmi

Please come here, oh Great Goddess, Giver of all wealth! Please remain sitting still until this vow of worship is not complete. With the offering of an invitation Oṁ I bow to the Goddess Lakṣmī.

seat

अनेकरत्नसंयुक्तं नानामणिगणान्वितम् ।
कार्तस्वरमयं दिव्यमासनं प्रतिगृह्यताम् ॥
ॐ श्रीं लक्ष्मयै नमः आसनं समर्पयामि

anekaratna saṁyuktaṁ nānāmaṇi gaṇānvitam
kārtasvaramayaṁ divyamāsanaṁ pratigṛhyatām
oṁ śrīṁ lakṣmyai namaḥ āsanaṁ samarpayāmi

United with many gems and a multitude of various jewels, voluntarily accept my offering of a divine seat. With the offering of a seat Oṁ I bow to the Goddess Lakṣmī.

foot bath

ॐ गङ्गादिसर्वतीर्थेभ्यो मया प्रार्थनयाहृतम् ।
तोयमेतत् सुखस्पर्शं पाद्यार्थं प्रतिगृह्यताम् ॥
ॐ श्रीं लक्ष्मयै नमः पाद्यं समर्पयामि

oṁ gaṅgādi sarva tīrthebhyo mayā prārthanayāhṛtam
toyametat sukha sparśaṁ pādyārthaṁ pratigṛhyatām
oṁ śrīṁ lakṣmyai namaḥ pādyaṁ samarpayāmi

The Gaṅges and other waters from all the places of pilgrimage are mingled together in this our prayer, that you please accept the comfortable touch of these waters offered to wash your lotus feet. With this offering of foot bath waters Oṁ I bow to the Goddess Lakṣmī.

water for washing hands and mouth

कर्पूरेण सुगन्धेन सुरभिस्वादु शीतलम् ।

तोयमाचमनीयार्थं देवीदं प्रतिगृह्यताम् ॥

ॐ श्रीं लक्ष्मयै नमः आचमनीयं समर्पयामि

karpūreṇa sugandhena surabhisvādu śītalam
toyamācamanīyārthaṁ devīdaṁ pratigṛhyatām
oṁ śrīṁ lakṣmyai namaḥ ācamanīyaṁ samarpayāmi

With camphor and excellent scent, cool with excellent taste, this water is being offered for washing, Oh Goddess, please accept. With this offering of washing waters Oṁ I bow to the Goddess Lakṣmī.

arghya

निधीनां सर्वदेवानां त्वमनर्घ्यगुणा ह्यसि ।

सिंहोपरिस्थिते देवि ! गृहाणार्घ्यं नमोऽस्तु ते ॥

ॐ श्रीं लक्ष्मयै नमः अर्घ्यं समर्पयामि

nidhīnāṁ sarvadevānāṁ tvamanarghyaguṇā hyasi
siṁhoparisthite devi ! gṛhāṇārghyaṁ namo-stu te
oṁ śrīṁ lakṣmyai namaḥ arghyaṁ samarpayāmi

Presented to all the Gods, you, oh Arghya, bring an abundance of pleasure. Oh Goddess who is seated upon the lion, accept this arghya. I bow to you. With this offering of arghya Oṁ I bow to the Goddess Lakṣmī.

madhuparka

दधिमधुघृतसमायुक्तं पात्रयुग्मं समन्वितम् ।

मधुपर्कं गृहाण त्वं शुभदा भव शोभने ॥

ॐ श्रीं लक्ष्मयै नमः मधुपर्कं समर्पयामि

dadhi madhu ghṛtasamāyuktaṁ
pātrayugmaṁ samanvitam
madhuparkaṁ gṛhāṇa tvaṁ śubhadā bhava śobhane
oṁ śrīṁ lakṣmyai namaḥ madhuparkaṁ samarpayāmi

Yogurt, honey, ghee mixed together, and blended fine in a vessel; please accept this madhuparka shining with radiant purity. With this offering of madhuparka Oṁ I bow to the Goddess Lakṣmī.

milk bath

ॐ कामधेनुसमुद्भूतं सर्वेषां जीवनं परम् ।
पावनं यज्ञहेतुश्च स्नानार्थं प्रतिगृह्यताम् ॥
ॐ श्रीं लक्ष्म्यै नमः पयस्नानं समर्पयामि

oṁ kāmadhenu samudbhūtaṁ sarveṣāṁ jīvanaṁ param
pāvanaṁ yajña hetuśca snānārthaṁ pratigṛhyatām
oṁ śrīṁ lakṣmyai namaḥ paya snānaṁ samarpayāmi

Coming from the ocean of being, the Fulfiller of all Desires, Grantor of Supreme Bliss to all souls. For the motive of purifying or sanctifying this holy union, we request you to accept this bath. With this offering of milk for your bath Oṁ I bow to the Goddess Lakṣmī.

yogurt bath

ॐ पयसस्तु समुद्भूतं मधुराम्लं शशिप्रभम् ।
दध्यानितं मया दत्तं स्नानार्थं प्रतिगृह्यताम् ॥
ॐ श्रीं लक्ष्म्यै नमः दधिस्नानं समर्पयामि

oṁ payasastu samudbhūtaṁ madhurāmlaṁ śaśiprabham
dadhyānitaṁ mayā dattaṁ snānārthaṁ pratigṛhyatām
oṁ śrīṁ lakṣmyai namaḥ dadhi snānaṁ samarpayāmi

Derived from milk from the ocean of being, sweet and pleasing like the glow of the moon, let these curds eternally be our ambassador, as we request you to accept this bath. With this offering of yogurt for your bath Oṁ I bow to the Goddess Lakṣmī.

ghee bath

ॐ नवनीतसमुत्पन्नं सर्वसन्तोषकारकम् ।
घृतं तुभ्यं प्रदास्यामि स्नानार्थं प्रतिगृह्यताम् ॥
ॐ श्रीं लक्ष्म्यै नमः घृतस्नानं समर्पयामि

oṁ navanīta samutpannaṁ sarvasantoṣakārakam
ghṛtaṁ tubhyaṁ pradāsyāmi snānārthaṁ pratigṛhyatām
oṁ śrīṁ lakṣmyai namaḥ ghṛta snānaṁ samarpayāmi

Freshly prepared from the ocean of being, causing all fulfillment, we offer this delightful ghee (clarified butter) and request you to accept this bath. With this offering of ghee for your bath Oṁ I bow to the Goddess Lakṣmī.

honey bath

ॐ तरुपुष्पसमुद्भूतं सुस्वादु मधुरं मधु ।
तेजोपुष्टिकरं दिव्यं स्नानार्थं प्रतिगृह्यताम् ॥
ॐ श्रीं लक्ष्म्यै नमः मधुस्नानं समर्पयामि

oṁ tarupuṣpa samudbhūtam susvādu madhuraṁ madhu
tejo puṣṭikaraṁ divyaṁ snānārtham pratigṛhyatām
oṁ śrīṁ lakṣmyai namaḥ madhu snānaṁ samarpayāmi

Prepared from flowers of the ocean of being, enjoyable as the sweetest of the sweet, causing the fire of divine nourishment to burn swiftly, we request you to accept this bath. With this offering of honey for your bath Oṁ I bow to the Goddess Lakṣmī.

sugar bath

ॐ इक्षुसारसमुद्भूता शर्करा पुष्टिकारिका ।
मलापहारिका दिव्या स्नानार्थं प्रतिगृह्यताम् ॥
ॐ श्रीं लक्ष्म्यै नमः शर्करास्नानं समर्पयामि

oṁ ikṣusāra samudbhūtā śarkarā puṣṭikārikā
malāpahārikā divyā snānārthaṁ pratigṛhyatām
oṁ śrīṁ lakṣmyai namaḥ śarkarā snānaṁ samarpayāmi

From the lake of sugar-cane, from the ocean of being, which causes the nourishment of sugar to give divine protection from all impurity, we request you to accept this bath. With this offering of sugar for your bath Oṁ I bow to the Goddess Lakṣmī.

five nectars bath

ॐ पयो दधि घृतं चैव मधु च शर्करायुतम् ।
पञ्चामृतं मयाऽऽनीतं स्नानार्थं प्रतिगृह्यताम् ॥
ॐ श्रीं लक्ष्म्यै नमः पञ्चामृतस्नानं समर्पयामि

oṁ payo dadhi ghṛtaṁ caiva madhu ca śarkarāyutam
pañcāmṛtaṁ mayā--nītaṁ snānārthaṁ pratigṛhyatām
oṁ śrīṁ lakṣmyai namaḥ pañcāmṛta snānaṁ samarpayāmi

Milk, curd, ghee and then honey and sugar mixed together; these five nectars are our ambassador, as we request you to accept this bath. With this offering of five nectars for your bath Oṁ I bow to the Goddess Lakṣmī.

scented oil

ॐ नानासुगन्धिद्रव्यं च चन्दनं रजनीयुतम् ।
उद्वर्तनं मया दत्तं स्नानार्थं प्रतिगृह्यताम् ॥
ॐ श्रीं लक्ष्म्यै नमः उद्वर्तनस्नानं समर्पयामि

oṁ nānāsugandhidravyaṁ ca candanaṁ rajanīyutam
udvartanaṁ mayā dattaṁ snānārthaṁ pratigṛhyatām
oṁ śrīṁ lakṣmyai namaḥ udvartana snānaṁ samarpayāmi

oṁ With various beautifully smelling ingredients, as well as the scent of sandal, we offer you this scented oil, Oh Lord. With this offering of scented oil Oṁ I bow to the Goddess Lakṣmī.

scent bath

गन्धद्वारां दुराधर्षां नित्यपुष्टां करीषिणीम् ।
ईश्वरीं सर्वभूतानां तामिहोपह्वये श्रियम् ॥
ॐ श्रीं लक्ष्म्यै नमः गन्धस्नानं समर्पयामि

gandhadvārāṁ durādharṣāṁ nityapuṣṭāṁ karīṣiṇīm
īśvarīṁ sarvabhūtānāṁ tāmihopahvaye śriyam
oṁ śrīṁ lakṣmyai namaḥ gandha snānaṁ samarpayāmi

She is the cause of the scent which is the door to religious ecstasy, unconquerable (never-failing), continually nurturing for all time. May we never tire from calling that manifestation of the Highest Respect, the Supreme Goddess of all existence. With this offering of scented bath Oṁ I bow to the Goddess Lakṣmī.

water bath

ॐ गङ्गे च जमुने चैव गोदावरि सरस्वति ।
नर्मदे सिन्धु कावेरि स्नानार्थं प्रतिगृह्यताम् ॥
ॐ श्रीं लक्ष्म्यै नमः गङ्गास्नानं समर्पयामि

oṁ gaṅge ca jamune caiva godāvari sarasvati
narmade sindhu kāveri snānārthaṁ pratigṛhyatām
oṁ śrīṁ lakṣmyai namaḥ gaṅgā snānaṁ samarpayāmi

Please accept the waters from the Gaṅges, the Jamunā, Godāvarī, Sarasvatī, Narmadā, Sindhu and Kāverī, which have been provided for your bath. With this offering of Ganges bath waters Oṁ I bow to the Goddess Lakṣmī.

cloth

ॐ शीतवातोष्णसंत्राणं लज्जायै रक्षणं परं ।
देहालंकरणं वस्त्रं अथ शान्तिं प्रयच्छ मे ॥
ॐ श्रीं लक्ष्मयै नमः वस्त्रं समर्पयामि

oṁ śīta vātoṣṇa saṁ trāṇaṁ lajjāyai rakṣaṇaṁ paraṁ
dehālaṅkaraṇaṁ vastraṁ atha śāntiṁ prayaccha me
oṁ śrīṁ lakṣmyai namaḥ vastraṁ samarpayāmi

To take away the cold and the wind and to fully protect your modesty, we adorn your body with this cloth, and thereby find the greatest Peace. With this offering of wearing apparel Oṁ I bow to the Goddess Lakṣmī.

sacred thread

ॐ यज्ञोपवीतं परमं पवित्रं प्रजापतेर्यत् सहजं पुरस्तात् ।
आयुष्यमग्रं प्रतिमुञ्च शुभ्रं यज्ञोपवीतं बलमस्तु तेजः ॥

oṁ yajñopavītaṁ paramaṁ pavitraṁ
prajāpateryat sahajaṁ purastāt
āyuṣyamagraṁ pratimuñca śubhraṁ
yajñopavītaṁ balamastu tejaḥ

Oṁ the sacred thread of the highest purity is given by Prajāpati, the Lord of Creation, for the greatest facility. You bring life and illuminate the greatness of liberation. Oh sacred thread, let your strength be of radiant light.

शमो दमस्तपः शौचं क्षान्तिरार्जवमेव च ।
ज्ञानं विज्ञानमास्तिक्यं ब्रह्मकर्म स्वभावजम् ॥

śamo damastapaḥ śaucaṁ kṣāntirārjavameva ca
jñānaṁ vijñānamāstikyaṁ brahmakarma svabhāvajam

Peacefulness, self-control, austerity, purity of mind and body, patience and forgiveness, sincerity and honesty, wisdom, knowledge, and self-realization, are the natural activities of a Brahmaṇa.

नवभिस्तन्तुभिर्युक्तं त्रिगुणं देवतामयं ।
उपवीतं मया दत्तं गृहाण त्वं सुरेश्वरि ॥
ॐ श्रीं लक्ष्म्यै नमः यज्ञोपवीतं समर्पयामि

navabhiṣṭantubhiryuktaṁ triguṇaṁ devatā mayaṁ
upavītaṁ mayā dattaṁ gṛhāṇa tvaṁ sureśvari
oṁ śrīṁ lakṣmyai namaḥ yajñopavītaṁ samarpayāmi

With nine desirable threads all united together, exemplifying the three guṇas (or three qualities of harmony of our deity), this sacred thread will be our ambassador. Oh Ruler of the Gods, please accept. With this offering of a sacred thread Oṁ I bow to the Goddess Lakṣmī.

rudrākṣa

त्र्यम्बकं यजामहे सुगन्धिं पुष्टिवर्द्धनम् ।
उर्वारुकमिव बन्धनान्मृत्योर्मुक्षीयमामृतात् ॥
ॐ श्रीं लक्ष्म्यै नमः रुद्राक्षं समर्पयामि

tryambakaṁ yajāmahe sugandhiṁ puṣṭivarddhanam
urvārukamiva bandhanānmṛtyormukṣīyamāmṛtāt
oṁ śrīṁ lakṣmyai namaḥ rudrākṣaṁ samarpayāmi

We adore the Father of the three worlds, of excellent fame, Grantor of Increase. As a cucumber is released from its bondage to the stem, so may we be freed from Death to dwell in immortality. With this offering of rudrākṣa Oṁ I bow to the Goddess Lakṣmī.

mālā

ॐ मां माले महामाये सर्वशक्तिस्वरूपिणि ।
चतुर्वर्गस्त्वयि न्यस्तस्तस्मान्मे सिद्धिदा भव ॥
ॐ श्रीं लक्ष्म्यै नमः मालां समर्पयामि

oṁ māṁ māle mahāmāye sarvaśaktisvarūpiṇi
caturvargastvayi nyastastasmānme siddhidā bhava
oṁ śrīṁ lakṣmyai namaḥ mālāṁ samarpayāmi

Oṁ my rosary, the Great Limitation of Consciousness, containing all energy within as your intrinsic nature, fulfilling the four desires of men, give us the attainment of your perfection. With this offering of a mālā Oṁ I bow to the Goddess Lakṣmī.

red powder

ॐ सिन्दूरमरुणाभासं जपाकुसुमसन्निभम् ।
पूजिताऽसि मया देवि प्रसीद परमेश्वरि ॥
ॐ श्रीं लक्ष्मयै नमः सिन्दूरं समर्पयामि

oṁ sindūramaruṇābhāsaṁ japākusumasannibham
pūjitā-si mayā devi prasīda parameśvari
oṁ śrīṁ lakṣmyai namaḥ sindūraṁ samarpayāmi

This red colored powder indicates Love, who drives the chariot of the Light of Wisdom, with which we are worshiping our Lord. Please be pleased, Oh Great Seer of All. With this offering of red colored powder Oṁ I bow to the Goddess Lakṣmī.

kuṅkum

ॐ कुङ्कुमं कान्तिदं दिव्यं कामिनीकामसम्भवम् ।
कुङ्कुमेनाऽर्चिते देवि प्रसीद परमेश्वरि ॥
ॐ श्रीं लक्ष्मयै नमः कुङ्कुमं समर्पयामि

oṁ kuṅkumaṁ kāntidaṁ divyaṁ
kāminī kāmasambhavam
kuṅkumenā-rcite devi prasīda parameśvari
oṁ śrīṁ lakṣmyai namaḥ kuṅkumaṁ samarpayāmi

You are being adorned with this divine red powder, which is made more beautiful by the love we share with you, and is so pleasing. Oh Lord, when we present this red powder be pleased, Oh Supreme Ruler of All. With this offering of red colored powder Oṁ I bow to the Goddess Lakṣmī.

sandal paste

ॐ श्रीखण्डचन्दनं दिव्यं गन्धाढ्यं सुमनोहरम् ।
विलेपनं च देवेशि चन्दनं प्रतिगृह्यताम् ॥
ॐ श्रीं लक्ष्मयै नमः चन्दनं समर्पयामि

oṁ śrīkhaṇḍacandanaṁ divyaṁ
gandhāḍhyaṁ sumano haram
vilepanaṁ ca deveśi candanaṁ pratigṛhyatām
oṁ śrīṁ lakṣmyai namaḥ candanaṁ samarpayāmi

You are being adorned with this beautiful divine piece of sandal wood, ground to a paste which is so pleasing. Please accept this offering of sandal paste, Oh Supreme Sovereign of all the Gods. With the offering of sandal paste Oṁ I bow to the Goddess Lakṣmī.

turmeric

ॐ हरिद्रारञ्जिता देवि सुख-सौभाग्यदायिनि ।

तस्मात्त्वं पूजयाम्यत्र दुःखशान्तिं प्रयच्छ मे ॥

ॐ श्रीं लक्ष्मयै नमः हरिद्रां समर्पयामि

oṁ haridrārañjitā devi sukha saubhāgyadāyini
tasmāttvaṁ pūjayāmyatra duḥkha śāntiṁ prayaccha me
oṁ śrīṁ lakṣmyai namaḥ haridrāṁ samarpayāmi

Oh Lord, you are being gratified by this turmeric, the giver of comfort and beauty. When you are worshiped like this, then you must bestow upon us the greatest peace. With the offering of turmeric Oṁ I bow to the Goddess Lakṣmī.

bracelets

ॐ माणिक्यमुक्ताखण्डयुक्ते सुवर्णकारेण च संस्कृते ये ।

ते किङ्किणीभिः स्वरिते सुवर्णे

मयाऽर्पिते देवि गृहाण कङ्कणे ॥

ॐ श्रीं लक्ष्मयै नमः कङ्कणे समर्पयामि

oṁ māṇikya muktā khaṇḍayukte
suvarṇakāreṇa ca saṁskṛte ye
te kiṅkiṇībhiḥ svarite suvarṇe
mayā-rpite devi gṛhāṇa kaṅkaṇe
oṁ śrīṁ lakṣmyai namaḥ kaṅkaṇe samarpayāmi

Oṁ United with gems and pearls, excellent gold and the alphabets of Saṁskṛta, this bracelet is yours and radiance I am offering. Oh Goddess, accept this bracelet. With this offering of a bracelet Oṁ I bow to the Goddess Lakṣmī.

conch ornaments

ॐ शङ्खञ्च विविधं चित्रं बाहूनाञ्च विभूषणम् ।
मया निवेदितं भक्त्या गृहाण परमेश्वरि ॥
ॐ श्रीं लक्ष्म्यै नमः शङ्खालङ्कारं समर्पयामि

oṁ śaṅkhañca vividhaṁ citraṁ bāhūnāñca vibhūṣaṇam
mayā niveditaṁ bhaktyā gṛhāṇa parameśvari
oṁ śrīṁ lakṣmyai namaḥ śaṅkhālaṅkāraṁ samarpayāmi

I am offering you with devotion ornaments worn upon the arms made of various qualities of conch shell. Please accept them, oh Supreme Divinity. With this offering of ornaments made of conch shell Oṁ I bow to the Goddess Lakṣmī.

ornaments

ॐ दिव्यरत्नसमायुक्ता वह्निभानुसमप्रभाः ।
गात्राणि शोभयिष्यन्ति अलङ्काराः सुरेश्वरि ॥
ॐ श्रीं लक्ष्म्यै नमः अलङ्कारान् समर्पयामि

oṁ divyaratnasamāyuktā vahnibhānusamaprabhāḥ
gātrāṇi śobhayiṣyanti alaṅkārāḥ sureśvari
oṁ śrīṁ lakṣmyai namaḥ alaṅkārān samarpayāmi

Oṁ United with divine jewels that are radiant like fire, and stones which are shining, please accept these ornaments, oh Supreme among the Gods. With this offering of ornaments Oṁ I bow to the Goddess Lakṣmī.

rice

अक्षतान् निर्मलान् शुद्धान् मुक्ताफलसमन्वितान् ।
गृहाणेमान् महादेवि देहि मे निर्मलां धियम् ॥
ॐ श्रीं लक्ष्म्यै नमः अक्षतान् समर्पयामि

akṣatān nirmalān śuddhān muktāphalasamanvitān
gṛhāṇemān mahādevi dehi me nirmalāṁ dhiyam
oṁ śrīṁ lakṣmyai namaḥ akṣatān samarpayāmi

Oh Great Goddess, please accept these grains of rice, spotlessly clean, bestowing the fruit of liberation, and give us a spotlessly clean mind. With this offering of grains of rice Oṁ I bow to the Goddess Lakṣmī.

food offering

ॐ सत्पात्रं शुद्धसुहविर्विविधानेकभक्षणम् ।
निवेदयामि देवेशि सर्वतृप्तिकरं परम् ॥

oṁ satpātraṁ śuddhasuhavir vividhānekabhakṣaṇam
nivedayāmi deveśi sarvatṛptikaraṁ param

Oṁ This ever-present platter containing varieties of the purest offerings of food we are presenting to the Lord of Gods to cause all satisfaction, most excellent and transcendental.

ॐ अन्नपूर्णे सदा पूर्णे शङ्करप्राणवल्लभे ।
ज्ञानवैराग्यसिद्ध्यर्थं भिक्षां देहि नमोऽस्तु ते ॥

oṁ annapūrṇe sadā pūrṇe śaṅkara prāṇavallabhe
jñānavairāgyasiddhyarthaṁ bhikṣāṁ dehi namo-stu te

Oṁ Goddess who is full, complete and perfect with food and grains, always full, complete and perfect, the strength of the life force of Śiva, the Cause of Peace. For the attainment of perfection in wisdom and renunciation, please give us offerings. We bow down to you.

माता च पार्वती देवी पिता देवो महेश्वरः ।
बान्धवाः शिवभक्ताश्च स्वदेशो भुवनत्रयम् ॥

mātā ca pārvatī devī pitā devo maheśvaraḥ
bāndhavāḥ śivabhaktāśca svadeśo bhuvanatrayam

Our Mother is the Goddess, Pārvatī, and our Father is the Supreme Lord, Maheśvara. The Consciousness of Infinite Goodness, Śiva, Lord of the three worlds, is being extolled by his devotees.

ॐ श्रीं लक्ष्म्यै नमः भोगनैवेद्यम् समर्पयामि

oṁ śrīṁ lakṣmyai namaḥ bhog-naivedyam samarpayāmi

With this presentation of food Oṁ I bow to the Goddess Lakṣmī.

drinking water

ॐ समस्तदेवदेवेशि सर्वतृप्तिकरं परम् ।
अखण्डानन्दसम्पूर्णं गृहाण जलमुत्तमम् ॥
ॐ श्रीं लक्ष्म्यै नमः पानार्थं जलम् समर्पयामि

oṁ samasta devadeveśi sarvatṛptikaraṁ param
akhaṇḍānanda sampūrṇaṁ gṛhāṇa jalamuttamam
oṁ śrīṁ lakṣmyai namaḥ pānārthaṁ jalam samarpayāmi

Oṁ Goddess of All the Gods and the fullness of Infinite Bliss, please accept this excellent drinking water. With this offering of drinking water Oṁ I bow to the Goddess Lakṣmī.

betel nuts

पूगीफलं महद्दिव्यं नागवल्ली दलैर्युतम् ।
एलादिचूर्णसंयुक्तं ताम्बूलं प्रतिगृह्यताम् ॥
ॐ श्रीं लक्ष्म्यै नमः ताम्बूलं समर्पयामि

pūgīphalaṁ mahaddivyaṁ nāgavallī dalairyutam
elādicūrṇasaṁyuktaṁ tāmbūlaṁ pratigṛhyatām
oṁ śrīṁ lakṣmyai namaḥ tāmbūlaṁ samarpayāmi

These betel nuts, which are great and divine, come from vines that creep like a snake. United with cardamom ground to a powder, please accept this offering of mouth-freshening betel nuts. With this offering of mouth freshening betel nuts Oṁ I bow to the Goddess Lakṣmī.

dakṣiṇā

ॐ पूजाफलसमृद्ध्यर्थं तवाग्रे स्वर्णमीश्वरि ।
स्थापितं तेन मे प्रीता पूर्णान् कुरु मनोरथान् ॥

oṁ pūjāphalasmṛddhyarthaṁ tavāgre svarṇamīśvari
sthāpitaṁ tena me prītā pūrṇān kuru manorathān

Oṁ For the purpose of increasing the fruits of worship, Oh Supreme Goddess of all Wealth, we establish this offering of that which is dear to me. Bring to perfection the journey of my mind.

हिरण्यगर्भगर्भस्थं हेमबीजं विभावसोः ।
अनन्तपुण्यफलदमतः शान्तिं प्रयच्छ मे ॥

hiraṅyagarbhagarbhasthaṁ hemabījaṁ vibhāvasoḥ
anantapuṇyaphaladamataḥ śāntiṁ prayaccha me

Oh Golden Womb, in whom all wombs are situated, shining brightly with the golden seed. Give infinite merits as fruits, we are wanting for peace.

ॐ श्रीं लक्ष्म्यै नमः दक्षिणां समर्पयामि

oṁ śrīṁ lakṣmyai namaḥ dakṣiṇāṁ samarpayāmi

Oṁ With this offering of wealth Oṁ I bow to the Goddess Lakṣmī.

umbrella

छत्रं देवि जगद्धात्रि ! घर्मवातप्रणाशनम् ।
गृहाण हे महामाये ! सौभाग्यं सर्वदा कुरु ॥
ॐ श्रीं लक्ष्म्यै नमः छत्रं समर्पयामि

chatraṁ devi jagaddhātri gharma vāta praṇāśanam
gṛhāṇa he mahāmāye saubhāgyaṁ sarvadā kuru
oṁ śrīṁ lakṣmyai namaḥ chatraṁ samarpayāmi

Oh Goddess, Creator of the Universe! This umbrella will protect you from heat and wind. Please accept it, oh Great Māyā, and remain always beautiful. With this offering of an umbrella Oṁ I bow to the Goddess Lakṣmī.

fly whisk

चामरं हे महादेवि चमरीपुच्छनिर्मितम् ।
गृहीत्वा पापराशीनां खण्डनं सर्वदा कुरु ॥
ॐ श्रीं लक्ष्म्यै नमः चामरं समर्पयामि

cāmaraṁ he mahādevi camarīpucchanirmitam
gṛhītvā pāparāśīnāṁ khaṇḍanaṁ sarvadā kuru
oṁ śrīṁ lakṣmyai namaḥ cāmaraṁ samarpayāmi

Oh Great Goddess, this fly whisk is made of yak's tail. Please accept it, and always whisk away all sin. With this offering of a fly whisk Oṁ I bow to the Goddess Lakṣmī.

fan

बर्हिर्बर्हकृताकारं मध्यदण्डसमन्वितम् ।
गृह्यतां व्यजनं देवि देहस्वेदापनुत्तये ॥
ॐ श्रीं लक्ष्मयै नमः तालवृन्तं समर्पयामि

barhirbarhakṛtākāraṁ madhyadaṇḍa samanvitam
gṛhyatāṁ vyajanaṁ devi dehasvedāpanuttaye
oṁ śrīṁ lakṣmyai namaḥ tālavṛntaṁ samarpayāmi

It moves back and forth with equanimity and has a stick in the middle. Please accept this fan, oh Goddess, to keep the perspiration from your body. With this offering of a fan Oṁ I bow to the Goddess Lakṣmī.

mirror

दर्पणं विमलं रम्यं शुद्धबिम्बप्रदायकम् ।
आत्मबिम्बप्रदर्शार्थमर्पयामि महेश्वरि ! ॥
ॐ श्रीं लक्ष्मयै नमः दर्पणं समर्पयामि

darpaṇaṁ vimalaṁ ramyaṁ śuddhabimbapradāyakam
ātmabimbapradarśanārtharpayāmi maheśvari
oṁ śrīṁ lakṣmyai namaḥ darpaṇaṁ samarpayāmi

This beautiful mirror will give a pure reflection. In order to reflect my soul, I am offering it to you, oh Great Seer of all. With this offering of a mirror Oṁ I bow to the Goddess Lakṣmī.

ārātrikam

ॐ चन्द्रादित्यौ च धरणी विद्युदग्निस्तथैव च ।
त्वमेव सर्वज्योतीषिं आरात्रिकं प्रतिगृह्यताम् ॥
ॐ श्रीं लक्ष्मयै नमः आरात्रिकं समर्पयामि

oṁ candrādityau ca dharaṇī vidyudagnistathaiva ca
tvameva sarvajyotīṣiṁ ārātrikaṁ pratigṛhyatām
oṁ śrīṁ lakṣmyai namaḥ ārātrikaṁ samarpayāmi

Oṁ All knowing as the Moon, the Sun and the Divine Fire, you alone are all light, and this light we request you to accept. With this offering of light Oṁ I bow to the Goddess Lakṣmī.

flower

मल्लिकादि सुगन्धीनि मालित्यादीनि वै प्रभो ।
मयाऽहृतानि पूजार्थं पुष्पाणि प्रतिगृह्यताम् ॥
ॐ श्रीं लक्ष्म्यै नमः पुष्पम् समर्पयामि

mallikādi sugandhīni mālityādīni vai prabho
mayā-hṛtāni pūjārthaṁ puṣpāṇi pratigṛhyatām
oṁ śrīṁ lakṣmyai namaḥ puṣpam samarpayāmi

Various flowers, such as mallikā and others of excellent scent, are being offered to you, Our Lord. All these flowers have come from the devotion of our hearts for your worship. Please accept them. With this offering of a flower Oṁ I bow to the Goddess Lakṣmī.

यज्ञेन यज्ञमयजन्त देवास्तानि धर्म्माणि प्रथमान्यासन् ।
ते ह नाकं महिमानः सचन्त यत्र पूर्वे साध्याः सन्ति देवाः ॥

yajñena yajñamayajanta devāstāni
dharmmāṇi prathamānyāsan
te ha nākaṁ mahimānaḥ sacanta yatra pūrve sādhyāḥ
santi devāḥ

By sacrifice, the Gods gave birth to sacrifice, and the first principles of eternal Dharma were established. Those who live according to the glorious way, ultimately reach the highest abode where the Gods dwell in that ancient perfection.

ॐ राजाधिराजाय प्रसह्य साहिने नमो वयं वैश्रवणाय कुर्महे
स मे कामान् कामकामाय मह्यं कामेश्वरो वैश्रवणो ददातु ।
कुबेराय वैश्रवणाय महाराजाय नमः ॥

oṁ rājādhirājāya prasahya sāhine namo vayaṁ
vaiśravaṇāya kurmahe sa me kāmān kāmakāmāya
mahyaṁ kāmeśvaro vaiśravaṇo dadātu kuberāya
vaiśravaṇāya mahārājāya namaḥ

Without any selfish interest we bow down to the universal being, the King of kings, the Lord of all desires, the Universal Being. May He grant to me the full and complete enjoyment of the desire of all desires dharma (the ideal of perfection), artha (material necessities), kāma (perfection of desire) and mokṣa (self realization).

ॐ स्वस्ति साम्राज्यं भौज्यं स्वाराज्यं वैराज्यं पारमेष्ठ्यं राज्यं महाराज्यमाधिपत्यमयं समन्तपर्यायि स्यात् । सार्वभौमः सार्वायुषां तदा परार्धात् पृथिव्यै समुद्रपर्यन्ताया एकराडिति । तदप्येष श्लोकोऽभिगीतो मरुतः परिवेष्टारो मरुत्तस्या ऽवस न् गृहे । आवीक्षितस्य कामप्रेर्विश्वेदेवाः सभासद इति ॥

oṁ svasti sāmrājyaṁ bhaujyaṁ svārājyaṁ vairājyaṁ pārameṣṭhyaṁ rājyaṁ mahārājyamādhipatyamayaṁ samantaparyāyai syāt sārvabhaumaḥ sārvāyuṣāṁ tadā parārdhāt pṛthivyai samudraparyantāyā-ekarāḍiti tadapyeṣa śloko-bhigīto marutaḥ pariveṣṭāro maruttasyā-vasan gṛhe āvīkṣitasya kāmaprerviśvedevāḥ sabhāsada iti

Oṁ Let blessings flow to all of the kingdom, His own kingdom, the universal kingdom, the kingdom of the Supreme Divinity, the great kingdom of our Lord greater than the greatest, in the equilibrium of spiritual austerities. All that lives in the heavens or on the earth or in the seas is thus united. Those spiritual aspirants who sing these verses can aspire to dwell in the home of the purified. Having no unfulfilled desires, only desiring as the Universal Gods always.

ॐ विश्वतश्चक्षुरुत विश्वतो मुखो विश्वतो बाहुरुत विश्वतस्पात् । सम्बाहुभ्यां धमति सम्पतत् त्रैर्द्यावा भूमिं जनयन् देव एकः ॥

oṁ viśvataścakṣuruta viśvato mukho viśvato bāhuruta viśvataspāt
sambāhubhyāṁ dhamati sampatat trairdyāvā bhūmiṁ janayan deva ekaḥ

Oṁ He who sees the universe, the mouth of the universe, the arms of the universe, the feet of the universe. He is One God, whose two arms and two wings make possible all the activities of all that lives in the heavens and on earth.

lakṣmī pūjā
worship of lakṣmī
lakṣmī gāyatrī

ॐ महालक्ष्म्यै च विद्महे सर्वशक्त्यै च धीमहे ।
तन्नो देवी प्रचोदयात् ॥

oṁ mahālakṣmyai ca vidmahe sarvaśaktyai ca dhīmahe
tanno devī pracodayāt

Oṁ We meditate upon the Great Goddess of True Wealth, we contemplate She Who Embodies all Energy. May that Goddess grant us increase.

एते गन्धपुष्पे ॐ श्रीं लक्ष्म्यै नमः

ete gandhapuṣpe oṁ śrīṁ lakṣmyai namaḥ

With these scented flowers Oṁ I bow to the Goddess Lakṣmī

dhyānam
meditation

ॐ पाशाक्षमालिकाम्बोज-सृणिभर्याम्यसौम्ययोः ।
पद्मासनस्तां ध्यायेच्च श्रियः त्रैलोक्यमातरम् ॥

oṁ pāśākṣamālikāmboja-sṛṇibharyāmyasaumyayoḥ
padmāsanastāṁ dhyāyecca śriyaḥ trailokyamātaram

Oṁ The bond, mālā of alphabets, a gourd, Her lovely hand gives freedom from fear of creation. We meditate upon the Goddess of the Highest Respect seated in the lotus posture, the Mother of the three worlds.

गौरवर्णां सुरूपाञ्च सर्वालङ्कार-भूषिताम् ।
रौक्मपद्मव्यग्रकरां वरदां दक्षिणेन तु ॥

gauravarṇāṁ surūpāñca sarvālaṅkāra-bhūṣitām
raukmapadmavyagrakarāṁ varadāṁ dakṣiṇena tu

She has a light color, with excellent form, all Her ornaments are shining. She holds a red lotus in Her hand, and Her right hand grants boons.

लक्ष्मिस्त्वं सर्वभूतानां नमस्ते विश्वभाविणी ।
देहि पुत्रं धानं देहि पाहि नित्यं नमोऽस्तु ते ॥

lakṣmistvaṁ sarvabhūtānāṁ namaste viśvabhāviṇī
dehi putraṁ dhānaṁ dehi pāhi nityaṁ namo-stu te

You are Lakṣmi and all existence bows to you, the Mother of the Universe. Give me children and give me wealth. Protect me eternally, I bow to you.

त्रैलोक्यपूजिते देवि कमले विष्णुवल्लभे ।
यथा त्वं सुस्थिरा कृष्णे तथा भव मयि स्थिरा ॥

trailokyapūjite devi kamale viṣṇuvallabhe
yathā tvaṁ susthirā kṛṣṇe tathā bhava mayi sthirā

The Goddess is worshipped in the three worlds as the Lotus One, the strength of Viṣṇu. Hey Energy of Kṛṣṇa, for as long as you sit still, let me be still as well.

ईश्वरी कमला लक्ष्मीश्चला भूतिर्हरिप्रिया ।
पद्मा पद्मालया सम्पद् हृष्ठिः श्रीः पद्मधारिणी ॥

īśvarī kamalā lakṣmīścalā bhūtirharipriyā
padmā padmālayā sampad
hṛṣṭhiḥ śrīḥ padmadhāriṇī

You are Īśvarī, Kamalā, Lakṣmī, She Who Moves All, All Existence, Beloved of Viṣṇu, Lotus, Who Resides in Lotuses, All Support, Joy, Respect, Who Holds a Lotus.

द्वादशैतानि नामानि लक्ष्मीं संपूज्य यः पठेत् ।
स्थिरा लक्ष्मीर्भवेत्तस्य पुत्रजायादिभिः सह ॥

dvādaśaitāni nāmāni lakṣmīṁ saṁpūjya yaḥ paṭhet
sthirā lakṣmīrbhavettasya putrajāyādibhiḥ saha

These are the twelve names of Lakṣmī. If one reads them in worship, Lakṣmī becomes fixed in your being and your children will always be victorious.

kara nyāsa
establishment in the hands

ॐ श्रां अंगुष्ठाभ्यां नमः

oṁ śrāṁ aṅguṣṭhābhyāṁ namaḥ thumb forefinger
Oṁ śrāṁ in the thumb I bow.

ॐ श्रीं तर्जनीभ्यां स्वाहा

oṁ śrīṁ tarjanībhyāṁ svāhā thumb forefinger
Oṁ śrīṁ in the forefinger, I am One with God!

ॐ श्रूं मध्यमाभ्यां वषट्

oṁ śrūṁ madhyamābhyāṁ vaṣaṭ thumb middlefinger
Oṁ śrūṁ in the middle finger, Purify!

ॐ श्रैं अनामिकाभ्यां हुं

oṁ śraiṁ anāmikābhyāṁ huṁ thumb ring finger
Oṁ śraiṁ in the ring finger, Cut the Ego!

ॐ श्रौं कनिष्ठिकाभ्यां बौषट्

oṁ śrauṁ kaniṣṭhikābhyāṁ vauṣaṭ thumb little finger
Oṁ śrauṁ in the little finger, Ultimate Purity!

Roll hand over hand forwards while reciting karatal kar,
and backwards while chanting pṛṣṭhābhyāṁ,
then clap hands when chanting astrāya phaṭ.

ॐ श्रः करतल कर पृष्ठाभ्यां अस्त्राय फट् ॥

oṁ śraḥ karatal kar pṛṣṭhābhyāṁ astrāya phaṭ
Oṁ śraḥ I bow to the Goddess Lakṣmī, with the weapon of Virtue.

ॐ श्रीं लक्ष्मयै नमः

oṁ śrīṁ lakṣmyai namaḥ
Oṁ I bow to the Goddess Lakṣmī

aṅga nyāsa

establishment in the body

Holding tattva mudrā, touch heart.

ॐ श्रां हृदयाय नमः

oṁ śrāṁ hṛdayāya namaḥ touch heart

Oṁ śrāṁ in the heart, I bow.

Holding tattva mudrā, touch top of head.

ॐ श्रीं शिरसे स्वाहा

oṁ śrīṁ śirase svāhā top of head

Oṁ śrīṁ on the top of the head, I am One with God!

With thumb extended, touch back of head.

ॐ श्रूं शिखायै वषट्

oṁ śrūṁ śikhāyai vaṣaṭ back of head

Oṁ śrūṁ on the back of the head, Purify!

Holding tattva mudrā, cross both arms.

ॐ श्रैं कवचाय हुं

oṁ śraiṁ kavacāya huṁ cross both arms

Oṁ śraiṁ crossing both arms, Cut the Ego!

Holding tattva mudrā, touch two eyes and in between at once with three middle fingers.

ॐ श्रौं नेत्रत्रयाय वौषट्

oṁ śrauṁ netratrayāya vauṣaṭ touch three eyes

Oṁ śrauṁ in the three eyes, Ultimate Purity!

Roll hand over hand forwards while reciting karatal kar,
and backwards while chanting pṛṣṭhābhyāṁ,
then clap hands when chanting astrāya phaṭ.

ॐ श्रः करतल कर पृष्ठाभ्यां अस्त्राय फट् ॥

oṁ śraḥ karatal kar pṛṣṭhābhyāṁ astrāya phaṭ

Oṁ śraḥ I bow to the Goddess Lakṣmī with the weapon of Virtue.

ॐ श्रीं लक्ष्म्यै नमः

oṁ śrīṁ lakṣmyai namaḥ
Oṁ I bow to the Goddess Lakṣmī.

mahālakṣmī aṣṭakaṁ
eight verses in praise of mahālakṣmī

नमस्तेऽस्तु महामाये श्रीपीठे सुरपूजिते ।
शङ्खचक्रगदाहस्ते महालक्ष्मि नमोऽस्तु ते ॥

namaste-stu mahāmāye śrīpīṭhe surapūjite
śaṅkhacakragadāhaste mahālakṣmi namo-stu te
The dwelling place of the highest respected wealth, worshipped by all divine beings, Oh Infinite Container of Consciousness, we bow to you. To you who holds the conch shell, discus and club (or mace) in your hands, to the Great Goddess of True Wealth, we bow.

नमस्ते गरुडारूढे कोलासुरभयंकरि ।
सर्वपापहरे देवि महालक्ष्मि नमोऽस्तु ते ॥

namaste garuḍārūḍhe kolāsurabhayaṁkari
sarvapāpahare devi mahālakṣmi namo-stu te
She who rides upon the eagle Garuḍa, filling the demon Kola (the Perverter of the Family or Destroyer of Excellence) with fear, the Goddess Who Eradicates Sin, to the Great Goddess of True Wealth we bow.

सर्वज्ञे सर्ववरदेसर्वदुष्टभयङ्करि ।
सर्वदुःखहरे देवि महालक्ष्मि नमोऽस्तु ते ॥

sarvajñe sarvavaradesarvaduṣṭabhayaṅkari
sarvaduḥkhahare devi mahālakṣmi namo-stu te
Knower of all, Grantor of all wishes, instilling the fear of all evil, the Goddess Who Takes Away All Pain, to the Great Goddess of True Wealth we bow.

सिद्धिबुद्धिप्रदे देवि भुक्तिमुक्तिप्रदायिनि ।
मन्त्रपूते सदा देवि महालक्ष्मि नमोऽस्तु ते ॥

siddhibuddhiprade devi bhuktimuktipradāyini
mantrapūte sadā devi mahālakṣmi namo-stu te
Grantor of perfection and intelligence, Giver of enjoyment and liberation, wearing mantra as your form, to the Great Goddess of True Wealth we bow.

आद्यन्तरहिते देवि आद्यशक्तिमहेश्वरि ।
योगजे योगसम्भूते महालक्ष्मि नमोऽस्तु ते ॥

ādyantarahite devi ādyaśaktimaheśvari
yogaje yogasambhūte mahālakṣmi namo-stu te
Without beginning or end, Oh Goddess, the primordial energy, the Great Seer of All (or Great Ruler of All), who dwells always in union, who is born of union, to the Great Goddess of True Wealth we bow.

स्थूलसूक्ष्ममहारौद्रे महाशक्तिमहोदरे ।
महापापहरे देवि महालक्ष्मि नमोऽस्तु ते ॥

sthūlasūkṣmamahāraudre mahāśaktimahodare
mahāpāpahare devi mahālakṣmi namo-stu te
Wearing the gross body, wearing the subtle body, as the Great Reliever of Suffering, the Great Energy, the Cosmic Source of All, the Goddess Who Takes Away Great Sin, to the Great Goddess of True Wealth we bow.

पद्मासनस्थिते देवि परब्रह्मस्वरूपिणि ।
परमेशि जगन्मातर्महालक्ष्मि नमोऽस्तु ते ॥

padmāsanasthite devi parabrahmasvarūpiṇi
parameśi jaganmātarmahālakṣmi namo-stu te
Situated upon a lotus seat, Oh Goddess, the Intrinsic Nature of the Universal Consciousness, the Supreme Ruler, Mother of the Universe, to the Great Goddess of True Wealth we bow.

श्वेताम्बरधरे देवि नानालङ्कारभूषिते ।
जगत्स्थिते जगन्मातर्महालक्ष्मि नमोऽस्तु ते ॥

svetāmbaradhare devi nānālaṅkārabhūṣite
jagatsthite jaganmātarmahālakṣmi namo-stu te

Wearing a white cloth, Oh Goddess, with various ornaments shining, the Residence of the Worlds, the Mother of the Worlds, to the Great Goddess of True Wealth we bow.

महालक्ष्म्यष्टकं स्तोत्रं यः पठेद्भक्तिमानरः ।
सर्वसिद्धिमवाप्नोति राज्यं प्राप्नोति सर्वदा ॥

mahālakṣmyaṣṭakaṁ stotraṁ yaḥ paṭhedbhaktimānaraḥ
sarvasiddhimavāpnoti rājyaṁ prāpnoti sarvadā

Whoever will recite these eight verses in praise of the Great Goddess of True Wealth with full devotion and attention, will attain to perfection for himself as well as for those who are under his influence.

एककाले पठेन्नित्यं महापापविनाशनम् ।
द्विकालं यः पठेन्नित्यं धनधान्यसमन्वितः ॥

ekakāle paṭhennityaṁ mahāpāpavināśanam
dvikālaṁ yaḥ paṭhennityaṁ dhanadhānyasamanvitaḥ

Whoever regularly recites this one time, will be freed even from great sins. Who regularly recites twice will have abundance of wealth and grains.

त्रिकालं यः पठेन्नित्यं महाशत्रुविनाशनम् ।
महालक्ष्मीर्भवेन्नित्यं प्रसन्ना वरदा शुभा ॥

trikālaṁ yaḥ paṭhennityaṁ mahāśatruvināśanam
mahālakṣmīrbhavennityaṁ prasannā varadā śubhā

Whoever regularly recites three times will witness the destruction of the Great Enemy (Ego), and the Great Goddess of True Wealth, the Grantor of Welfare, the Giver of Boons, will always be pleased.

ॐ विश्वरूपस्य भार्य्यासि पद्मे पद्मालये शुभे ।
सर्वतः पाहि मां देवी महालक्ष्मि नमोऽस्तु ते ॥

oṁ viśvarūpasya bhārjyāsi padme padmālaye śubhe
sarvataḥ pāhi māṁ devī mahālakṣmi namo-stu te

Oṁ the form of the universe, you are the wife of the universe, Lotus One, Who Resides in Lotuses, Pure One; always protect me, oh Goddess. Oh Great Goddess of True Wealth, I bow to you.

॥ अथ श्रीलक्ष्मीसहस्रनामस्तोत्रम् ॥
|| atha śrīlakṣmīsahasranāmastotram ||

श्रीर्वासुदेवमहिषी पुंप्रधानेश्वरेश्वरी ।
अचिन्त्यानन्तविभवा भावाभावविभाविनी ॥१॥
śrīrvāsudevamahiṣī puṁpradhāneśvareśvarī |
acintyānantavibhavā bhāvābhāvavibhāvinī || 1 ||

अहंभावात्मिका पद्मा शान्तानन्तजितात्मिका ।
ब्रह्मभावं गता त्यक्तभीता सर्वजगन्मयी ॥२॥
ahaṁbhāvātmikā padmā śāntānantajitātmikā |
brahmabhāvaṁ gatā tyaktabhītā sarvajaganmayī || 2 ||

षाड्गुण्यपूर्णा त्रय्यन्तरूपाऽऽत्मनपगामिनी ।
एकयोग्याऽशून्य भावाकृतिस्तेजः प्रभाविनी ॥३॥
ṣāḍguṇyapūrṇā trayyantarūpā--tmanapagāminī |
ekayogyā-śūnya bhāvākṛtistejaḥ prabhāvinī || 3 ||

भाव्यभावकभावाऽऽत्माव्या कामधुगात्मभू ।
भावाभावमयी दिव्या भेद्याभेदकभावगा ॥४॥
bhāvyabhāvakabhāvā--tmāvyā kāmadhugātmabhū |
bhāvābhāvamayī divyā bhedyabhedakabhāvagā || 4 ||

जगत्कुटुम्बिन्यखिलाधारा कामविजृम्भणी ।
पञ्चकृत्यकरी पञ्चशक्तिमय्यात्मवल्लभा ॥५॥
jagatkuṭumbinyakhilādhārā kāmavijṛmbhaṇī |
pañcakṛtyakarī pañcaśaktimayyātmavallabhā || 5 ||

भावाभावानुगा सर्वसम्मताऽऽत्मोपगूहिनी ।
अपृथक्चारिणी सौम्या सौम्यरूपाऽव्यवस्थिता ॥६॥
bhāvābhāvānugā sarvasammatā--tmopagūhinī |
apṛthakcāriṇī saumyā saumyarūpā-vyavasthitā || 6 ||

आद्यन्तरहिता देवी भवभाव्यस्वरूपिणी ।
महाविभूतिस्समतां गता ज्योतिर्गणेश्वरी ॥७॥
ādyantarahitā devī bhavabhāvyasvarūpiṇī |
mahāvibhūtissamatāṁ gatā jyotirgaṇeśvarī || 7 ||

सर्वकार्यकरी धर्मस्वभावात्माऽग्रतः स्थिता ।
आज्ञासमविभक्ताङ्गी ज्ञानानन्दक्रियामयी ॥८॥
sarvakāryakarī dharmasvabhāvātmā-grataḥ sthitā |
ājñāsamavibhaktāṅgī jñānānandakriyāmayī || 8 ||

स्वातन्त्र्यरूपा देवोरःस्थिता तद्धर्मधर्मिणी ।
सर्वभूतेश्वरी सर्वभूतमाताऽऽत्ममोहिनी ॥९॥
svātantryarūpā devoraḥsthitā taddharmadharmiṇī |
sarvabhūteśvarī sarvabhūtamātā--tmamohinī || 9 ||

सर्वाङ्गसुन्दरी सर्वव्यापिनी प्राप्तयोगिनी ।
विमुक्तिदायिनी भक्तगम्या संसारतारिणी ॥१०॥
sarvāṅgasundarī sarvavyāpinī prāptayoginī |
vimuktidāyinī bhaktagamyā saṁsāratāriṇī || 10 ||

धर्मार्थवादिनि व्योमनिलया व्योमविग्रहा ।
पञ्चव्योमपदी रक्षव्यावृत्तिः प्राप्यपूरिणी ॥११॥
dharmārthavādini vyomanilayā vyomavigrahā |
pañcavyomapadī rakṣavyāvṛttiḥ prāpyapūriṇī || 11 ||

आनन्दरूपा सर्वाप्तिशालिनी शक्तिनायिका ।
हिरण्यवर्णा हैरण्यप्राकारा हेममालिनी ॥१२॥
ānandarūpā sarvāptiśālinī śaktināyikā |
hiraṇyavarṇā hairaṇyaprākārā hemamālinī || 12 ||

प्रस्फुरत्ता भद्रहोमा वेशिनी रजतस्रजा ।
स्वाज्ञाकार्यमरा नित्यसुरभिर्व्योमचारिणी ॥१३॥
prasphurattā bhadrahomā veśinī rajatasrajā |
svājñākāryamarā nityasurabhirvyomacāriṇī || 13 ||

योगक्षेमावहा सर्वसुलभेच्छाक्रियात्मिका ।
महासमूहा निखिलप्ररोहा वेदगोचरा ॥१४॥
yogakṣemāvahā sarvasulabhecchākriyātmikā |
mahāsamūhā nikhilaprarohā vedagocarā || 14 ||

विस्मयाधायिनी ब्रह्मसंहिता सुगुणोत्तरा ।
प्रज्ञापरिमिताऽऽत्मानुरूपा सत्योपयार्जिता ॥१५॥
vismayādhāyinī brahmasaṁhitā suguṇottarā |
prajñāparimitā--tmānurūpā satyopayārjitā || 15 ||

मनोज्ञेया ज्ञानगम्या नित्यमुक्ताऽऽत्मसेविनी ।
कर्तृशक्तिः सुगहना भोक्तृशक्तिर्गुणप्रिया ॥१६॥
manojñeyā jñānagamyā nityamuktā--tmasevinī |
kartṛśaktiḥ sugahanā bhoktṛśaktirguṇapriyā || 16 ||

ज्ञान शक्तिरनौपम्या परशक्तिर्निरामया ।
अकलङ्का महाशक्तिर्निराधारा विकासिनी ॥१७॥
jñāna śaktiranaupamyā paraśaktirnirāmayā |
akalaṅkā mahāśaktirnirādhārā vikāsinī || 17 ||

महामाया महानन्दा ब्रह्मनीतिर्निराश्रया ।
एकस्वरूपा त्रिविधा सङ्ख्यातीता निरञ्जना ॥१८॥
mahāmāyā mahānandā brahmanītirnirāśrayā |
ekasvarūpā trividhā saṅkhyātītā nirañjanā || 18 ||

आत्मसक्ता नित्यशुचिर्निर्विकल्पा सुखोचिता ।
नित्यशान्ता निस्तरङ्गा निर्भिन्ना सर्वभेदिनी ॥१९॥
ātmasaktā nityaśucirnirvikalpā sukhocitā |
nityaśāntā nistaraṅgā nirbhinnā sarvabhedinī || 19 ||

असङ्कीर्णाऽविधेयात्मा निषेद्ध्या सर्वपावनी ।
निष्कामना सर्वरसाऽभेद्या सर्वार्थसाधिनी ॥२०॥
asaṅkīrṇā-vidheyātmā niṣeddhyā sarvapāvanī |
niṣkāmanā sarvarasā-bhedyā sarvārthasādhinī || 20 ||

अनिर्देश्याऽपरिमिता निर्विकारा त्रिलक्षणा ।
अभयङ्करी स्त्रीस्वरूपाऽव्यक्ता सदसदाकृतिः ॥२१॥
anirdeśyā-parimitā nirvikārā trilakṣaṇā |
abhayaṅkarī strīsvarūpā-vyaktā sadasadākṛtiḥ || 21 ||

अप्रतर्क्याऽप्रतिहता नियन्त्री यन्त्रवाहिनी ।
हार्दमूर्तिर्महामूर्तिरव्यक्ता विश्वगोपिनी ॥२२॥
apratarkyā-pratihatā niyantrī yantravāhinī |
hārdamūrtirmahāmūrtiravyaktā viśvagopinī || 22 ||

वर्धमानाऽनवद्याङ्गी निरवद्या त्रिवर्गदा ।
अप्रमेयाऽमृतदुघा कूटस्था कुलनन्दिनी ॥२३॥
vardhamānā-navadyāṅgī niravadyā trivargadā |
aprameyā-mṛtadughā kūṭasthā kulanandinī || 23 ||

अविगीता तन्त्रसिद्धा योगसिद्धाऽमरेश्वरी ।
विश्वसूतिस्तर्पयन्ती नित्यतृप्ता महौषधिः ॥२४॥
avigītā tantrasiddhā yogasiddhā-mareśvarī |
viśvasūtistarpayantī nityatṛptā mahauṣadhiḥ || 24 ||

शब्दात्यया शब्दसहा कृतज्ञा कृतलक्षणा ।
त्रिवर्तिनी त्रिलोकस्था भूर्भुवस्स्वरयोनिजा ॥२५॥
śabdātyayā śabdasahā kṛtajñā kṛtalakṣaṇā |
trivartinī trilokasthā bhūrbhuvassvarayonijā || 25 ||

अग्राह्याऽग्राहिकाऽनन्ताह्वया सर्वातिशायिनी ।
व्योमपद्मा कृतधुरा पूर्णकामा महेश्वरी ॥२६॥
agrāhyā-grāhikā-nantāhvayā sarvātiśāyinī |
vyomapadmā kṛtadhurā pūrṇakāmā maheśvarī || 26 ||

सुवाच्या वाचिका सत्यकथना सर्वपावनी ।
लक्ष्यमाणा लक्षयन्ती जगज्ज्येष्ठा शुभावहा ॥२७॥
suvācyā vācikā satyakathanā sarvapāvanī |
lakṣyamāṇā lakṣayantī jagajjyeṣṭhā śubhāvahā || 27 ||

जगत्प्रतिष्ठा भुवनभर्त्री गूढप्रभाविनी ।
क्रियायोगात्मिका मूर्ता हृदब्जस्था महाक्रमा ॥२८॥
jagatpratiṣṭhā bhuvanabhartrī gūḍhaprabhāvinī |
kriyāyogātmikā mūrtā hṛdabjasthā mahākramā || 28 ||

परमद्यौः प्रथमजा परमाप्ता जगन्निधिः ।
आत्मानपायिनी तुल्यस्वरूपा समलक्षणा ॥२९॥
paramadyauḥ prathamajā paramāptā jagannidhiḥ |
ātmānapāyinī tulyasvarūpā samalakṣaṇā || 29 ||

तुल्यवृत्ता समवया मोदमाना खगध्वजा ।
तुल्यचेष्टा तुल्यशीला वरदा कामरूपिणी ॥३०॥
tulyavṛttā samavayā modamānā khagadhvajā |
tulyaceṣṭā tulyaśīlā varadā kāmarūpiṇī || 30 ||

समग्रलक्षणाऽनन्ता तुल्यभूतिः सनातना ।
महर्द्धिः सत्यसङ्कल्पा भूमिजा परमेश्वरी ॥३१॥
samagralakṣaṇā-nantā tulyabhūtiḥ sanātanā |
maharddhiḥ satyasaṅkalpā bhūmijā parameśvarī || 31 ||

जगन्माता सूत्रवती भूतधात्री यशस्विनी ।
महाभिलाषा सावित्री प्रधाना सर्वभासिनी ॥३२॥
jaganmātā sūtravatī bhūtadhātrī yaśasvinī |
mahābhilāṣā sāvitrī pradhānā sarvabhāsinī || 32 ||

नानावपुर्बहुविधा सर्वज्ञा पुण्यकीर्तना ।
भूताश्रया हृषीकेशा अशोका स्वाङ्गिवाहिका ॥३३॥
nānāvapurbahuvidhā sarvajñā puṇyakīrtanā |
bhūtāśrayā hṛṣīkeśā aśokā svāṅgivāhikā || 33 ||

ब्रह्मात्मिका पुण्यजनी सत्यकामा समाधिभूः ।
हिरण्यगर्भा गम्भीरा गोधूली कमलासना ॥३४॥
brahmātmikā puṇyajanī satyakāmā samādhibhūḥ |
hiraṇyagarbhā gambhīrā godhūlī kamalāsanā || 34 ||

जितक्रोधा कुमुदिनी वैजयन्ती मनोजवा ।
धनलक्ष्मीः स्वस्तिकरी राज्यलक्ष्मीर्महासती ॥३५॥
jitakrodhā kumudinī vaijayantī manojavā |
dhanalakṣmīḥ svastikarī rājyalakṣmīrmahāsatī || 35 ||

जयलक्ष्मीर्महागोष्ठी मघोनी माधवप्रिया ।
पद्मगर्भा वेदवती विविक्ता परमेष्ठिनी ॥३६॥
jayalakṣmīrmahāgoṣṭhī maghonī mādhavapriyā |
padmagarbhā vedavatī viviktā parameṣṭhinī || 36 ||

सुवर्णबिन्दुर्महती महायोगिप्रियाऽनघा ।
पद्मे स्थिता वेदमयी कुमुदा जयवाहिनी ॥३७॥
suvarṇabindurmahatī mahāyogipriyā-naghā |
padme sthitā vedamayī kumudā jayavāhinī || 37 ||

संहतिर्निर्मिता ज्योतिर्नियतिर्विविधोत्सवा ।
रुद्रवन्द्या सिन्धुमती वेदमाता मधुव्रता ॥३८॥
saṁhatirnirmitā jyotirniyatirvividhotsavā |
rudravandyā sindhumatī vedamātā madhuvratā || 38 ||

विश्वम्भरा हैमवती समुद्रेच्छाविहारिणी ।
अनुकूला यज्ञवती शतकोटिः सुपेशला ॥३९॥
viśvambharā haimavatī samudrecchāvihāriṇī |
anukūlā yajñavatī śatakoṭiḥ supeśalā || 39 ||

धर्मोदया धर्मसेवा सुकुमारी सभावती ।
भीमा ब्रह्मस्तुता मध्यप्रभा देवर्षिवन्दिता ॥४०॥
dharmodayā dharmasevā sukumārī sabhāvatī |
bhīmā brahmastutā madhyaprabhā devarṣivanditā || 40 ||

देवभोग्या महाभागा प्रतिज्ञा पूर्णशेवधिः ।
सुवर्णा रूचिरप्रख्या भोगिनी भोगदायिनी ॥४१॥
devabhogyā mahābhāgā pratijñā pūrṇaśevadhiḥ |
suvarṇā rūciraprakhyā bhoginī bhogadāyinī || 41 ||

वसुप्रणोत्तमवधूर्गायत्री कमलोद्भवा ।
विद्वत्प्रिया पद्मचिह्ना वरिष्ठा कमलेक्षणा ॥४२॥

**vasupraṇottamavadhūrgāyatrī kamalodbhavā |
vidvatpriyā padmacihnā variṣṭhā kamalekṣaṇā || 42 ||**

पद्मप्रिया सुप्रसन्ना प्रमोदा प्रियपार्श्वगा ।
विश्वभूषा कान्तिमती कृष्णा वीणारवोत्सुका ॥४३॥

**padmapriyā suprasannā pramodā priyapārśvagā |
viśvabhūṣā kāntimatī kṛṣṇā vīṇāravotsukā || 43 ||**

रोचिष्करी स्वप्रकाशा शोभमाना विहङ्गमा ।
देवाङ्गस्था परिणतिः कामवत्सा महामतिः ॥४४॥

**rociṣkarī svaprakāśā śobhamānā vihaṅgamā |
devāṅgasthā pariṇatiḥ kāmavatsā mahāmatiḥ || 44 ||**

इल्वलोत्पलनाभाऽधिशमनी वरवर्णिनी ।
स्वनिष्ठा पद्मनिलया सद्गतिः पद्मगन्धिनी ॥४५॥

**ilvalotpalanābhā-dhiśamanī varavarṇinī |
svaniṣṭhā padmanilayā sadgatiḥ padmagandhinī || 45 ||**

पद्मवर्णा कामयोनिश्चण्डिका चारुकोपना ।
रतिस्नुषा पद्मधरा पूज्या त्रैलोक्यमोहिनी ॥४६॥

**padmavarṇā kāmayoniścaṇḍikā cārukopanā |
ratisnuṣā padmadharā pūjyā trailokyamohinī || 46 ||**

नित्यकन्या बिन्दुमालिन्यक्षया सर्वगन्धिनी ।
गन्धात्मिका सुरसिका दीप्तमूर्तिः सुमध्यमा ॥४७॥

**nityakanyā bindumālinyakṣayā sarvagandhinī |
gandhātmikā surasikā dīptamūrtiḥ sumadhyamā || 47 ||**

पृथुश्रोणी सौम्यमुखी सुभगा विष्टरश्रुतिः ।
स्मितानना चारुगतिर्निम्ननाभिर्महास्तनी ॥४८॥

pṛthuśroṇī saumyamukhī subhagā viṣṭaraśrutiḥ I
smitānanā cārugatirnimnanābhirmahāstanī II 48 II

स्निग्धवेणी भगवती सुकान्ता वामलोचना ।
पल्लवाङ्घ्रिः पद्ममनाः पद्मबोधा महाप्सराः ॥४९॥

snigdhaveṇī bhagavatī sukāntā vāmalocanā I
pallavāṅghriḥ padmamanāḥ padmabodhā mahāpsarāḥ II 49 II

सरस्वती चारुहासा शुभदृष्टिः ककुद्मिनी ।
कम्बुग्रीवा सुजघना रक्तपाणि मनोरमा ॥५०॥

sarasvatī cāruhāsā śubhadṛṣṭiḥ kakudminī I
kambugrīvā sujaghanā raktapāṇi manoramā II 50 II

पद्मिनी मन्दगमना चतुर्दंष्ट्रा चतुर्भुजा ।
शुभरेखा विलासभ्रूः शुकवाणी कलावती ॥५१॥

padminī mandagamanā caturdaṁṣṭrā caturbhujā I
śubharekhā vilāsabhrūḥ śukavāṇī kalāvatī II 51 II

ऋजुनासा कलरवा वरारोहा तलोदरी ।
सन्ध्या बिम्बाधरा पूर्वभाषिणी श्रीसमाह्वया ॥५२॥

ṛjunāsā kalaravā varārohā talodarī I
sandhyā bimbādharā pūrvabhāṣiṇī śrīsamāhvayā II 52 II

इक्षुचापा सुमशरा दिव्यभूषा मनोहरा ।
वासवी पाण्डरच्छत्रा करभोरुस्तिलोत्तमा ॥५३॥

ikṣucāpā sumaśarā divyabhūṣā manoharā I
vāsavī pāṇḍaracchatrā karabhorustilottamā II 53 II

सीमन्तिनी प्राणशक्तिर्विभीषिण्यसुधारिणी ।
भद्रा जयावहा चन्द्रवदना कुटिलालका ॥५४॥
sīmantinī prāṇaśaktirvibhīṣiṇyasudhāriṇī |
bhadrā jayāvahā candravadanā kuṭilālakā || 54 ||

चित्राम्बरा चित्रगन्धा रत्नमौलिसमुज्ज्वला ।
दिव्यायुधा दिव्यमाल्या विशाखा चित्रवाहना ॥५५॥
citrāmbarā citragandhā ratnamaulisamujjvalā |
divyāyudhā divyamālyā viśākhā citravāhanā || 55 ||

अम्बिका सिन्धुतनया निश्रेणी सुमहासिनी ।
सामप्रिया नवमृगी सर्वसेव्या वराङ्गना ॥५६॥
ambikā sindhutanayā niśreṇī sumahāsinī |
sāmapriyā navamṛgī sarvasevyā varāṅganā || 56 ||

गन्धद्वारा दुराधर्षा नित्यपुष्टा करीषिणी ।
देवजुष्टाऽऽदिव्यवर्णा दिव्यगन्धा स्वकर्दमा ॥५७॥
gandhadvārā durādharṣā nityapuṣṭā karīṣiṇī |
devajuṣṭā--divyavarṇā divyagandhā svakardamā || 57 ||

अनन्तरूपाऽनन्तस्था सर्वदाऽनन्तसङ्गमा ।
यज्ञाशिनी महावृष्टिः सर्वपूज्या वषट्क्रिया ॥५८॥
anantarūpā-nantasthā sarvadā-nantasaṅgamā |
yajñāśinī mahāvṛṣṭiḥ sarvapūjyā vaṣaṭkriyā || 58 ||

योगप्रिया वियन्नाभिरनन्तश्रीरतीन्द्रिया ।
योगिसेव्या सत्यरता योगमाया पुरातनी ॥५९॥
yogapriyā viyannābhiranantaśrīratīndriyā |
yogisevyā satyaratā yogamāyā purātanī || 59 ||

सर्वेश्वरी सुतरुणी शरण्या धर्मदेवता ।
सुतरा संवृतज्योतिर्योगिनी योगसिद्धिदा ॥६०॥
sarveśvarī sutaruṇī śaraṇyā dharmadevatā |
sutarā saṁvṛtajyotiryoginī yogasiddhidā || 60 ||

सृष्टिशक्तिर्द्योतमानाभूता मङ्गलदेवता ।
संहारशक्तिः प्रबला निरुपाधिः परावरा ॥६१॥
sṛṣṭiśaktirdyotamānābhūtā maṅgaladevatā |
saṁhāraśaktiḥ prabalā nirupādhiḥ parāvarā || 61 ||

उत्तारिणी तारयन्ती शाश्वती समितिञ्जया ।
महाश्रीरजहत्कीर्तिर्योगश्रीः सिद्धिसाधनी ॥६२॥
uttāriṇī tārayantī śāśvatī samitiñjayā |
mahāśrīrajahatkīrtiryogaśrīḥ siddhisādhanī || 62 ||

पुण्यश्रीः पुण्यनिलया ब्रह्मश्रीर्ब्राह्मणप्रिया ।
राजश्री राजकलिता फलश्रीः स्वर्गदायिनी ॥६३॥
puṇyaśrīḥ puṇyanilayā brahmaśrīrbrāhmaṇapriyā |
rājaśrī rājakalitā phalaśrīḥ svargadāyinī || 63 ||

देवश्रीरद्भुतकथा वेदश्रीः श्रुतिमार्गिणी ।
तमोपहाऽव्ययनिधिर्लक्ष्मणा हृदयङ्गमा ॥६४॥
devaśrīradbhutakathā vedaśrīḥ śrutimārgiṇī |
tamopahā-vyayanidhirlakṣmaṇā hṛdayaṅgamā || 64 ||

मृतसञ्जीविनी शुभ्रा चन्द्रिका सर्वतोमुखी ।
सर्वोत्तमा मित्रविन्दा मैथिली प्रियदर्शना ॥६५॥
mṛtasañjīvinī śubhrā candrikā sarvatomukhī |
sarvottamā mitravindā maithilī priyadarśanā || 65 ||

सत्यभामा वेदवेद्या सीता प्रणतपोषिणी ।
मूलप्रकृतिरीशाना शिवदा दीप्रदीपिनी ॥६६॥
satyabhāmā vedavedyā sītā praṇatapoṣiṇī |
mūlaprakṛtirīśānā śivadā dīpradīpinī || 66 ||

अभिप्रिया स्वैरवृत्ती रुक्मिणी सर्वसाक्षिणी ।
गान्धारिणी परगतिस्तत्त्वगर्भा भवाभवा ॥६७॥
abhipriyā svairavṛttī rukmiṇī sarvasākṣiṇī |
gāndhāriṇī paragatistattvagarbhā bhavābhavā || 67 ||

अन्तर्वर्तिर्महामुद्रा विष्णुदुर्गा महाबला ।
मदयन्ती लोकधारिण्यदृश्या सर्वनिष्कृतिः ॥६८॥
antarvartirmahāmudrā viṣṇudurgā mahābalā |
madayantī lokadhāriṇyadṛśyā sarvaniṣkṛtiḥ || 68 ||

देवसेनाऽऽत्मफलदा वसुधा मुख्यमातृका ।
क्षीरधारा घृतमयी जुह्वती यज्ञदक्षिणा ॥६९॥
devasenā--tmaphaladā vasudhā mukhyamātṛkā |
kṣīradhārā ghṛtamayī juhvatī yajñadakṣiṇā || 69 ||

योगनिद्रा योगरता ब्रह्मचर्या दुरत्यया ।
सिंहपिच्छा महादुर्गा जयन्ती खगवाहिनी ॥७०॥
yoganidrā yogaratā brahmacaryā duratyayā |
siṁhapicchā mahādurgā jayantī khagavāhinī || 70 ||

जगत्प्रिया विरूपाक्षी सुवर्णा क्रूरतापिनी ।
कात्यायनी कालरात्रिर्निशिदृष्टा करालिका ॥७१॥
jagatpriyā virūpākṣī suvarṇā krūratāpinī |
kātyāyanī kālarātrirniśidṛṣṭā karālikā || 71 ||

त्रिशूलिनी खड्गधरा महाकालीन्द्रमालिनी ।
एकवीरा भद्रकाली सौनन्दी उल्लसद्गदा ॥७२॥
triśūlinī khaḍgadharā mahākālīndramālinī |
ekavīrā bhadrakālī saunandī ullasadgadā || 72 ||

नारायणी जगत्पूरिण्युर्वरा द्रुहिणप्रसूः ।
यज्ञकामा लेलिहाना तीर्थकर्युग्रविक्रमा ॥७३॥
nārāyaṇī jagatpūriṇyurvarā druhiṇaprasūḥ |
yajñakāmā lelihānā tīrthakaryugravikramā || 73 ||

गरुत्मदुदयाऽत्युग्रा वाराही मातृभीषिणी ।
अश्वक्रान्ता रथक्रान्ता विष्णुक्रान्तोरुचारिणी ॥७४॥
garutmadudayā-tyugrā vārāhī mātṛbhīṣiṇī |
aśvakrāntā rathakrāntā viṣṇukrāntorucāriṇī || 74 ||

वैरोचिनी नारसिंही जीमूता शुभदेक्षणा ।
दीक्षाविधा विश्वशक्तिर्निजशक्तिः सुदर्शिनी ॥७५॥
vairocinī nārasiṁhī jīmūtā śubhadekṣaṇā |
dīkṣāvidhā viśvaśaktirnijaśaktiḥ sudarśinī || 75 ||

प्रतीतिर्जगती वन्यधारिणी कलिनाशिनी ।
अयोध्याऽच्छिन्नसन्ताना महारत्ना सुखावहा ॥७६॥
pratītirjagatī vanyadhāriṇī kalināśinī |
ayodhyā-cchinnasantānā mahāratnā sukhāvahā || 76 ||

राजवर्त्यर्कप्रतिभा विनयत्री महाशना ।
अमृतस्यन्दिनी सीमा यज्ञगर्भा समीक्षणा ॥७७॥
rājavartyarkapratibhā vinayatrī mahāśanā |
amṛtasyandinī sīmā yajñagarbhā samīkṣaṇā || 77 ||

आकूतिर्ऋग्यजुस्सामघोषाऽऽरामवधूत्सुका ।
सोमपा माधवी नित्यकल्याणी कमलार्चिता ॥७८॥
ākūtirṛgyajussāmaghoṣā--rāmavadhūtsukā |
somapā mādhavī nityakalyāṇī kamalārcitā || 78 ||

योगरूढिः स्वार्थजुष्टा वह्निवर्णा जितासुरा ।
यज्ञविद्या गुह्यविद्याऽध्यात्मविद्या कृतागमा ॥७९॥
yogarūḍhiḥ svārthajuṣṭā vahnivarṇā jitāsurā |
yajñavidyā guhyavidyā-dhyātmavidyā kṛtāgamā || 79 ||

आप्यायिनी कलातीता सुमित्रा परभक्तीदा ।
काङ्क्षमाणा महामाया कोलकामाऽमरावती ॥८०॥
āpyāyinī kalātītā sumitrā parabhaktīdā |
kāṅkṣamāṇā mahāmāyā kolakāmā-marāvatī || 80 ||

सुवीर्या दुःस्वप्नहरा देवकी वसुदेवता ।
सौदामिनी मेघरथा ऋद्धिदा दैत्यमर्दिनी ॥८१॥
suvīryā duḥsvapnaharā devakī vasudevatā |
saudāminī megharathā ṛddhidā daityamardinī || 81 ||

श्रेयस्करी चित्रलीलैकायिनी रत्नपादुका ।
मनस्यमाना तुलसी रोगनाशिन्युरुप्रथा ॥८२॥
śreyaskarī citralīlaikāyinī ratnapādukā |
manasyamānā tulasī roganāśinyurupratha || 82 ||

तेजस्विनी सुखोज्ज्वाला मन्दरेखाऽमृताशिनी ।
ब्रह्मिष्ठा वह्निशमनी जुषमाणा गुणात्यया ॥८३॥
tejasvinī sukhojjvālā mandarekhā-mṛtāśinī |
brahmiṣṭhā vahniśamanī juṣamāṇā guṇātyayā || 83 ||

कादम्बरी ब्रह्मरता विधात्र्युज्ज्वलहस्तिका ।
अक्षोभ्या सर्वतोभद्रा वयस्या स्वस्तिदाक्षिणा ॥८४॥
kādambarī brahmaratā vidhātryujjvalahastikā |
akṣobhyā sarvatobhadrā vayasyā svastidākṣiṇā || 84 ||

सहस्रास्या ज्ञानमाता वैश्वानर्यक्षवर्तिनी ।
प्रत्यग्वरा वारणवत्यनसूया दुरासदा ॥८५॥
sahasrāsyā jñānamātā vaiśvānaryakṣavartinī |
pratyagvarā vāraṇavatyanasūyā durāsadā || 85 ||

अरुन्धती कुण्डलिनी भव्या दुर्गतिनाशिनी ।
मृत्युञ्जया त्रासहरा निर्भया शत्रुसूदिनी ॥८६॥
arundhatī kuṇḍalinī bhavyā durgatināśinī |
mṛtyuñjayā trāsaharā nirbhayā śatrusūdinī || 86 ||

एकाक्षरा सुपुरन्ध्री सुरपक्षा वरातुला ।
सकृद्विभासा प्रद्युम्ना हरिभद्रा धुरन्धरा ॥८७॥
ekākṣarā supurandhrī surapakṣā varātulā |
sakṛdvibhāsā pradyumnā haribhadrā dhurandharā || 87 ||

बिल्वप्रियाऽवनी चक्रहृदया कम्बुतीर्थगा ।
सर्वमन्त्रात्मिका विद्युद्यशोदा सर्वरञ्जिनी ॥८८॥
bilvapriyā-vanī cakrahṛdayā kambutīrthagā |
sarvamantrātmikā vidyudyaśodā sarvarañjinī || 88 ||

ध्वजच्छत्राश्रया भूमिर्वैष्णवी सद्गुणोज्ज्वला ।
सुषेणा लोकविदिता कामसूर्जगदादिभूः ॥८९॥
dhvajacchatrāśrayā bhūmirvaiṣṇavī sadguṇojjvalā |
suṣeṇā lokaviditā kāmasūrjagadādibhūḥ || 89 ||

वेदान्तयोनिर्जिज्ञासा मनीषा समदर्शिनी ।
सहस्रशक्तिरावृतिः सुस्थिरा श्रेयसां निधिः ॥९०॥

**vedāntayonirjijñāsā manīṣā samadarśinī |
sahasraśaktirāvṛtiḥ susthirā śreyasāṁ nidhiḥ || 90 ||**

रोहिणी रेवती चन्द्रसोदरी भद्रमोदिनी ।
आर्या गव्यप्रिया विश्वभाविनी सुविभाविनी ॥९१॥

**rohiṇī revatī candrasodarī bhadramodinī |
āryā gavyapriyā viśvabhāvinī suvibhāvinī || 91 ||**

सुप्रदृश्या कामचारिण्यप्रमत्ता ललन्तिका ।
मोक्षलक्ष्मीर्जगद्योनिर्व्योमलक्ष्मीः सुदुर्लभा ॥९२॥

**supradṛśyā kāmacāriṇyapramattā lalantikā |
mokṣalakṣmīrjagadyonirvyomalakṣmīḥ sudurlabhā || 92 ||**

भास्करी पुण्यगेहस्था मनोज्ञा विभवप्रदा ।
लोकस्वामिन्यच्युतार्था पुष्कला जगदाकृतिः ॥९३॥

**bhāskarī puṇyagehasthā manojñā vibhavapradā |
lokasvāminyacyutārthā puṣkalā jagadākṛtiḥ || 93 ||**

विचित्रहारिणी कान्ता पाविनी भूतभाविनी ।
प्राणिनी प्राणदा विद्वद्विश्वब्रह्माण्डवासिनी ॥९४॥

**vicitrahāriṇī kāntā pāvinī bhūtabhāvinī |
prāṇinī prāṇadā vidvadviśvabrahmāṇḍavāsinī || 94 ||**

सम्पूर्णा परमोत्साहा श्रीपतिः श्रीमतिः श्रुतिः ।
श्रयन्ती श्रयमाणा क्ष्मा विश्वरूपा प्रसादिनि ॥९५॥

**sampūrṇā paramotsāhā śrīpatiḥ śrīmatiḥ śrutiḥ |
śrayantī śrayamāṇā kṣmā viśvarūpā prasādini || 95 ||**

हर्षणी प्रथमा सर्वा विशाला कामवर्षिणी ।
सुप्रतीका पृश्निमतीर्निवृत्तिर्विविधा परा ॥९६॥
harṣaṇī prathamā sarvā viśālā kāmavarṣiṇī |
supratīkā pṛśnimatīrnivṛttirvividhā parā || 96 ||

सुयज्ञा मधुरा श्रीदा देवरातिर्महामनाः ।
स्थूला सर्वाकृतिः सूक्ष्मा निम्नगव्या तमोनुदा ॥९७॥
suyajñā madhurā śrīdā devarātirmahāmanāḥ |
sthūlā sarvākṛtiḥ sūkṣmā nimnagavyā tamonudā || 97 ||

तुष्टिर्वागीश्वरी पुष्टिः सर्वाद्या स्वरुशोषिणी ।
शक्त्यात्मिका शब्दशक्तिर्विशिष्टा वायुमत्युमा ॥९८॥
tuṣṭirvāgīśvarī puṣṭiḥ sarvādyā svaruśoṣiṇī |
śaktyātmikā śabdaśaktirviśiṣṭā vāyumatyumā || 98 ||

आन्वीक्षिकी त्रयी वार्ता दण्डनीतिर्नियामिका ।
व्याली सङ्कर्षणी द्योता महादेव्यपराजिता ॥९९॥
ānvīkṣikī trayī vārtā daṇḍanītirniyāmikā |
vyālī saṅkarṣaṇī dyotā mahādevyaparājitā || 99 ||

कपिला पिङ्गला स्वस्था बलाकी घोषनन्दिनी ।
अजिता कर्षणी क्षान्तिर्गरुडा गरुडासना ॥१००॥
kapilā piṅgalā svasthā balākī ghoṣanandinī |
ajitā karṣaṇī kṣāntirgaruḍā garuḍāsanā || 100 ||

ह्लादिन्यनुग्रहा नित्या ब्रह्मविद्या हिरण्मयी ।
मही शुद्धविदा पृथ्वी शतानन्दांशुमालिनी ॥१०१॥
hlādinyanugrahā nityā brahmavidyā hiraṇmayī |
mahī śuddhavidā pṛthvī śatānandāṁśumālinī || 101 ||

यज्ञाश्रया ख्यातिपरा स्तव्या घृष्टिस्त्रिकालगा ।
सम्बोधिनी शब्दपूर्णा विजयांशुमती कला ॥१०२॥

yajñāśrayā khyātiparā stavyā ghṛṣṭistrikālagā |
sambodhinī śabdapūrṇā vijayāṁśumatī kalā || 102 ||

शिवा स्तुतिप्रिया ख्यातिर्जीवयन्ती पुनर्वसुः ।
दीक्षा भक्तार्तिहा रक्षा परीक्षा यज्ञसंभवा ॥१०३॥

śivā stutipriyā khyātirjīvayantī punarvasuḥ |
dīkṣā bhaktārtihā rakṣā parīkṣā yajñasaṁbhavā || 103 ||

आद्रा पुष्करिणी पुण्या गण्या दारिद्र्यभञ्जिनी ।
धन्या मान्या पद्मनेमी भार्गवी वंशवर्धिनी ॥१०४॥

ārdrā puṣkariṇī puṇyā gaṇyā dāridryabhañjinī |
dhanyā mānyā padmanemī bhārgavī vaṁśavardhinī || 104 ||

तीक्ष्णप्रवृत्तिः सत्कीर्तिर्निधिसेव्याऽघनाशिनी ।
सञ्ज्ञा निस्संशया पूर्वा वनमाला वसुन्धरा ॥१०५॥

tīkṣṇapravṛttiḥ satkīrtirnidhisevyā-ghanāśinī |
sañjñā nissaṁśayā pūrvā vanamālā vasundharā || 105 ||

पृथ्वी महोत्कटाऽहल्या मण्डलाश्रितमानदा ।
सर्वा नित्योदितोदारा जृम्भमाणा महोदया ॥१०६॥

pṛthvī mahotkaṭā-halyā maṇḍalāśritamānadā |
sarvā nityoditodārā jṛmbhamāṇā mahodayā || 106 ||

चन्द्रकान्तोदिता सूर्या चतुरश्रा मनोजवा ।
बाला कुमारी युवती करुणा भक्तवत्सला ॥१०७॥

candrakāntoditā sūryā caturaśrā manojavā |
bālā kumārī yuvatī karuṇā bhaktavatsalā || 107 ||

मेदिन्युपनिषन्मिश्रा सुमवीरुर्धनेश्वरी ।
दुर्मर्षणी सुचरिता बोधा शोभा सुवर्चला ॥१०८॥
medinyupaniṣanmiśrā sumavīrurdhaneśvarī |
durmarṣaṇī sucaritā bodhā śobhā suvarcalā || 108 ||

यमुनाक्षौहिणी गङ्गा मन्दाकिन्यमलाशया ।
गोदा गोदावरी चन्द्रभागा कावेर्युदन्वती ॥१०९॥
yamunākṣauhiṇī gaṅgā mandākinyamalāśayā |
godā godāvarī candrabhāgā kāveryudanvatī || 109 ||

सिनीवाली कुहू राका वारणा सिन्धुमत्यमा ।
पूर्तिर्मायात्मिका स्फूर्तिर्व्याख्या सूत्रा प्रजावती ॥११०॥
sinīvālī kuhū rākā vāraṇā sindhumatyamā |
pūrtirmāyātmikā sphūrtirvyākhyā sūtrā prajāvatī || 110 ||

वृद्धिः स्थितिर्ध्रुवा बुद्धिस्त्रिगुणा गुणगह्वरा ।
अमोघा शान्तिदा सत्या ज्ञानदोत्कर्षिणी शिवा ॥१११॥
vṛddhiḥ sthitirdhruvā buddhistriguṇā guṇagahvarā |
amoghā śāntidā satyā jñānadotkarṣiṇī śivā || 111 ||

प्रकृतिर्भामिनी लोला कमला कामधुग्विधिः ।
प्रज्ञा रामा परा सन्ध्या सुभद्रा सर्वमङ्गला ॥११२॥
prakṛtirbhāminī lolā kamalā kāmadhugvidhiḥ |
prajñā rāmā parā sandhyā subhadrā sarvamaṅgalā || 112 ||

नन्दा भद्रा जया रिक्ता तिथिपूर्णा ऋतंभरा ।
काष्ठा कामेश्वरी निष्ठा काम्या रम्या धरा स्मृतिः ॥११३॥

nandā bhadrā jayā riktā tithipūrṇā ṛtaṁbharā |
kāṣṭhā kāmeśvarī niṣṭhā kāmyā ramyā dharā smṛtiḥ || 113 ||

शङ्खिनी चक्रिणी श्यामा समा गोत्रा रमा द्युतिः ।
शान्तिदा स्तुतिः सिद्धिश्च विरजाऽत्युज्ज्वलाऽव्यया ॥११४॥

śaṅkhinī cakriṇī śyāmā samā gotrā ramā dyutiḥ |
śāntidā stutiḥ siddhiśca virajā-tyujjvalā-vyayā || 114 ||

वाणी गौरीन्दिरा लक्ष्मीः मेधा श्रद्धाऽप्रमा द्युतिः ।
स्वधा स्वाहा रतिरुषा वसुर्विद्या धृतिः सभा ॥११५॥

vāṇī gaurīndirā lakṣmīḥ medhā śraddhā-pramā dyutiḥ |
svadhā svāhā ratiruṣā vasurvidyā dhṛtiḥ sabhā || 115 ||

शिष्टा इष्टा शुची धात्री सुधाराऽक्षोण्यजाऽमृता ।
रमण्येका शारदाम्बा समेधाऽऽद्या शुभाक्षरा ॥११६॥

śiṣṭā iṣṭā śucī dhātrī sudhārā-kṣoṇyajā-mṛtā |
ramaṇyekā śāradāmbā samedhā--dyā śubhākṣarā || 116 ||

रत्नावली भारतीडा धीर धीः केवलाऽऽत्मदा ।
या सा शुद्धिः सोस्मित का नीला राधाऽमृतोद्भवा ॥११७॥

ratnāvalī bhāratīḍā dhīra dhīḥ kevalā--tmadā |
yā sā śuddhiḥ sosmita kā nīlā rādhā-mṛtodbhavā || 117 ||

विभूतिर्निष्कला रम्या रक्षा सुविमला क्षमा ।
प्राप्तिर्वासन्तिका लेखा भूरिबीजा महाङ्गदा ॥११८॥

vibhūtirniṣkalā ramyā rakṣā suvimalā kṣamā |
prāptirvāsantikā lekhā bhūribījā mahāṅgadā || 118 ||

वरधुर्या स्वधा ह्रीर्भूः कामिनी शोकनाशिनी ।
माया प्रीतिरसहना नर्मदा गोकुलाश्रया ॥११९॥

varadhuryā svadhā hrīrbhūḥ kāminī śokanāśinī |
māyā prītirasahanā narmadā gokulāśrayā || 119 ||

अर्कप्रभा रसेभा श्रीनिलयेन्दुप्रभाऽद्भुता ।
श्रीः कृशानु प्रभा वज्रलम्भना सर्वभूमिदा ॥१२०॥

arkaprabhā rasebhā śrīnilayenduprabhā-dbhutā |
śrīḥ kṛśānu prabhā vajralambhanā sarvabhūmidā || 120 ||

भोगप्रिया भोगवती भोगीन्द्रशयनासना ।
अश्वपूर्वा रथमध्या हस्तिनादप्रबोधिनी ॥१२१॥

bhogapriyā bhogavatī bhogīndraśayanāsanā |
aśvapūrvā rathamadhyā hastinādaprabodhinī || 121 ||

सर्वलक्षणलक्ष्ण्या सर्वलोकप्रियङ्करी ।
सर्वमङ्गलमाङ्गल्या दृष्टादृष्टफलप्रदा ॥१२२॥

sarvalakṣaṇalakṣṇyā sarvalokapriyaṅkarī |
sarvamaṅgalamāṅgalyā dṛṣṭādṛṣṭaphalapradā || 122 ||

॥ इति श्रीलक्ष्मीसहस्रनामस्तोत्रम् संपूर्णम् ॥

|| iti śrīlakṣmīsahasranāmastotram saṁpūrṇam ||

अथ लक्ष्मीसहस्रनामावल्या:

atha lakṣmīsahasranāmāvalyāḥ

\- 1 -

ॐ श्रियै स्वाहा

oṁ śriyai svāhā
She who is the Ultimate Respect, peace in the mind, peace in the heart.

\- 2 -

ॐ वासुदेवमहिष्यै स्वाहा

oṁ vāsudevamahiṣyai svāhā
She who is the greatness of the Lord of the Earth.

\- 3 -

ॐ पुंप्रधानेश्वरेश्वर्यै स्वाहा

oṁ puṁpradhāneśvareśvaryai svāhā
She who is the highest above all Gods and Goddesses.

\- 4 -

ॐ अचिन्त्यानन्तविभवायै स्वाहा

oṁ acintyānantavibhavāyai svāhā
She who is the manifestation of the unthinkable infinity of creation.

\- 5 -

ॐ भावाभावविभाविन्यै स्वाहा

oṁ bhāvābhāvavibhāvinyai svāhā
She who displays all attitudes both good and bad.

\- 6 -

ॐ अहंभावात्मिकायै स्वाहा

oṁ ahaṁbhāvātmikāyai svāhā
She who gives the capacity of the soul to express the attitude of I.

\- 7 -

ॐ पद्मायै स्वाहा

oṁ padmāyai svāhā
She who is a lotus.

- 8 -

ॐ शान्तानन्तजितात्मिकायै स्वाहा

oṁ śāntānantajitātmikāyai svāhā
She who gives the capacity for the soul to attain infinite peace.

- 9 -

ॐ ब्रह्मभावंगतायै स्वाहा

oṁ brahmabhāvaṁgatāyai svāhā
She who is the substance of the many attitudes of the supreme.

- 10 -

ॐ त्यक्तभीत्यै स्वाहा

oṁ tyaktabhītyai svāhā
She who is beyond all fear.

- 11 -

ॐ सर्वजगन्मय्यै स्वाहा

oṁ sarvajaganmayyai svāhā
She who is the manifestation of the entire perceivable world.

- 12 -

ॐ षाडगुण्यपूर्णायै स्वाहा

oṁ ṣāḍaguṇyapūrṇāyai svāhā
She who is full of pure qualities.

- 13 -

ॐ त्रय्यन्तरूपायै स्वाहा

oṁ trayyantarūpāyai svāhā
She who is the form of the ultimate three.

- 14 -

ॐ आत्मानपगामिन्यै स्वाहा

oṁ ātmānapagāminyai svāhā
She who travels with the soul.

- 15 -

ॐ एकयोग्यायै स्वाहा

oṁ ekayogyāyai svāhā
She who is in union.

- 16 -

ॐ अशून्यभावाकृत्यै स्वाहा

oṁ aśūnyabhāvākṛtyai svāhā
She who is the uncreated attitude that fills the silence.

- 17 -

ॐ तेजःप्रभाविन्यै स्वाहा

oṁ tejaḥprabhāvinyai svāhā
She who spreads Her lustrous light.

- 18 -

ॐ भाव्याभावकभावायै स्वाहा

oṁ bhāvyābhāvakabhāvāyai svāhā
She whose attitude is the attitude of all attitudes.

- 19 -

ॐ आत्मभाव्यायै स्वाहा

oṁ ātmabhāvyāyai svāhā
She who is the attitude of the soul.

- 20 -

ॐ कामदुहे स्वाहा

oṁ kāmaduhe svāhā
She who destroys desire.

- 21 -

ॐ आत्मभुवे स्वाहा

oṁ ātmabhuve svāhā
She who is the being of the soul.

- 22 -

ॐ भावाभावमय्यै स्वाहा

oṁ bhāvābhāvamayyai svāhā
She who is the manifestation of all attitudes, both good and bad.

- 23 -

ॐ दिव्यायै स्वाहा

oṁ divyāyai svāhā
She who is divine.

- 24 -

ॐ भेद्याभेदकभावगायै स्वाहा

oṁ bhedyabhedakabhāvagāyai svāhā

She who expresses the attitude of that which can be divided and that which cannot be divided.

- 25 -

ॐ जगत्कुटुम्बिन्यै स्वाहा

oṁ jagatkuṭumbinyai svāhā

She who is head of the family of the perceivable universe.

- 26 -

ॐ अखिलाधारायै स्वाहा

oṁ akhilādhārāyai svāhā

She who supports the entire creation.

- 27 -

ॐ कामविजृम्भिण्यै स्वाहा

oṁ kāmavijṛmbhiṇyai svāhā

She who has conquered all desires.

- 28 -

ॐ पञ्चकृत्यकर्यै स्वाहा

oṁ pañcakṛtyakaryai svāhā

She who creates the universe composed of five elements.

- 29 -

ॐ पञ्चशक्तिमय्यै स्वाहा

oṁ pañcaśaktimayyai svāhā

She who is the manifestation of the five energies.

- 30 -

ॐ आत्मवल्लभायै स्वाहा

oṁ ātmavallabhāyai svāhā

She who is the strength of the soul.

- 31 -

ॐ भावाभावानुगायै स्वाहा

oṁ bhāvābhāvānugāyai svāhā

She who is beyond all attitudes, both good and bad.

- 32 -

ॐ सर्वसम्मतायै स्वाहा

oṁ sarvasammatāyai svāhā
She who is all wealth.

- 33 -

ॐ आत्मोपगूहिन्यै स्वाहा

oṁ ātmopagūhinyai svāhā
She who dwells within the secret place of the soul.

- 34 -

ॐ अपृथक्चारिण्यै स्वाहा

oṁ apṛthakcāriṇyai svāhā
She who moves without separation.

- 35 -

ॐ सौम्यायै स्वाहा

oṁ saumyāyai svāhā
She who is beautiful.

- 36 -

ॐ सौम्यरूपायै स्वाहा

oṁ saumyarūpāyai svāhā
She who is the form of beauty.

- 37 -

ॐ अव्यवस्थितायै स्वाहा

oṁ avyavasthitāyai svāhā
She who resides in the imperishable creation.

- 38 -

ॐ आद्यन्तरहितायै स्वाहा

oṁ ādyantarahitāyai svāhā
She who shines from beginning to end.

- 39 -

ॐ देव्यै स्वाहा

oṁ devyai svāhā
She who is the goddess.

- 40 -

ॐ भवभाव्यस्वरूपिण्यै स्वाहा

oṁ bhavabhāvyasvarūpiṇyai svāhā
She who is the intrinsic nature of the attitude of existence.

- 41 -

ॐ महाविभूत्यै स्वाहा

oṁ mahāvibhūtyai svāhā
She who is the great expression.

- 42 -

ॐ समतांगतायै स्वाहा

oṁ samatāṁgatāyai svāhā
She whose body is in equilibrium.

- 43 -

ॐ ज्योतिर्गणेश्वर्यै स्वाहा

oṁ jyotirgaṇeśvaryai svāhā
She who is the supreme of the multitude of lights.

- 44 -

ॐ सर्वकार्यकर्यै स्वाहा

oṁ sarvakāryakaryai svāhā
She who is the performer of all causes.

- 45 -

ॐ धर्मस्वभावायै स्वाहा

oṁ dharmasvabhāvāyai svāhā
She who is the intrinsic nature of the ideal of perfection.

- 46-

ॐ आत्माग्रतःस्थितायै स्वाहा

oṁ ātmāgrataḥsthitāyai svāhā
She who is situated in the advancement of the soul.

- 47 -

ॐ आज्ञासमविभक्ताङ्ग्यै स्वाहा

oṁ ājñāsamavibhaktāṅgyai svāhā
She who brings equality to the limbs of devotion in the ājna cākra.

- 48 -

ॐ ज्ञानानन्दक्रियामय्यै स्वाहा

oṁ jñānānandakriyāmayyai svāhā
She who is the manifestation of the bliss of wisdom in all action.

- 49 -

ॐ स्वातन्त्र्यरूपायै स्वाहा

oṁ svātantryarūpāyai svāhā
She who is the form of independence.

- 50 -

ॐ देवोरःस्थितायै स्वाहा

oṁ devoraḥsthitāyai svāhā
She who is situated above the Gods.

- 51 -

ॐ तद्धर्मधर्मिण्यै स्वाहा

oṁ taddharmadharmiṇyai svāhā
She who is that ideal of all ideals of perfection.

- 52 -

ॐ सर्वभूतेश्वर्यै स्वाहा

oṁ sarvabhūteśvaryai svāhā
She who is the supreme Goddess of all existence.

- 53 -

ॐ सर्वभूतमात्रे स्वाहा

oṁ sarvabhūtamātre svāhā
She who is the Mother of all existence.

- 54 -

ॐ आत्ममोहिन्यै स्वाहा

oṁ ātmamohinyai svāhā
She who creates the ignorance of the soul.

- 55 -

ॐ सर्वाङ्गसुन्दर्यै स्वाहा

oṁ sarvāṅgasundaryai svāhā
She whose every limb is beautiful.

- 56 -

ॐ सर्वव्यापिन्यै स्वाहा

oṁ sarvavyāpinyai svāhā
She who distinguishes the individuals of existence.

- 57 -

ॐ प्राप्तयोगिन्यै स्वाहा

oṁ prāptayoginyai svāhā
She who has attained the highest union.

- 58 -

ॐ विमुक्तिदायिन्यै स्वाहा

oṁ vimuktidāyinyai svāhā
She who gives liberation.

- 59 -

ॐ भक्तगम्यायै स्वाहा

oṁ bhaktagamyāyai svāhā
She who goes to devotees.

- 60 -

ॐ संसारतारिण्यै स्वाहा

oṁ saṁsāratāriṇyai svāhā
She who takes across the ocean of worldliness.

- 61 -

ॐ धर्मार्थवादिन्यै स्वाहा

oṁ dharmārthavādinyai svāhā
She who explains the meaning of the ideal of perfection.

- 62 -

ॐ व्योमनिलयायै स्वाहा

oṁ vyomanilayāyai svāhā
She who creates the atmosphere.

- 63 -

ॐ व्योमविग्रहायै स्वाहा

oṁ vyomavigrahāyai svāhā
She who is the form of the atmosphere.

- 64 -

ॐ पञ्चव्योमपद्यै स्वाहा

oṁ pañcavyomapadyai svāhā
She who is the attributes of the elements like ether.

- 65 -

ॐ रक्षव्यावृत्यै स्वाहा

oṁ rakṣavyāvṛtyai svāhā
She who protects and does not change.

- 66 -

ॐ प्राप्यपूरिण्यै स्वाहा

oṁ prāpyapūriṇyai svāhā
She who has the fullest attainment.

- 67 -

ॐ आनन्दरूपायै स्वाहा

oṁ ānandarūpāyai svāhā
She who is the form of bliss.

- 68 -

ॐ सर्वाप्तिशालिन्यै स्वाहा

oṁ sarvāptiśālinyai svāhā
She who resides in consciousness.

- 69 -

ॐ शक्तिनायिकायै स्वाहा

oṁ śaktināyikāyai svāhā
She who is the foremost energy.

- 70 -

ॐ हिरण्यवर्णायै स्वाहा

oṁ hiraṇyavarṇāyai svāhā
She who has a golden color.

- 71 -

ॐ हैरण्यप्राकारायै स्वाहा

oṁ hairaṇyaprākārāyai svāhā
She who resides in all kinds of wealth.

- 72 -

ॐ हेममालिन्यै स्वाहा

oṁ hemamālinyai svāhā
She who cultivates all that is valuable.

- 73 -

ॐ प्रस्फुरत्तायै स्वाहा

oṁ prasphurattāyai svāhā
She who illuminates all.

- 74 -

ॐ भद्रहोमायै स्वाहा

oṁ bhadrahomāyai svāhā
She who is the excellent fire sacrifice.

- 75 -

ॐ वेशिन्यै स्वाहा

oṁ veśinyai svāhā
She who is abundance.

- 76 -

ॐ रजतस्रजायै स्वाहा

oṁ rajatasrajāyai svāhā
She who gives birth to the flow of wealth.

- 77 -

ॐ स्वाज्ञाकार्यमरायै स्वाहा

oṁ svājñākāryamarāyai svāhā
She who follows her own orders.

- 78 -

ॐ नित्यसुरभ्यै स्वाहा

oṁ nityasurabhyai svāhā
She who is eternally divine.

- 79 -

ॐ व्योमचारिण्यै स्वाहा

oṁ vyomacāriṇyai svāhā
She who moves through the ether.

- 80 -

ॐ योगक्षेमवहायै स्वाहा

oṁ yogakṣemavahāyai svāhā
She who is the vehicle of liberation in union.

- 81 -

ॐ सर्वसुलभायै स्वाहा

oṁ sarvasulabhāyai svāhā
She for whom all is easy of attainment.

- 82 -

ॐ इच्छाक्रियात्मिकायै स्वाहा

oṁ icchākriyātmikāyai svāhā
She who is the capacity of desire and action.

- 83 -

ॐ महासमूहायै स्वाहा

oṁ mahāsamūhāyai svāhā
She who is the great creation.

- 84 -

ॐ निखिलप्ररोहायै स्वाहा

oṁ nikhilaprarohāyai svāhā
She who administers the entire existence.

- 85 -

ॐ वेदगोचरायै स्वाहा

oṁ vedagocarāyai svāhā
She who moves with the light of wisdom.

- 86 -

ॐ विस्मयाधायिन्यै स्वाहा

oṁ vismayādhāyinyai svāhā
She who gives all that is wonderful.

- 87 -

ॐ ब्रह्मसंहितायै स्वाहा

oṁ brahmasaṁhitāyai svāhā
She who is the text of the Supreme.

- 88 -

ॐ सुगुणोत्तरायै स्वाहा

oṁ suguṇottarāyai svāhā
She who is the highest excellent quality.

- 89 -

ॐ प्रज्ञापरिमितायै स्वाहा

oṁ prajñāparimitāyai svāhā
She who has the highest enjoyment of the foremost wisdom.

- 90 -

ॐ आत्मानुरूपायै स्वाहा

oṁ ātmānurūpāyai svāhā
She who is the smallest form of the soul.

- 91 -

ॐ सत्योपायार्जितायै स्वाहा

oṁ satyopāyārjitāyai svāhā
She who utilizes the way of truth.

- 92 -

ॐ मनोज्ञेयायै स्वाहा

oṁ manojñeyāyai svāhā
She whose mind is filled with wisdom.

- 93 -

ॐ ज्ञानगम्यायै स्वाहा

oṁ jñānagamyāyai svāhā
She who moves with wisdom.

- 94 -

ॐ नित्यमुक्तायै स्वाहा

oṁ nityamuktāyai svāhā
She who is eternally liberated.

- 95 -

ॐ आत्मसेविन्यै स्वाहा

oṁ ātmasevinyai svāhā
She who is served by the soul.

- 96 -

ॐ कर्तृशक्त्यै स्वाहा

oṁ kartṛśaktyai svāhā
She who is the energy of action.

- 97 -

ॐ सुगहनायै स्वाहा

oṁ sugahanāyai svāhā
She who is extremely deep.

- 98 -

ॐ भोक्तृशक्त्यै स्वाहा

oṁ bhoktṛśaktyai svāhā
She who is the energy of enjoyment.

- 99 -

ॐ गुणप्रियायै स्वाहा

oṁ guṇapriyāyai svāhā
She who loves all qualities or attributes.

- 100 -

ॐ ज्ञानशक्त्यै स्वाहा

oṁ jñānaśaktyai svāhā
She who is the energy of wisdom.

- 101 -

ॐ अनौपम्यायै स्वाहा

oṁ anaupamyāyai svāhā
She who has no comparison.

- 102 -

ॐ परशक्त्यै स्वाहा

oṁ paraśaktyai svāhā
She who is the supreme energy.

- 103 -

ॐ निरामयायै स्वाहा

oṁ nirāmayāyai svāhā
She who cures all disease.

- 104 -

ॐ अकलङ्कायै स्वाहा

oṁ akalaṅkāyai svāhā

She who is without stain or imperfection.

- 105 -

ॐ महाशक्त्यै स्वाहा

oṁ mahāśaktyai svāhā

She who is the great energy.

- 106 -

ॐ निराधारायै स्वाहा

oṁ nirādhārāyai svāhā

She who supports all without any other support.

- 107 -

ॐ विकासिन्यै स्वाहा

oṁ vikāsinyai svāhā

She who illuminates all.

- 108 -

ॐ महामायायै स्वाहा

oṁ mahāmāyāyai svāhā

She who is the great measurement of consciousness.

- 109 -

ॐ महानन्दायै स्वाहा

oṁ mahānandāyai svāhā

She who gives the great bliss.

- 110 -

ॐ ब्रह्मनीत्यै स्वाहा

oṁ brahmanītyai svāhā

She who is the supreme discipline.

- 111 -

ॐ निराश्रयायै स्वाहा

oṁ nirāśrayāyai svāhā

She who has no other refuge.

- 112 -

ॐ एकस्वरूपायै स्वाहा

oṁ ekasvarūpāyai svāhā
She who is the intrinsic nature of all.

- 113 -

ॐ त्रिविधायै स्वाहा

oṁ trividhāyai svāhā
She who is the three kinds of knowledge.

- 114 -

ॐ संख्यातीतायै स्वाहा

oṁ saṁkhyātītāyai svāhā
She who is beyond the Saṁkhya philosophy.

- 115 -

ॐ निरंजनायै स्वाहा

oṁ niraṁjanāyai svāhā
She who delights all.

- 116 -

ॐ आत्मसक्तायै स्वाहा

oṁ ātmasaktāyai svāhā
She who is the friend of the soul.

- 117 -

ॐ नित्यशुचये स्वाहा

oṁ nityaśucaye svāhā
She who is eternally pure.

- 118 -

ॐ निर्विकल्पायै स्वाहा

oṁ nirvikalpāyai svāhā
She who is without idea.

- 119 -

ॐ सुखोचितायै स्वाहा

oṁ sukhocitāyai svāhā
She whose consciousness is comfortable.

\- 120 -

ॐ नित्यशान्तायै स्वाहा

oṁ nityaśāntāyai svāhā
She who is always at peace.

\- 121 -

ॐ निस्तरङ्गायै स्वाहा

oṁ nistaraṅgāyai svāhā
She who has no waves.

\- 122 -

ॐ निर्भिन्नायै स्वाहा

oṁ nirbhinnāyai svāhā
She who has no separation.

\- 123 -

ॐ सर्वभेदिन्यै स्वाहा

oṁ sarvabhedinyai svāhā
She who is all distinctions.

\- 124 -

ॐ असंकीर्णायै स्वाहा

oṁ asaṁkīrṇāyai svāhā
She who is beyond measurement.

\- 125 -

ॐ अविधेयात्मने स्वाहा

oṁ avidheyātmane svāhā
She who is the soul beyond all rules.

\- 126 -

ॐ निषेद्ध्यायै स्वाहा

oṁ niṣeddhyāyai svāhā
She who cannot be known.

\- 127 -

ॐ सर्वपावन्यै स्वाहा

oṁ sarvapāvanyai svāhā
She who purifies all.

- 128 -

ॐ निष्कामनायै स्वाहा

oṁ niṣkāmanāyai svāhā
She who has no desire.

- 129 -

ॐ सर्वरसायै स्वाहा

oṁ sarvarasāyai svāhā
She who has all flavors and tastes.

- 130 -

ॐ अभेद्यायै स्वाहा

oṁ abhedyāyai svāhā
She who cannot be divided.

- 131 -

ॐ सर्वार्थसाधिन्यै स्वाहा

oṁ sarvārthasādhinyai svāhā
She who defines all.

- 132 -

ॐ अनिर्देश्यायै स्वाहा

oṁ anirdeśyāyai svāhā
She who no one can order.

- 133 -

ॐ अपरिमितायै स्वाहा

oṁ aparimitāyai svāhā
She who is beyond measurement.

- 134 -

ॐ निर्विकारायै स्वाहा

oṁ nirvikārāyai svāhā
She who never changes.

- 135 -

ॐ त्रिलक्षणायै स्वाहा

oṁ trilakṣaṇāyai svāhā
She who defines the three.

- 136 -

ॐ अभयङ्कर्यै स्वाहा

oṁ abhayaṅkaryai svāhā
She who is beyond fear.

- 137 -

ॐ स्त्रीस्वरूपायै स्वाहा

oṁ strīsvarūpāyai svāhā
She who is the intrinsic nature of women.

- 138 -

ॐ अव्यक्तायै स्वाहा

oṁ avyaktāyai svāhā
She who cannot be divided.

- 139 -

ॐ सदसदाकृत्यै स्वाहा

oṁ sadasadākṛtyai svāhā
She who creates the world of truth and untruth.

- 140 -

ॐ अप्रतर्क्यायै स्वाहा

oṁ apratarkyāyai svāhā
She who is not perceived through the senses.

- 141 -

ॐ अप्रतिहतायै स्वाहा

oṁ apratihatāyai svāhā
She who cannot be apprehended.

- 142 -

ॐ नियन्त्र्यै स्वाहा

oṁ niyantryai svāhā
She who is beyond all tools.

- 143 -

ॐ यन्त्रवाहिन्यै स्वाहा

oṁ yantravāhinyai svāhā
She who carries all tools.

- 144 -

ॐ हार्दमूर्त्यै स्वाहा

oṁ hārdamūrtyai svāhā
She who is the divine image within the heart.

- 145 -

ॐ महामूर्त्यै स्वाहा

oṁ mahāmūrtyai svāhā
She who is the great divine image.

- 146 -

ॐ अव्यक्तायै स्वाहा

oṁ avyaktāyai svāhā
She who cannot be divided.

- 147 -

ॐ विश्वगोपिन्यै स्वाहा

oṁ viśvagopinyai svāhā
She who is hidden within the universe.

- 148 -

ॐ वर्धमानायै स्वाहा

oṁ vardhamānāyai svāhā
She who always increases.

- 149 -

ॐ अनवद्याङ्ग्यै स्वाहा

oṁ anavadyāṅgyai svāhā
She whose body is immortal.

- 150 -

ॐ निरवद्यायै स्वाहा

oṁ niravadyāyai svāhā
She who is without death.

- 151 -

ॐ त्रिवर्गदायै स्वाहा

oṁ trivargadāyai svāhā
She who unites the three worlds.

- 152 -

ॐ अप्रमेयायै स्वाहा

oṁ aprameyāyai svāhā
She who is beyond explanation.

- 153 -

ॐ अमृतदुघायै स्वाहा

oṁ amṛtadughāyai svāhā
She who is the milk of the nectar of immortal bliss.

- 154 -

ॐ कूटस्थायै स्वाहा

oṁ kūṭasthāyai svāhā
She who is seated on the back of her carrier.

- 155-

ॐ कुलनन्दिन्यै स्वाहा

oṁ kulanandinyai svāhā
She who is the delight of the family.

- 156 -

ॐ अविगीतायै स्वाहा

oṁ avigītāyai svāhā
She whose praises cannot be sung.

- 157 -

ॐ तन्त्रसिद्धायै स्वाहा

oṁ tantrasiddhāyai svāhā
She who has attained perfection in the synthesis of all knowledge.

- 158 -

ॐ योगसिद्धायै स्वाहा

oṁ yogasiddhāyai svāhā
She who has attained the perfection of union.

- 159 -

ॐ अमरेश्वर्यै स्वाहा

oṁ amareśvaryai svāhā
She who is the supreme Goddess beyond death.

- 160 -

ॐ विश्वसूत्यै स्वाहा

oṁ viśvasūtyai svāhā

She who is the daughter of the universe.

- 161 -

ॐ तर्पयन्त्यै स्वाहा

oṁ tarpayantyai svāhā

She who is the offering of respect.

- 162 -

ॐ नित्यतृप्तायै स्वाहा

oṁ nityatṛptāyai svāhā

She who is always delighted.

- 163 -

ॐ महोषध्यै स्वाहा

oṁ mahoṣadhyai svāhā

She who is the great medicine.

- 164 -

ॐ शब्दात्ययायै स्वाहा

oṁ śabdātyayāyai svāhā

She who is all words.

- 165 -

ॐ शब्दसहायै स्वाहा

oṁ śabdasahāyai svāhā

She who communicates all words.

- 166 -

ॐ कृतज्ञायै स्वाहा

oṁ kṛtajñāyai svāhā

She who knows all action.

- 167 -

ॐ कृतलक्षणायै स्वाहा

oṁ kṛtalakṣaṇāyai svāhā

She who is the definition of all action.

- 168 -

ॐ त्रिवर्तिन्यै स्वाहा

oṁ trivartinyai svāhā
She who is the three times.

- 169 -

ॐ त्रिलोकस्थायै स्वाहा

oṁ trilokasthāyai svāhā
She who resides in the three worlds.

- 170 -

ॐ भूर्भुवःस्वरयोनिजायै स्वाहा

oṁ bhūrbhuvaḥsvarayonijāyai svāhā
She whose womb gives birth to the gross body, subtle body and causal body.

- 171 -

ॐ अग्राह्मायै स्वाहा

oṁ agrāhmāyai svāhā
She who accepts nothing for herself.

- 172 -

ॐ अग्राह्मकायै स्वाहा

oṁ agrāhmakāyai svāhā
She who causes others to renounce.

- 173 -

ॐ अनन्ताह्वयायै स्वाहा

oṁ anantāhvayāyai svāhā
She who is called infinitely.

- 174 -

ॐ सर्वातिशायिन्यै स्वाहा

oṁ sarvātiśāyinyai svāhā
She who allows all to rest.

- 175 -

ॐ व्योमपद्मायै स्वाहा

oṁ vyomapadmāyai svāhā
She who is a lotus in the atmosphere.

- 176 -

ॐ कृतधुरायै स्वाहा

oṁ kṛtadhurāyai svāhā
She who is far from all action.

- 177 -

ॐ पूर्णकामायै स्वाहा

oṁ pūrṇakāmāyai svāhā
She who fulfills all desires.

- 178 -

ॐ महेश्वर्यै स्वाहा

oṁ maheśvaryai svāhā
She who is the great supreme Goddess.

- 179 -

ॐ सुवाच्यायै स्वाहा

oṁ suvācyāyai svāhā
She who is the excellence of speech.

- 180 -

ॐ वाचिकायै स्वाहा

oṁ vācikāyai svāhā
She who is all vibrations.

- 181 -

ॐ सत्यकथनायै स्वाहा

oṁ satyakathanāyai svāhā
She who tells the truth.

- 182 -

ॐ सर्वपाविन्यै स्वाहा

oṁ sarvapāvinyai svāhā
She who drinks all.

- 183 -

ॐ लक्ष्यमाणायै स्वाहा

oṁ lakṣyamāṇāyai svāhā
She who sticks to the goal.

- 184 -

ॐ लक्षयन्त्यै स्वाहा

oṁ lakṣayantyai svāhā
She who is all criteria.

- 185 -

ॐ जगज्ज्येष्ठायै स्वाहा

oṁ jagajjyeṣṭhāyai svāhā
She who is the oldest in the world.

- 186 -

ॐ शुभावहायै स्वाहा

oṁ śubhāvahāyai svāhā
She who invites all auspiciousness.

- 187 -

ॐ जगत्प्रतिष्ठायै स्वाहा

oṁ jagatpratiṣṭhāyai svāhā
She who establishes the perceivable universe.

- 188 -

ॐ भुवनभर्त्र्यै स्वाहा

oṁ bhuvanabhatryai svāhā
She who is the wife of the perceivable world.

- 189 -

ॐ गूढप्रभाविन्यै स्वाहा

oṁ gūḍhaprabhāvinyai svāhā
She who illuminates all secrets.

- 190 -

ॐ क्रियायोगात्मिकायै स्वाहा

oṁ kriyāyogātmikāyai svāhā
She who is the capacity of the soul to unite in action.

- 191 -

ॐ मूर्तायै स्वाहा

oṁ mūrtāyai svāhā
She who is the image of divinity.

- 192 -

ॐ हृदब्जस्थायै स्वाहा

oṁ hṛdabjasthāyai svāhā
She who resides within the heart.

- 193 -

ॐ महाक्रमायै स्वाहा

oṁ mahākramāyai svāhā
She who is the great organizer.

- 194 -

ॐ परमदिवे स्वाहा

oṁ paramadive svāhā
She who is the supreme divinity.

- 195 -

ॐ प्रथमजायै स्वाहा

oṁ prathamajāyai svāhā
She who was first to be born.

- 196 -

ॐ परमाप्तायै स्वाहा

oṁ paramāptāyai svāhā
She who is the supreme seer of truth.

- 197 -

ॐ जगन्निधये स्वाहा

oṁ jagannidhaye svāhā
She who is the discipline of the perceivable world.

- 198 -

ॐ आत्मानपायिन्यै स्वाहा

oṁ ātmānapāyinyai svāhā
She within whom all souls reside.

- 199 -

ॐ तुल्यस्वरूपायै स्वाहा

oṁ tulyasvarūpāyai svāhā
She who is the intrinsic nature of equality.

- 200 -

ॐ समलक्षणायै स्वाहा

oṁ samalakṣaṇāyai svāhā
She who contains all the criteria.

- 201 -

ॐ तुल्यवृत्तायै स्वाहा

oṁ tulyavṛttāyai svāhā
She who is equal in all changes.

- 202 -

ॐ समवयसे स्वाहा

oṁ samavayase svāhā
She whose age is always the same.

- 203 -

ॐ मोदमानायै स्वाहा

oṁ modamānāyai svāhā
She who banishes ignorance.

- 204 -

ॐ खगध्वजायै स्वाहा

oṁ khagadhvajāyai svāhā
She who holds the ether as Her flag.

- 205 -

ॐ तुल्यचेष्टायै स्वाहा

oṁ tulyaceṣṭāyai svāhā
She who is equal in all effort.

- 206 -

ॐ तुल्यशीलायै स्वाहा

oṁ tulyaśīlāyai svāhā
She who is equal in stillness.

- 207 -

ॐ वरदायै स्वाहा

oṁ varadāyai svāhā
She who gives boons.

- 208 -

ॐ कामरूपिण्यै स्वाहा

oṁ kāmarūpiṇyai svāhā

She who is the intrinsic nature of desire.

- 209 -

ॐ समग्रलक्षणायै स्वाहा

oṁ samagralakṣaṇāyai svāhā

She who evaluates all criteria equally.

- 210 -

ॐ अनन्तायै स्वाहा

oṁ anantāyai svāhā

She who is infinite.

- 211 -

ॐ तुल्यभूत्यै स्वाहा

oṁ tulyabhūtyai svāhā

She who is equal in all elements.

- 212 -

ॐ सनातनायै स्वाहा

oṁ sanātanāyai svāhā

She who is eternal.

- 213 -

ॐ महर्द्धर्यै स्वाहा

oṁ maharddharyai svāhā

She who has great patience.

- 214 -

ॐ सत्यसंकल्पायै स्वाहा

oṁ satyasaṁkalpāyai svāhā

She who is true to her vow.

- 215 -

ॐ भूमिजायै स्वाहा

oṁ bhūmijāyai svāhā

She who gives birth to the earth.

- 216 -

ॐ परमेश्वर्यै स्वाहा

oṁ parameśvaryai svāhā
She who is the supreme Goddess of all.

- 217 -

ॐ जगन्मात्रे स्वाहा

oṁ jaganmātre svāhā
She who is the Mother of the perceivable world.

- 218 -

ॐ सूत्रवत्यै स्वाहा

oṁ sūtravatyai svāhā
She who is the thread of all explanation.

- 219 -

ॐ भुतधात्र्यै स्वाहा

oṁ bhutadhātryai svāhā
She who is the Mother of the five elements.

- 220 -

ॐ यशस्विन्यै स्वाहा

oṁ yaśasvinyai svāhā
She who has all fame.

- 221 -

ॐ महाभिलाषायै स्वाहा

oṁ mahābhilāṣāyai svāhā
She who is the great desire.

- 222 -

ॐ सावित्र्यै स्वाहा

oṁ sāvitryai svāhā
She who is the daughter of the light.

- 223 -

ॐ प्रधानायै स्वाहा

oṁ pradhānāyai svāhā
She who is foremost.

- 224 -

ॐ सर्वभासिन्यै स्वाहा

oṁ sarvabhāsinyai svāhā
She who illuminates all.

- 225 -

ॐ नानावपुषे स्वाहा

oṁ nānāvapuṣe svāhā
She who is all nourishment.

- 226 -

ॐ बहुविधायै स्वाहा

oṁ bahuvidhāyai svāhā
She who supports many disciplines.

- 227 -

ॐ सर्वज्ञायै स्वाहा

oṁ sarvajñāyai svāhā
She who knows all.

- 228 -

ॐ पुण्यकीर्तनायै स्वाहा

oṁ puṇyakīrtanāyai svāhā
She who is celebrated in meritorious song.

- 229 -

ॐ भूताश्रयायै स्वाहा

oṁ bhūtāśrayāyai svāhā
She within whom all elements take refuge.

- 230 -

ॐ हृषीकेशायै स्वाहा

oṁ hṛṣīkeśāyai svāhā
She who has controlled the senses.

- 231 -

ॐ अशोकायै स्वाहा

oṁ aśokāyai svāhā
She who has no sorrow.

- 232 -

ॐ स्वाङ्गिवाहिकायै स्वाहा

oṁ svāṅgivāhikāyai svāhā
She who comes with Her friends.

- 233 -

ॐ ब्रह्मात्मिकायै स्वाहा

oṁ brahmātmikāyai svāhā
She who has the capacity to express supreme divinity.

- 234 -

ॐ पुण्यजन्यै स्वाहा

oṁ puṇyajanyai svāhā
She who gives birth to merit.

- 235 -

ॐ सत्यकामायै स्वाहा

oṁ satyakāmāyai svāhā
She whose desire is truth.

- 236 -

ॐ समाधिभुवे स्वाहा

oṁ samādhibhuve svāhā
She whose every idea is in pure, intuitive vision.

- 237 -

ॐ हिरण्यगर्भायै स्वाहा

oṁ hiraṇyagarbhāyai svāhā
She from whose golden womb existence is born.

- 238 -

ॐ गम्भीरायै स्वाहा

oṁ gambhīrāyai svāhā
She who is serious.

- 239 -

ॐ गोधूल्यै स्वाहा

oṁ godhūlyai svāhā
She who is the evening.

- 240 -

ॐ कमलासनायै स्वाहा

oṁ kamalāsanāyai svāhā
She whose seat is upon a lotus.

- 241 -

ॐ जितक्रोधायै स्वाहा

oṁ jitakrodhāyai svāhā
She who has conquered anger.

- 242 -

ॐ कुमुदिन्यै स्वाहा

oṁ kumudinyai svāhā
She who shines like the full moon.

- 243 -

ॐ वैजयन्त्यै स्वाहा

oṁ vaijayantyai svāhā
She who is always victorious.

- 244 -

ॐ मनोजवायै स्वाहा

oṁ manojavāyai svāhā
She who creates in the mind.

- 245 -

ॐ धनलक्ष्म्यै स्वाहा

oṁ dhanalakṣmyai svāhā
She who is the highest goal of wealth.

- 246 -

ॐ स्वस्तिकर्यै स्वाहा

oṁ svastikaryai svāhā
She who gives the effects of blessings.

- 247 -

ॐ राज्यलक्ष्म्यै स्वाहा

oṁ rājyalakṣmyai svāhā
She who is the highest goal in the kingdom.

- 248 -

ॐ महासत्यै स्वाहा

oṁ mahāsatyai svāhā
She who is the great, true existence.

- 249 -

ॐ जयलक्ष्म्यै स्वाहा

oṁ jayalakṣmyai svāhā
She who is the highest goal of victory.

- 250 -

ॐ महागोष्ठ्यै स्वाहा

oṁ mahāgoṣṭhyai svāhā
She who is the illumination of the great desire.

- 251 -

ॐ मघोन्यै स्वाहा

oṁ maghonyai svāhā
She who has the deepest contemplation.

- 252 -

ॐ माधवप्रियायै स्वाहा

oṁ mādhavapriyāyai svāhā
She who is beloved of the sweet form of Viṣṇu.

- 253 -

ॐ पद्मगर्भायै स्वाहा

oṁ padmagarbhāyai svāhā
She who has the lotus womb.

- 254 -

ॐ वेदवत्यै स्वाहा

oṁ vedavatyai svāhā
She who is the spirit of wisdom.

- 255 -

ॐ विविक्तायै स्वाहा

oṁ viviktāyai svāhā
She who is remembered in a special way.

- 256 -

ॐ परमेष्ठिन्यै स्वाहा

oṁ parameṣṭhinyai svāhā
She who is the supreme desire.

- 257 -

ॐ सुवर्णविन्दवे स्वाहा

oṁ suvarṇavindave svāhā
She who is the center of excellent being.

- 258 -

ॐ महत्यै स्वाहा

oṁ mahatyai svāhā
She who is great.

- 259 -

ॐ महायोगिप्रियायै स्वाहा

oṁ mahāyogipriyāyai svāhā
She who is beloved of the great yogi Lord Śiva.

- 260 -

ॐ अनघायै स्वाहा

oṁ anaghāyai svāhā
She who is sinless.

- 261 -

ॐ पद्मेस्थितायै स्वाहा

oṁ padmesthitāyai svāhā
She who is always situated in the lotus.

- 262 -

ॐ वेदमय्यै स्वाहा

oṁ vedamayyai svāhā
She who is the manifestation of wisdom.

- 263 -

ॐ कुमुदायै स्वाहा

oṁ kumudāyai svāhā
She who is the full moon.

- 264 -

ॐ जयवाहिन्यै स्वाहा

oṁ jayavāhinyai svāhā
She who is the conveyance of victory.

- 265 -

ॐ संहृत्यै स्वाहा

oṁ saṁhṛtyai svāhā
She who is hymns of praise.

- 266 -

ॐ निर्मितायै स्वाहा

oṁ nirmitāyai svāhā
She who is the cause of everything.

- 267 -

ॐ ज्योतिषे स्वाहा

oṁ jyotiṣe svāhā
She who resides in light.

- 268 -

ॐ नियत्यै स्वाहा

oṁ niyatyai svāhā
She who resides in space.

- 269 -

ॐ विविधोत्सवायै स्वाहा

oṁ vividhotsavāyai svāhā
She who is the festival of life.

- 270 -

ॐ रुद्रवन्द्यायै स्वाहा

oṁ rudravandyāyai svāhā
She who is worshipped by Rudra.

- 271 -

ॐ सिन्धुमत्यै स्वाहा

oṁ sindhumatyai svāhā
She whose mind is unfathomable.

- 272 -

ॐ वेदमात्रे स्वाहा

oṁ vedamātre svāhā
She who is the Mother of wisdom.

- 273 -

ॐ मधुव्रतायै स्वाहा

oṁ madhuvratāyai svāhā
She whose vow is sweet.

- 274 -

ॐ विश्वम्भरायै स्वाहा

oṁ viśvambharāyai svāhā
She who brings fulfillment to the universe.

- 275 -

ॐ हैमवत्यै स्वाहा

oṁ haimavatyai svāhā
She who is the spirit of all wealth.

- 276 -

ॐ समुद्रायै स्वाहा

oṁ samudrāyai svāhā
She who is as vast as the ocean.

- 277 -

ॐ इच्छाविहारिण्यै स्वाहा

oṁ icchāvihāriṇyai svāhā
She who takes away all desire.

- 278 -

ॐ अनुकूलायै स्वाहा

oṁ anukūlāyai svāhā
She who is always agreeable.

- 279 -

ॐ यज्ञवत्यै स्वाहा

oṁ yajñavatyai svāhā
She who is the spirit of sacrifice.

- 280 -

ॐ शतकोट्यै स्वाहा

oṁ śatakoṭyai svāhā
She who is innumerable.

- 281 -

ॐ सुपेशलायै स्वाहा

oṁ supeśalāyai svāhā
She who has a large body.

- 282 -

ॐ धर्मोदयायै स्वाहा

oṁ dharmodayāyai svāhā
She who gives rise to the ideal of perfection.

- 283 -

ॐ धर्मसेवायै स्वाहा

oṁ dharmsevāyai svāhā
She who serves the ideal of perfection.

- 284 -

ॐ सुकुमार्यै स्वाहा

oṁ sukumāryai svāhā
She who is excellent and ever pure.

- 285 -

ॐ सभावत्यै स्वाहा

oṁ sabhāvatyai svāhā
She who is the spirit of the assembly.

- 286 -

ॐ भीमायै स्वाहा

oṁ bhīmāyai svāhā
She who is terrible.

- 287 -

ॐ ब्रह्मस्तुतायै स्वाहा

oṁ brahmastutāyai svāhā
She who is the song of the supreme.

- 288 -

ॐ मध्यप्रभायै स्वाहा

oṁ madhyaprabhāyai svāhā
She who is surrounded by luster.

- 289 -

ॐ देवर्षिवन्दितायै स्वाहा

oṁ devarṣivanditāyai svāhā
She who is worshipped by godly ṛṣis.

- 290 -

ॐ देवभोग्यायै स्वाहा

oṁ devabhogyāyai svāhā
She who enjoys divinity.

- 291 -

ॐ महाभागायै स्वाहा

oṁ mahābhāgāyai svāhā
She who is the great wealth.

- 292 -

ॐ प्रतिज्ञायै स्वाहा

oṁ pratijñāyai svāhā
She who is the promise.

- 293 -

ॐ पूणशेवध्यै स्वाहा

oṁ pūṇaśevadhyai svāhā
She who continuously slays enemies.

- 294 -

ॐ सुवर्णायै स्वाहा

oṁ suvarṇāyai svāhā
She who has excellent color.

- 295 -

ॐ रुचिरप्रख्यायै स्वाहा

oṁ ruciraprakhyāyai svāhā
She whose taste is delightful.

- 296 -

ॐ भोगिन्यै स्वाहा

oṁ bhoginyai svāhā
She who is the enjoyer of all.

- 297 -

ॐ भोगदायिन्यै स्वाहा

oṁ bhogadāyinyai svāhā
She who gives all enjoyment.

- 298 -

ॐ वसुप्राणायै स्वाहा

oṁ vasuprāṇāyai svāhā
She who is the life of the Earth.

- 299 -

ॐ उत्तमवध्वै स्वाहा

oṁ uttamavadhvai svāhā
She who is most excellent.

- 300 -

ॐ गायत्र्यै स्वाहा

oṁ gāyatryai svāhā
She who is the song of the three forms of wisdom.

- 301 -

ॐ कमलोद्भवायै स्वाहा

oṁ kamalodbhavāyai svāhā
She whose existence is in the lotus of peace.

- 302 -

ॐ विद्वत्प्रियायै स्वाहा

oṁ vidvatpriyāyai svāhā
She who loves knowledge.

- 303 -

ॐ पद्मचिह्नायै स्वाहा

oṁ padmacihnāyai svāhā
She who is recognized by the lotus.

- 304 -

ॐ वरिष्ठायै स्वाहा

oṁ variṣṭāyai svāhā
She who is the desired boon.

- 305 -

ॐ कमलेक्षणायै स्वाहा

oṁ kamalekṣaṇāyai svāhā
She who is defined by the lotus.

- 306 -

ॐ पद्मप्रियायै स्वाहा

oṁ padmapriyāyai svāhā
She who is the beloved lotus.

- 307 -

ॐ सुप्रसन्नायै स्वाहा

oṁ suprasannāyai svāhā
She who is excellently pleased.

- 308 -

ॐ प्रमोदायै स्वाहा

oṁ pramodāyai svāhā
She who is extremely delighted.

- 309 -

ॐ प्रियपार्श्वगायै स्वाहा

oṁ priyapārśvagāyai svāhā
She who is loved on all sides.

- 310 -

ॐ विश्वभूषायै स्वाहा

oṁ viśvabhūṣāyai svāhā
She who is the ornament of the universe.

- 311 -

ॐ कान्तिमत्यै स्वाहा

oṁ kāntimatyai svāhā
She whose every thought is beauty enhanced by love.

- 312 -

ॐ कृष्णायै स्वाहा

oṁ kṛṣṇāyai svāhā
She who is the doer of all.

- 313 -

ॐ वीणारवोन्सुकायै स्वाहा

oṁ vīṇāravonsukāyai svāhā
She whose musical instrument vīnā makes delightful tones.

- 314 -

ॐ रोचिष्कर्यै स्वाहा

oṁ rociṣkaryai svāhā
She who is the cause of delight.

- 315 -

ॐ स्वप्रकाशायै स्वाहा

oṁ svaprakāśāyai svāhā
She who illuminates herself.

- 316 -

ॐ शोभमानायै स्वाहा

oṁ śobhamānāyai svāhā
She whose thoughts shine.

- 317 -

ॐ विहङ्गमायै स्वाहा

oṁ vihaṅgamāyai svāhā
She who has no obstruction.

- 318 -

ॐ देवाङ्गस्थायै स्वाहा

oṁ devāṅgasthāyai svāhā
She who is situated in the limbs of the Gods.

- 319 -

ॐ परिणत्यै स्वाहा

oṁ pariṇatyai svāhā
She who is the Supreme Spirit.

- 320 -

ॐ कामवत्सायै स्वाहा

oṁ kāmavatsāyai svāhā
She who is the child of desire.

- 321 -

ॐ महामत्यै स्वाहा

oṁ mahāmatyai svāhā
She who is the great mind.

- 322 -

ॐ इल्वलायै स्वाहा

oṁ ilvalāyai svāhā
She who is the repository of respect.

- 323 -

ॐ उत्पलनाभायै स्वाहा

oṁ utpalanābhāyai svāhā
She who is the one who springs from the navel.

- 324 -

ॐ आधिशमन्यै स्वाहा

oṁ ādhiśamanyai svāhā
She who has the supreme mind of peace.

- 325 -

ॐ वरवर्णिन्यै स्वाहा

oṁ varavarṇinyai svāhā
She who defines boons.

- 326 -

ॐ स्वनिष्ठायै स्वाहा

oṁ svaniṣṭhāyai svāhā
She who has Her own discipline.

- 327 -

ॐ पद्मनिलयायै स्वाहा

oṁ padmanilayāyai svāhā
She who resides on a lotus.

- 328 -

ॐ सद्गत्यै स्वाहा

oṁ sadgatyai svāhā
She who takes refuge in truth.

- 329 -

ॐ पद्मगन्धिन्यै स्वाहा

oṁ padmaganvinyai svāhā
She who moves in the lotus.

- 330 -

ॐ पद्मवर्णायै स्वाहा

oṁ padmavarṇāyai svāhā
She who is the color of the lotus.

- 331 -

ॐ कामयोन्यै स्वाहा

oṁ kāmayonyai svāhā
She who is the womb of desire.

- 332 -

ॐ चण्डिकायै स्वाहा

oṁ caṇḍikāyai svāhā
She who tears apart thought.

- 333 -

ॐ चारुकोपनायै स्वाहा

oṁ cārukopanāyai svāhā
She who has extreme anger.

- 334 -

ॐ रतिस्नुषायै स्वाहा

oṁ ratisnuṣāyai svāhā
She who illuminates the spring.

- 335-

ॐ पद्मधरायै स्वाहा

oṁ padmadharāyai svāhā
She who holds a lotus.

- 336 -

ॐ पूज्यायै स्वाहा

oṁ pūjyāyai svāhā
She who is worshipped.

- 337 -

ॐ त्रैलोक्यमोहिन्यै स्वाहा

oṁ trailokyamohinyai svāhā
She who thrusts the three worlds into the ignorance of attachment.

- 338 -

ॐ नित्यकन्यायै स्वाहा

oṁ nityakanyāyai svāhā
She who is eternally young.

- 339 -

ॐ विन्दुमालिन्यै स्वाहा

oṁ vindumālinyai svāhā
She who cultivates from the center.

- 340 -

ॐ अक्षयायै स्वाहा

oṁ akṣayāyai svāhā
She who is the sum of all parts.

- 341 -

ॐ सर्वगन्धिन्यै स्वाहा

oṁ sarvagandhinyai svāhā
She who exudes all fragrances.

- 342 -

ॐ गन्धात्मिकायै स्वाहा

oṁ gandhātmikāyai svāhā
She who is the capacity of the sense of smell.

- 343 -

ॐ सुरसिकायै स्वाहा

oṁ surasikāyai svāhā
She who is above the Gods.

- 344 -

ॐ दीप्तमूर्त्यै स्वाहा

oṁ dīptamūrtyai svāhā
She who is the image of light.

- 345 -

ॐ सुमध्यमायै स्वाहा

oṁ sumadhyamāyai svāhā
She who manifests in the midst of excellence.

- 346 -

ॐ पृथुश्रोण्यै स्वाहा

oṁ pṛthuśroṇyai svāhā
She who is the sound of the earth.

- 347 -

ॐ सोम्यमुख्यै स्वाहा

oṁ somyamukhyai svāhā
She who has a beautiful face.

- 348 -

ॐ सुभगायै स्वाहा

oṁ subhagāyai svāhā
She who gives excellent fortune.

- 349 -

ॐ विष्टरश्रुत्यै स्वाहा

oṁ viṣṭaraśrutyai svāhā
She who hears all.

- 350 -

ॐ स्मितााननायै स्वाहा

oṁ smitānanāyai svāhā
She who is the embodiment of memories.

- 351 -

ॐ चारुगत्यै स्वाहा

oṁ cārugatyai svāhā
She who moves with great speed.

- 352 -

ॐ निम्ननाभ्यै स्वाहा

oṁ nimnanābhyai svāhā
She who has a deep navel.

- 353 -

ॐ महास्तन्यै स्वाहा

oṁ mahāstanyai svāhā
She who has large breasts.

- 354 -

ॐ स्निग्धवेन्यै स्वाहा

oṁ snigdhavenyai svāhā
She who is gentle and friendly.

- 355 -

ॐ भगवत्यै स्वाहा

oṁ bhagavatyai svāhā
She who is the supreme Goddess.

- 356 -

ॐ सुकान्तायै स्वाहा

oṁ sukāntāyai svāhā
She who has excellent beauty enhanced by love.

- 357 -

ॐ वामलोचनायै स्वाहा

oṁ vāmalocanāyai svāhā
She who has eyes of love.

- 358 -

ॐ पल्लवाङ्घ्यै स्वाहा

oṁ pallavāṅghyai svāhā
She who is the new shoots of vegetation.

- 359 -

ॐ पद्ममनसे स्वाहा

oṁ padmamanase svāhā
She who has the lotus of peace in Her mind.

- 360 -

ॐ पद्मबोधायै स्वाहा

oṁ padmabodhāyai svāhā
She who knows the lotus of peace.

- 361 -

ॐ महाप्सारसे स्वाहा

oṁ mahāpsarase svāhā
She who is the great heavenly damsel.

- 362 -

ॐ सरस्वत्यै स्वाहा

oṁ sarasvatyai svāhā
She who is the Goddess of knowledge.

- 363 -

ॐ चारुहासायै स्वाहा

oṁ cāruhāsāyai svāhā
She who has a great laugh.

- 364 -

ॐ शुभदृष्टयै स्वाहा

oṁ śubhadṛṣṭyai svāhā
She who has pure perception.

- 365 -

ॐ ककुद्मिन्यै स्वाहा

oṁ kakudminyai svāhā
She who rides upon a bull.

- 366 -

ॐ कम्बुग्रीवायै स्वाहा

oṁ kambugrīvāyai svāhā
She who has lotus marks upon Her neck.

- 367 -

ॐ सुजघनायै स्वाहा

oṁ sujaghanāyai svāhā
She who has beautiful ideas.

- 368 -

ॐ रक्तपाण्यै स्वाहा

oṁ raktapāṇyai svāhā
She who has red on the palms of Her hands.

- 369 -

ॐ मनोरमायै स्वाहा

oṁ manoramāyai svāhā
She who is beautiful.

- 370 -

ॐ पद्मिन्यै स्वाहा

oṁ padminyai svāhā
She who is a lotus.

- 371 -

ॐ मन्दगमनायै स्वाहा

oṁ mandagamanāyai svāhā
She who moves in an intoxicated state.

- 372 -

ॐ चतुर्दंष्ट्रायै स्वाहा

oṁ caturdaṁṣṭrāyai svāhā
She who has four tusks.

- 373 -

ॐ चतुर्भुजायै स्वाहा

oṁ caturbhujāyai svāhā
She who has four arms.

- 374 -

ॐ शुभरैखायै स्वाहा

oṁ śubharaikhāyai svāhā
She who has auspicious lines in Her palm.

- 375 -

ॐ विलासभ्रुवे स्वाहा

oṁ vilāsabhruve svāhā
She whose eyebrows evoke love.

- 376 -

ॐ शुकवाण्यै स्वाहा

oṁ śukavāṇyai svāhā

She whose voice is sweet like a parrot.

- 377 -

ॐ कलावत्यै स्वाहा

oṁ kalāvatyai svāhā

She who is the spirit of art.

- 378 -

ॐ ऋजुतासायै स्वाहा

oṁ ṛjutāsāyai svāhā

She who expresses the imperishable truth.

- 379 -

ॐ कलरवायै स्वाहा

oṁ kalaravāyai svāhā

She who is always praised in song.

- 380 -

ॐ वरारोहायै स्वाहा

oṁ varārohāyai svāhā

She who is always giving boons.

- 381 -

ॐ तलोदर्यै स्वाहा

oṁ talodaryai svāhā

She who raises the lowly.

- 382 -

ॐ सन्ध्यायै स्वाहा

oṁ sandhyāyai svāhā

She who is the time of prayer.

- 383 -

ॐ बिम्बाधरायै स्वाहा

oṁ bimbādharāyai svāhā

She who holds the reflection.

- 384 -

ॐ पूर्वभाषिण्यै स्वाहा

oṁ pūrvabhāṣiṇyai svāhā
She who speaks the old language.

- 385 -

ॐ श्रीसमाह्वयायै स्वाहा

oṁ śrīsamāhvayāyai svāhā
She who invites with equal respect.

- 386 -

ॐ इक्षुचापायै स्वाहा

oṁ ikṣucāpāyai svāhā
She who is sweet like sugarcane.

- 387 -

ॐ सुमशरायै स्वाहा

oṁ sumaśarāyai svāhā
She who is the excellent arrow of the mind.

- 388 -

ॐ दिव्यभूषायै स्वाहा

oṁ divyabhūṣāyai svāhā
She who radiates divinity.

- 389 -

ॐ मनोहरायै स्वाहा

oṁ manoharāyai svāhā
She who steals away the mind.

- 390 -

ॐ वासव्यै स्वाहा

oṁ vāsavyai svāhā
She who controls all.

- 391 -

ॐ पाण्डरच्छत्रायै स्वाहा

oṁ pāṇḍaracchatrāyai svāhā
She who has a white umbrella.

- 392 -

ॐ करभोरवे स्वाहा

oṁ karabhorave svāhā
She who has beautiful fingernails.

- 393 -

ॐ तिलोत्तमायै स्वाहा

oṁ tilottamāyai svāhā
She who is extremely beautiful.

- 394 -

ॐ सीमन्तिन्यै स्वाहा

oṁ sīmantinyai svāhā
She who wears a part in Her hair.

- 395 -

ॐ प्राणशक्त्यै स्वाहा

oṁ prāṇaśaktyai svāhā
She who is the energy of life.

- 396 -

ॐ विभीषिण्यै स्वाहा

oṁ vibhīṣiṇyai svāhā
She who is discrimination.

- 397 -

ॐ असुधारिण्यै स्वाहा

oṁ asudhāriṇyai svāhā
She who tolerates the impure.

- 398 -

ॐ भद्रायै स्वाहा

oṁ bhadrāyai svāhā
She who is excellent.

- 399 -

ॐ जयावहायै स्वाहा

oṁ jayāvahāyai svāhā
She who conveys victory.

- 400 -

ॐ चन्द्रवदनायै स्वाहा

oṁ candravadanāyai svāhā
She whose face is like the moon.

- 401 -

ॐ कुटिलालकायै स्वाहा

oṁ kuṭilālakāyai svāhā
She who loves those of humble abode.

- 402 -

ॐ चित्राम्बरायै स्वाहा

oṁ citrāmbarāyai svāhā
She who wears various colored clothes.

- 403 -

ॐ चित्रगन्धायै स्वाहा

oṁ citragandhāyai svāhā
She who emits various scents.

- 404 -

ॐ रत्नमौलिसमुज्ज्वलायै स्वाहा

oṁ ratnamaulisamujjvalāyai svāhā
She for whom all gems and jewels shine equally.

- 405 -

ॐ दिव्यायुधायै स्वाहा

oṁ divyāyudhāyai svāhā
She who gives divine life.

- 406 -

ॐ दिव्यमाल्यायै स्वाहा

oṁ divyamālyāyai svāhā
She who wears a divine garland.

- 407 -

ॐ विशाखायै स्वाहा

oṁ viśākhāyai svāhā
She who has united all parts.

- 408 -

ॐ चित्रवाहनायै स्वाहा

oṁ citravāhanāyai svāhā

She who moves by various conveyances.

- 409 -

ॐ अम्बिकायै स्वाहा

oṁ ambikāyai svāhā

She who is the Mother of the universe.

- 410 -

ॐ सिन्धुतनयायै स्वाहा

oṁ sindhutanayāyai svāhā

She who is the embodiment of the ocean of existence.

- 411 -

ॐ निःश्रेण्यै स्वाहा

oṁ niḥśreṇyai svāhā

She who cannot be classified.

- 412 -

ॐ सुमहासिन्यै स्वाहा

oṁ sumahāsinyai svāhā

She whose excellence is great.

- 413 -

ॐ सामप्रियायै स्वाहा

oṁ sāmapriyāyai svāhā

She who loves song.

- 414 -

ॐ नवमृग्यै स्वाहा

oṁ navamṛgyai svāhā

She who comes as nine deers.

- 415 -

ॐ सर्वसेव्यायै स्वाहा

oṁ sarvasevyāyai svāhā

She who is served by all.

- 416 -

ॐ वराङ्गनायै स्वाहा

oṁ varāṅganāyai svāhā
She who gives blessings to all bodies.

- 417 -

ॐ गन्धद्वारायै स्वाहा

oṁ gandhadvārāyai svāhā
She whose body exudes fragrant scent.

- 418 -

ॐ दुराधर्षायै स्वाहा

oṁ durādharṣāyai svāhā
She who is difficult to perceive.

- 419 -

ॐ नित्यपुष्टायै स्वाहा

oṁ nityapuṣṭāyai svāhā
She who always gives nourishment.

- 420 -

ॐ करीषिण्यै स्वाहा

oṁ karīṣiṇyai svāhā
She who is the supreme ruler of nonviolence.

- 421 -

ॐ देवजुष्टायै स्वाहा

oṁ devajuṣṭāyai svāhā
She who is foremost among the gods.

- 422 -

ॐ दिव्यावर्णायै स्वाहा

oṁ divyāvarṇāyai svāhā
She whose color is divine.

- 423 -

ॐ दिव्यगन्धायै स्वाहा

oṁ divyagandhāyai svāhā
She whose scent is divine.

- 424 -

ॐ स्वकर्दमायै स्वाहा

oṁ svakardamāyai svāhā
She whose body is earth.

- 425 -

ॐ अनन्तरूपायै स्वाहा

oṁ anantarūpāyai svāhā
She who is the form of infinity.

- 426 -

ॐ अनन्तस्थायै स्वाहा

oṁ anantasthāyai svāhā
She who resides in infinity.

- 427 -

ॐ सर्वदानन्तसङ्गमायै स्वाहा

oṁ sarvadānantasaṅgamāyai svāhā
She who is always in infinite communion.

- 428 -

ॐ यज्ञाशन्यै स्वाहा

oṁ yajñāśanyai svāhā
She who is the fire of sacrifice.

- 429 -

ॐ महावृष्ट्यै स्वाहा

oṁ mahāvṛṣṭyai svāhā
She who gives great rain.

- 430 -

ॐ सर्वपूज्यायै स्वाहा

oṁ sarvapūjyāyai svāhā
She who is worshipped by all.

- 431 -

ॐ वषट्क्रियायै स्वाहा

oṁ vaṣaṭkriyāyai svāhā
She who loves purification.

- 432 -

ॐ योगप्रियायै स्वाहा

oṁ yogapriyāyai svāhā
She who loves union.

- 433 -

ॐ वियन्नाभ्यै स्वाहा

oṁ viyannābhyai svāhā
She whose navel is varied.

- 434 -

ॐ अनन्तश्रियै स्वाहा

oṁ anantaśriyai svāhā
She who is infinite respect.

- 435 -

ॐ अतीन्द्रियायै स्वाहा

oṁ atīndriyāyai svāhā
She who is beyond the five senses.

- 436 -

ॐ योगिसेव्यायै स्वाहा

oṁ yogisevyāyai svāhā
She who is served by those who are in union.

- 437 -

ॐ सत्यरतायै स्वाहा

oṁ satyaratāyai svāhā
She who is delighted by Truth.

- 438 -

ॐ योगमायायै स्वाहा

oṁ yogamāyāyai svāhā
She who is the measurement of Consciousness in union.

- 439 -

ॐ पुरातन्यै स्वाहा

oṁ purātanyai svāhā
She who is old.

- 440 -

ॐ सर्वेश्वर्यै स्वाहा

oṁ sarveśvaryai svāhā
She who is the supreme goddess of all.

- 441 -

ॐ सुतरुण्यै स्वाहा

oṁ sutaruṇyai svāhā
She who is the excellent young lady of purity.

- 442 -

ॐ शरण्यायै स्वाहा

oṁ śaraṇyāyai svāhā
She who is refuge.

- 443 -

ॐ धर्मदेवतायै स्वाहा

oṁ dharmadevatāyai svāhā
She who is the goddess who manifests the ideal of Perfection.

- 444 -

ॐ सुतरायै स्वाहा

oṁ sutarāyai svāhā
She who has excellent children.

- 445 -

ॐ संवृतज्योतिषे स्वाहा

oṁ saṁvṛtajyotiṣe svāhā
She who contains all the lights of heaven.

- 446 -

ॐ योगिन्यै स्वाहा

oṁ yoginyai svāhā
She who is the Supreme Being of union.

- 447 -

ॐ योगसिद्धिदायै स्वाहा

oṁ yogasiddhidāyai svāhā
She who grants the perfection of union.

- 448 -

ॐ सृष्टिशक्त्यै स्वाहा

oṁ sṛṣṭiśaktyai svāhā
She who is the energy of existence.

- 449 -

ॐ द्योतमानभूतायै स्वाहा

oṁ dyotamānabhūtāyai svāhā
She who illuminates the elements.

- 450 -

ॐ मङ्गलदेवतायै स्वाहा

oṁ maṅgaladevatāyai svāhā
She who is the god of welfare.

- 451 -

ॐ सहारशक्त्यै स्वाहा

oṁ sahāraśaktyai svāhā
She who is the energy that protects.

- 452 -

ॐ प्रबलायै स्वाहा

oṁ prabalāyai svāhā
She who has great strength.

- 453 -

ॐ निरुपाध्यै स्वाहा

oṁ nirupādhyai svāhā
She who is without attribute.

- 454 -

ॐ परावरायै स्वाहा

oṁ parāvarāyai svāhā
She who is the supreme blessing.

- 455 -

ॐ उत्तारिण्यै स्वाहा

oṁ uttāriṇyai svāhā
She who is the energy in the North.

- 456 -

ॐ तारयन्त्यै स्वाहा

oṁ tārayantyai svāhā
She who takes across the ocean of worldliness.

- 457 -

ॐ शाश्वत्यै स्वाहा

oṁ śāśvatyai svāhā
She who is eternal.

- 458 -

ॐ समितिञ्जयायै स्वाहा

oṁ samitiñjayāyai svāhā
She who is victorious in the community.

- 459 -

ॐ महाश्रियै स्वाहा

oṁ mahāśriyai svāhā
She who is greatly respected.

- 460 -

ॐ अजहत्कीर्त्यै स्वाहा

oṁ ajahatkīrtyai svāhā
She whose fame is unconquerable.

- 461 -

ॐ योगश्रियै स्वाहा

oṁ yogaśriyai svāhā
She who is respect in union.

- 462 -

ॐ सिद्धिसाधन्यै स्वाहा

oṁ siddhisādhanyai svāhā
She who performs discipline to Perfection.

- 463 -

ॐ पुण्यश्रियै स्वाहा

oṁ puṇyaśriyai svāhā
She whose merit is respected.

- 464 -

ॐ पुण्यनिलयायै स्वाहा

oṁ puṇyanilayāyai svāhā
She who is the repository of merit.

- 465 -

ॐ ब्रह्मश्रियै स्वाहा

oṁ brahmaśriyai svāhā
She who is the respect of the supreme divinity.

- 466 -

ॐ ब्रह्मणप्रियायै स्वाहा

oṁ brahmaṇapriyāyai svāhā
She who is the beloved of the supreme divinity.

- 467 -

ॐ राजश्रियै स्वाहा

oṁ rājaśriyai svāhā
She who is the respect of the king.

- 468 -

ॐ राजकलितायै स्वाहा

oṁ rājakalitāyai svāhā
She who is the family of the king.

- 469 -

ॐ फलश्रियै स्वाहा

oṁ phalaśriyai svāhā
She who is the fruit of respect.

- 470 -

ॐ स्वर्गदायिन्यै स्वाहा

oṁ svargadāyinyai svāhā
She who grants heaven.

- 471 -

ॐ देवश्रियै स्वाहा

oṁ devaśriyai svāhā
She who is divine respect.

- 472 -

ॐ अद्भुतकथायै स्वाहा

oṁ adbhutakathāyai svāhā
She whose words are wonderful.

- 473 -

ॐ वेदश्रियै स्वाहा

oṁ vedaśriyai svāhā
She who has the wisdom of respect.

- 474 -

ॐ श्रुतिमार्गिण्यै स्वाहा

oṁ śrutimārgiṇyai svāhā
She who is the path of wisdom that is heard.

- 475 -

ॐ तमोपहायै स्वाहा

oṁ tamopahāyai svāhā
She who banishes darkness.

- 476 -

ॐ अव्ययनिधये स्वाहा

oṁ avyayanidhaye svāhā
She who is the external discipline.

- 477 -

ॐ लक्ष्मणायै स्वाहा

oṁ lakṣmaṇāyai svāhā
She who is the criteria of all.

- 478 -

ॐ हृदयङ्गमायै स्वाहा

oṁ hṛdayaṅgamāyai svāhā
She who resides in the heart of all bodes.

- 479 -

ॐ मृतसंजीविन्यै स्वाहा

oṁ mṛtasaṁjīvinyai svāhā
She who brings from death to life.

- 480 -

ॐ शुभ्रायै स्वाहा

oṁ śubhrāyai svāhā
She who is radiant purity.

- 481 -

ॐ चन्द्रिकायै स्वाहा

oṁ candrikāyai svāhā
She who is the rays of light from the moon.

- 482 -

ॐ सर्वतोमुख्यै स्वाहा

oṁ sarvatomukhyai svāhā
She who is the chief of all.

- 483 -

ॐ सर्वोत्तमायै स्वाहा

oṁ sarvottamāyai svāhā
She who is most excellent of all.

- 484 -

ॐ मित्रविन्दायै स्वाहा

oṁ mitravindāyai svāhā
She who is the center of all friendship.

- 485 -

ॐ मैथिल्यै स्वाहा

oṁ maithilyai svāhā
She who resides in mithila.

- 486 -

ॐ प्रियदर्शनायै स्वाहा

oṁ priyadarśanāyai svāhā
She whose vision is loved.

- 487 -

ॐ सत्यभामायै स्वाहा

oṁ satyabhāmāyai svāhā
She who resides in truth.

- 488 -

ॐ वेदवेद्यायै स्वाहा

oṁ vedavedyāyai svāhā
She who cures with wisdom.

- 489 -

ॐ सीतायै स्वाहा

oṁ sītāyai svāhā
She who is the pure energy of the perfect manifestation of consciousness.

- 490 -

ॐ प्रणतपोषिण्यै स्वाहा

oṁ praṇatapoṣiṇyai svāhā
She who nourishes those who surrender.

- 491 -

ॐ मूलप्रकृत्यै स्वाहा

oṁ mūlaprakṛtyai svāhā
She who is the root of all nature.

- 492 -

ॐ ईशानायै स्वाहा

oṁ īśānāyai svāhā
She who is the supreme divinity.

- 493 -

ॐ शिवदायै स्वाहा

oṁ śivadāyai svāhā
She who bestows the consciousness of infinite goodness.

- 494 -

ॐ दीपप्रदीपिन्यै स्वाहा

oṁ dīpapradīpinyai svāhā
She who illuminates the light.

- 495 -

ॐ अभिप्रियायै स्वाहा

oṁ abhipriyāyai svāhā
She who is beloved of all.

- 496 -

ॐ स्वैरवृत्त्यै स्वाहा

oṁ svairavṛttyai svāhā
She who changes of Her own volition.

- 497 -

ॐ रुक्मिण्यै स्वाहा

oṁ rukmiṇyai svāhā
She who is the light of the jewel.

- 498 -

ॐ सर्वसाक्षिण्यै स्वाहा

oṁ sarvasākṣiṇyai svāhā
She who is the witness of all.

- 499 -

ॐ गान्धारिण्यै स्वाहा

oṁ gāndhāriṇyai svāhā
She who is the support of all scents.

- 500 -

ॐ परगत्यै स्वाहा

oṁ paragatyai svāhā
She who is supreme refuge.

- 501 -

ॐ तत्त्वगर्भायै स्वाहा

oṁ tattvagarbhāyai svāhā
She who is the womb of all principles.

- 502 -

ॐ भवाभवायै स्वाहा

oṁ bhavābhavāyai svāhā
She who is both good and bad attitudes.

- 503 -

ॐ अन्तर्वर्त्यै स्वाहा

oṁ antarvartyai svāhā
She whose spirit is within.

- 504 -

ॐ महामुद्रायै स्वाहा

oṁ mahāmudrāyai svāhā

She who is the great mystical symbol.

- 505 -

ॐ विष्णुदुर्गायै स्वाहा

oṁ viṣṇudurgāyai svāhā

She who removes all obstacles from the all-pervading consciousness.

- 506 -

ॐ महाबलायै स्वाहा

oṁ mahābalāyai svāhā

She who has great strength.

- 507 -

ॐ मदयन्त्यै स्वाहा

oṁ madayantyai svāhā

She who is the ultimate intoxication.

- 508 -

ॐ लोकधारिण्यै स्वाहा

oṁ lokadhāriṇyai svāhā

She who supports all the worlds.

- 509 -

ॐ अदृश्यायै स्वाहा

oṁ adṛśyāyai svāhā

She who is imperceivable.

- 510 -

ॐ सर्वनिष्कृत्यै स्वाहा

oṁ sarvaniṣkṛtyai svāhā

She who gives liberation to all.

- 511 -

ॐ देवसेनायै स्वाहा

oṁ devasenāyai svāhā

She who is the commander of the army of gods.

- 512 -

ॐ आत्मफलदायै स्वाहा

oṁ ātmaphaladāyai svāhā
She who gives the soul the fruits of karma (action).

- 513 -

ॐ वसुधायै स्वाहा

oṁ vasudhāyai svāhā
She who is the earth.

- 514 -

ॐ मुख्यमातृकायै स्वाहा

oṁ mukhyamātṛkāyai svāhā
She who is the foremost Mother.

- 515 -

ॐ क्षीरधारायै स्वाहा

oṁ kṣīradhārāyai svāhā
She who supports the ocean of pure consciousness.

- 516 -

ॐ घृतमय्यै स्वाहा

oṁ ghṛtamayyai svāhā
She who manifests illumination.

- 517 -

ॐ जुह्वत्यै स्वाहा

oṁ juhvatyai svāhā
She who cuts through negativity.

- 518 -

ॐ यज्ञदक्षिणायै स्वाहा

oṁ yajñadakṣiṇāyai svāhā
She who is the offering to the priest in sacrifice.

- 519 -

ॐ योगनिद्रायै स्वाहा

oṁ yoganidrāyai svāhā
She who is the sleep of union.

- 520 -

ॐ योगरतायै स्वाहा

oṁ yogaratāyai svāhā
She who is delighted in union.

- 521 -

ॐ ब्रह्मचर्यायै स्वाहा

oṁ brahmacaryāyai svāhā
She who moves with God.

- 522 -

ॐ दुरत्ययायै स्वाहा

oṁ duratyayāyai svāhā
She who is seen from afar.

- 523 -

ॐ सिह्मपिच्छायै स्वाहा

oṁ sihmapicchāyai svāhā
She who sits upon a lion.

- 524 -

ॐ महादुर्गायै स्वाहा

oṁ mahādurgāyai svāhā
She who is the great reliever of difficulty.

- 525 -

ॐ जयन्त्यै स्वाहा

oṁ jayantyai svāhā
She who is always victorious.

- 526 -

ॐ खगवाहिन्यै स्वाहा

oṁ khagavāhinyai svāhā
She who supports the sky.

- 527 -

ॐ जगत्प्रियायै स्वाहा

oṁ jagatpriyāyai svāhā
She who is the beloved of the perceivable world.

- 528 -

ॐ विरूपाक्ष्यै स्वाहा

oṁ virūpākṣyai svāhā
She who sees beyond form.

- 529 -

ॐ सुवर्णायै स्वाहा

oṁ suvarṇāyai svāhā
She who is of excellent color.

- 530 -

ॐ क्रूरतापिन्यै स्वाहा

oṁ krūratāpinyai svāhā
She who gives strong discipline.

- 531 -

ॐ कात्यायन्यै स्वाहा

oṁ kātyāyanyai svāhā
She who is always pure.

- 532 -

ॐ कालरात्र्यै स्वाहा

oṁ kālarātryai svāhā
She who is the dark night of overcoming the ego.

- 533 -

ॐ निशिदृष्टायै स्वाहा

oṁ niśidṛṣṭāyai svāhā
She who sees in the darkness.

- 534 -

ॐ करालिकायै स्वाहा

oṁ karālikāyai svāhā
She who is formidable.

- 535 -

ॐ त्रिशूलिन्यै स्वाहा

oṁ triśūlinyai svāhā
She who holds a trident.

- 536 -

ॐ खड्गधरायै स्वाहा

oṁ khaṅgadharāyai svāhā
She who holds a sword.

- 537 -

ॐ महाकाल्यै स्वाहा

oṁ mahākālyai svāhā
She who takes away the darkness.

- 538 -

ॐ इन्द्रमालिन्यै स्वाहा

oṁ indramālinyai svāhā
She who cultivates for Indra.

- 539 -

ॐ एकवीरायै स्वाहा

oṁ ekavīrāyai svāhā
She who is attentive to the battle.

- 540 -

ॐ भद्रकाल्यै स्वाहा

oṁ bhadrakālyai svāhā
She who is the excellent remover of darkness.

- 541 -

ॐ सौनन्द्यै स्वाहा

oṁ saunandyai svāhā
She who is the excellent young lady.

- 542 -

ॐ उल्लसद्गदायै स्वाहा

oṁ ullasadgadāyai svāhā
She whose mace brings great bliss.

- 543 -

ॐ नारायण्यै स्वाहा

oṁ nārāyaṇyai svāhā
She who exposes consciousness.

- 544 -

ॐ जगत्पूरिण्यै स्वाहा

oṁ jagatpūriṇyai svāhā

She who gives fulfillment to the perceivable world.

- 545 -

ॐ उर्वरायै स्वाहा

oṁ urvarāyai svāhā

She who is nutrients to the soil.

- 546 -

ॐ द्रुहिणप्रसवे स्वाहा

oṁ drfihiṇaprasave svāhā

She who raises the lowly.

- 547 -

ॐ यज्ञकामायै स्वाहा

oṁ yajñakāmāyai svāhā

She who is the desire of union.

- 548 -

ॐ लेलिहानायै स्वाहा

oṁ lelihānāyai svāhā

She whose tongue is sticking out.

- 549 -

ॐ तीर्थकर्यै स्वाहा

oṁ tīrthakaryai svāhā

She who gives the effects of the places of pilgrimage.

- 550 -

ॐ उग्रविक्रमायै स्वाहा

oṁ ugravikramāyai svāhā

She who has a difficult discipline.

- 551 -

ॐ गरुत्मदुदयायै स्वाहा

oṁ garutmadudayāyai svāhā

She who makes devotion increase.

- 552 -

ॐ अत्युग्रायै स्वाहा

oṁ atyugrāyai svāhā
She who is extremely fierce.

- 553 -

ॐ वाराह्यै स्वाहा

oṁ vārāhyai svāhā
She who is the boon of sacrifice.

- 554 -

ॐ मातृभाषिण्यै स्वाहा

oṁ mātṛbhāṣiṇyai svāhā
She who speaks as a Mother.

- 555 -

ॐ अश्वक्रान्तायै स्वाहा

oṁ aśvakrāntāyai svāhā
She who moves with the gait of a horse.

- 556 -

ॐ रथक्रान्तायै स्वाहा

oṁ rathakrāntāyai svāhā
She who moves by chariot.

- 557 -

ॐ विष्णुक्रान्तायै स्वाहा

oṁ viṣṇukrāntāyai svāhā
She who moves with the all-pervading consciousness.

- 558 -

ॐ उरुचारिण्यै स्वाहा

oṁ urucāriṇyai svāhā
She who moves by Her legs.

- 559 -

ॐ वैरोचिन्यै स्वाहा

oṁ vairocinyai svāhā
She who explains the essence.

- 560 -

ॐ नारसिंह्यै स्वाहा

oṁ nārasiṁhyai svāhā
She who is half-human and half-lion.

- 561 -

ॐ जीमूतायै स्वाहा

oṁ jīmūtāyai svāhā
She who is all sounds.

- 562 -

ॐ शुभदेक्षणायै स्वाहा

oṁ śubhadekṣaṇāyai svāhā
She who constantly gives welfare.

- 563 -

ॐ दीक्षाविधायै स्वाहा

oṁ dīkṣāvidhāyai svāhā
She who is the procedure of mantra initiation.

- 564 -

ॐ विश्वशक्त्यै स्वाहा

oṁ viśvaśaktyai svāhā
She who is the energy of the universe.

- 565 -

ॐ निजशक्त्यै स्वाहा

oṁ nijaśaktyai svāhā
She who is Her own energy.

- 566 -

ॐ सुदर्शिन्यै स्वाहा

oṁ sudarśinyai svāhā
She whose vision is excellent.

- 567 -

ॐ प्रतीत्यै स्वाहा

oṁ pratītyai svāhā
She who is the same in all.

- 568 -

ॐ जगत्यै स्वाहा

oṁ jagatyai svāhā
She who is the perceivable world.

- 569 -

ॐ वन्यधारिण्यै स्वाहा

oṁ vanyadhāriṇyai svāhā
She who supports the forests.

- 570 -

ॐ कलिनाशिन्यै स्वाहा

oṁ kalināśinyai svāhā
She who destroys the age of darkness.

- 571 -

ॐ अयोध्यायै स्वाहा

oṁ ayodhyāyai svāhā
She who dwells in the places of peace.

- 572 -

ॐ अच्छिन्नसन्तानायै स्वाहा

oṁ acchinnasantānāyai svāhā
She whose children cannot be divided.

- 573 -

ॐ महारत्नायै स्वाहा

oṁ mahāratnāyai svāhā
She who is the great jewel.

- 574 -

ॐ सुखावहायै स्वाहा

oṁ sukhāvahāyai svāhā
She who carries happiness.

- 575 -

ॐ राजवत्यै स्वाहा

oṁ rājavatyai svāhā
She who is the spirit of the king.

- 576 -

ॐ अर्कप्रतिभायै स्वाहा

oṁ arkapratibhāyai svāhā
She who is the illumination of the sun.

- 577 -

ॐ विनयित्र्यै स्वाहा

oṁ vinayitryai svāhā
She who displays humility.

- 578 -

ॐ महाशनायै स्वाहा

oṁ mahāśanāyai svāhā
She who is the great thunder.

- 579 -

ॐ अमृतस्यन्दिन्यै स्वाहा

oṁ amṛtasyandinyai svāhā
She who is the wish for immortal nectar.

- 580 -

ॐ सीमायै स्वाहा

oṁ sīmāyai svāhā
She who is the limit.

- 581 -

ॐ यज्ञगर्भायै स्वाहा

oṁ yajñagarbhāyai svāhā
She who is the womb of the sacrificial union.

- 582 -

ॐ समीक्षणायै स्वाहा

oṁ samīkṣaṇāyai svāhā
She who examines all equally.

- 583 -

ॐ आकूत्यै स्वाहा

oṁ ākūtyai svāhā
She who is the image of prayer.

- 584 -

ॐ ऋग्यजुःसामघोषायै स्वाहा

oṁ ṛgyajuḥsāmaghoṣāyai svāhā
She who illuminates the three Vedas.

- 585 -

ॐ आरामवधूत्सुकायै स्वाहा

oṁ ārāmavadhūtsukāyai svāhā
She who desires every wife to be in comfort.

- 586 -

ॐ सोमपायै स्वाहा

oṁ somapāyai svāhā
She who drinks the nectar of devotion.

- 587 -

ॐ माधव्यै स्वाहा

oṁ mādhavyai svāhā
She who is sweet.

- 588 -

ॐ नित्यकल्याण्यै स्वाहा

oṁ nityakalyāṇyai svāhā
She who is eternal welfare.

- 589 -

ॐ कमलार्चितायै स्वाहा

oṁ kamalārcitāyai svāhā
She who is offered lotuses.

- 590 -

ॐ योगरूढायै स्वाहा

oṁ yogarūḍhāyai svāhā
She who rides in union.

- 591 -

ॐ स्वार्थजुष्टायै स्वाहा

oṁ svārthajuṣṭāyai svāhā
She who enjoys Her own meanings.

- 592 -

ॐ वह्निवर्णायै स्वाहा

oṁ vahnivarṇāyai svāhā
She who is the color of fire.

- 593 -

ॐ जितासुरायै स्वाहा

oṁ jitāsurāyai svāhā
She who defeats the asuras.

- 594 -

ॐ यज्ञविद्यायै स्वाहा

oṁ yajñavidyāyai svāhā
She who is the knowledge of sacrifice.

- 595 -

ॐ गुह्यविद्यायै स्वाहा

oṁ guhyavidyāyai svāhā
She who has secret knowledge.

- 596 -

ॐ अध्यात्मविद्यायै स्वाहा

oṁ adhyātmavidyāyai svāhā
She who is spiritual knowledge.

- 597 -

ॐ कृतागमायै स्वाहा

oṁ kṛtāgamāyai svāhā
She who moves in action.

- 598 -

ॐ आप्यायिन्यै स्वाहा

oṁ āpyāyinyai svāhā
She who gives love and respect.

- 599 -

ॐ कलातीतायै स्वाहा

oṁ kalātītāyai svāhā
She who is beyond attributes.

- 600 -

ॐ सुमित्रायै स्वाहा

oṁ sumitrāyai svāhā
She who is an excellent friend.

- 601 -

ॐ परभक्तिदायै स्वाहा

oṁ parabhaktidāyai svāhā
She who gives supreme devotion.

- 602 -

ॐ काङ्क्षमाणायै स्वाहा

oṁ kāṅkṣamāṇāyai svāhā
She whose mind is filled with desire.

- 603 -

ॐ महामायायै स्वाहा

oṁ mahāmāyāyai svāhā
She who is the great the limitation of consciousness.

- 604 -

ॐ कोलकामायै स्वाहा

oṁ kolakāmāyai svāhā
She who is excellent desire.

- 605 -

ॐ अमरावत्यै स्वाहा

oṁ amarāvatyai svāhā
She who is the dwelling place of immortal gods.

- 606 -

ॐ सुवीर्यायै स्वाहा

oṁ suvīryāyai svāhā
She who is an excellent hero.

- 607 -

ॐ दुःस्वप्नहरायै स्वाहा

oṁ duḥsvapnaharāyai svāhā
She who takes away bad dreams.

- 608 -

ॐ देवक्यै स्वाहा

oṁ devakyai svāhā
She who makes the Gods shine.

- 609 -

ॐ वसुदेवतायै स्वाहा

oṁ vasudevatāyai svāhā
She who is the Goddess of the earth.

- 610 -

ॐ सौदामिन्यै स्वाहा

oṁ saudāminyai svāhā
She who is beautiful like a flower.

- 611 -

ॐ मेघरथायै स्वाहा

oṁ megharathāyai svāhā
She who rides upon the clouds.

- 612 -

ॐ ऋद्धिदायै स्वाहा

oṁ ṛddhidāyai svāhā
She who gives increase and fulfillment.

- 613 -

ॐ दैत्यमर्दिन्यै स्वाहा

oṁ daityamardinyai svāhā
She who destroys duality.

- 614 -

ॐ श्रेयस्कर्यै स्वाहा

oṁ śreyaskaryai svāhā
She who causes respect.

- 615 -

ॐ चित्रलीलायै स्वाहा

oṁ citralīlāyai svāhā
She who presents various plays on the stage of life.

- 616 -

ॐ एकायिन्यै स्वाहा

oṁ ekāyinyai svāhā
She who is the only one.

- 617 -

ॐ रत्नपादुकायै स्वाहा

oṁ ratnapādukāyai svāhā
She whose shoes are covered with gems.

- 618 -

ॐ मनस्यमानायै स्वाहा

oṁ manasyamānāyai svāhā
She who is the thoughts of the mind.

- 619 -

ॐ तुलस्यै स्वाहा

oṁ tulasyai svāhā
She who is the basil plant.

- 620 -

ॐ रोगनाशिन्यै स्वाहा

oṁ roganāśinyai svāhā
She who destroys all illness.

- 621 -

ॐ उरुप्रथायै स्वाहा

oṁ uruprathāyai svāhā
She who was born from the thigh.

- 622 -

ॐ तेजस्विन्यै स्वाहा

oṁ tejasvinyai svāhā
She who is heat and light.

- 623 -

ॐ सुखोज्ज्वलायै स्वाहा

oṁ sukhojjvalāyai svāhā
She who is luminous comfort.

- 624 -

ॐ मन्दरेखायै स्वाहा

oṁ mandarekhāyai svāhā
She who writes upon the mind.

- 625 -

ॐ अमृतनाशिन्यै स्वाहा

oṁ amṛtanāśinyai svāhā
She who destroys the nectar of immortal bliss.

- 626 -

ॐ ब्रह्मिष्ठायै स्वाहा

oṁ brahmiṣṭhāyai svāhā
She who desires supreme divinity.

- 627 -

ॐ वह्निशमन्यै स्वाहा

oṁ vahniśamanyai svāhā
She who is the same as fire.

- 628 -

ॐ जुषमाणायै स्वाहा

oṁ juṣamāṇāyai svāhā
She who is always happy.

- 629 -

ॐ गुणात्ययायै स्वाहा

oṁ guṇātyayāyai svāhā
She who is beyond all qualities.

- 630 -

ॐ कादम्बर्यै स्वाहा

oṁ kādambaryai svāhā
She who is a flower.

- 631 -

ॐ ब्रह्मरतायै स्वाहा

oṁ brahmaratāyai svāhā
She who takes delight in supreme divinity.

- 632 -

ॐ विधात्र्यै स्वाहा

oṁ vidhātryai svāhā
She who is the Creator.

- 633 -

ॐ उज्ज्वलहस्तिकायै स्वाहा

oṁ ujjvalahastikāyai svāhā
She who is a shining elephant.

- 634 -

ॐ अक्षोभ्यायै स्वाहा

oṁ akṣobhyāyai svāhā
She who is both finite and infinite.

- 635 -

ॐ सर्वतोभद्रायै स्वाहा

oṁ sarvatobhadrāyai svāhā
She who is the most excellent of all.

- 636 -

ॐ वयस्यायै स्वाहा

oṁ vayasyāyai svāhā
She who has no age.

- 637 -

ॐ स्वस्तिदक्षिणायै स्वाहा

oṁ svastidakṣiṇāyai svāhā
She who gives imperishable blessings.

- 638 -

ॐ सहस्रास्यायै स्वाहा

oṁ sahasrāsyāyai svāhā
She who is thousands.

- 639 -

ॐ ज्ञानमात्रे स्वाहा

oṁ jñānamātre svāhā
She who is the Mother of wisdom.

- 640 -

ॐ वैश्वानर्यै स्वाहा

oṁ vaiśvānaryai svāhā
She who is the universal person.

- 641 -

ॐ अक्षवर्तिन्यै स्वाहा

oṁ akṣavartinyai svāhā
She who rules manifested existence.

- 642 -

ॐ प्रत्यग्वरायै स्वाहा

oṁ pratyagvarāyai svāhā
She who blesses the promise.

- 643 -

ॐ वारणवत्यै स्वाहा

oṁ vāraṇavatyai svāhā
She who guides along the right path.

- 644 -

ॐ अनसूयायै स्वाहा

oṁ anasūyāyai svāhā
She who is a devoted follower.

- 645 -

ॐ दुरासदायै स्वाहा

oṁ durāsadāyai svāhā
She who banishes untruth.

- 646 -

ॐ अरुन्धत्यै स्वाहा

oṁ arundhatyai svāhā
She who is the ambassador of love.

- 647 -

ॐ कुण्डलिन्यै स्वाहा

oṁ kuṇḍalinyai svāhā
She who is individual energy.

- 648 -

ॐ भव्यायै स्वाहा

oṁ bhavyāyai svāhā
She who is manifested existence.

- 649 -

ॐ दुर्गतिनाशिन्यै स्वाहा

oṁ durgatināśinyai svāhā
She who destroys difficulties.

- 650-

ॐ मृत्युञ्जयायै स्वाहा

oṁ mṛtyuñjayāyai svāhā
She who conquers death.

- 651 -

ॐ त्रासहरायै स्वाहा

oṁ trāsaharāyai svāhā
She who dispels fear.

- 652 -

ॐ निर्भयायै स्वाहा

oṁ nirbhayāyai svāhā
She who is without fear.

- 653 -

ॐ शत्रुसूदिन्यै स्वाहा

oṁ śatrusūdinyai svāhā
She who destroys enemies.

- 654 -

ॐ एकाक्षरायै स्वाहा

oṁ ekākṣarāyai svāhā
She who is one and whole.

- 655 -

ॐ सुपुरन्त्र्यै स्वाहा

oṁ supurantryai svāhā
She who brings fulfillment to the city.

- 656 -

ॐ सुरपक्षायै स्वाहा

oṁ surapakṣāyai svāhā
She who is on the side of the gods.

- 657 -

ॐ वरातुलायै स्वाहा

oṁ varātulāyai svāhā
She who gives imcomparable blessings.

- 658 -

ॐ सकृद्विभासायै स्वाहा

oṁ sakṛdvibhāsāyai svāhā
She who gives a beautiful illumination through action.

- 659 -

ॐ प्रद्युम्नायै स्वाहा

oṁ pradyumnāyai svāhā
She who is of the nature of the sky.

- 660 -

ॐ हरिभद्रायै स्वाहा

oṁ haribhadrāyai svāhā
She who is the excellence of Hari.

- 661 -

ॐ धुरन्धरायै स्वाहा

oṁ dhurandharāyai svāhā
She who is most clever.

- 662 -

ॐ बिल्वप्रियायै स्वाहा

oṁ bilvapriyāyai svāhā
She who loves bel.

- 663 -

ॐ अवन्यै स्वाहा

oṁ avanyai svāhā
She who shines like the sun.

- 664 -

ॐ चक्रहृदयायै स्वाहा

oṁ cakrahṛdayāyai svāhā
She who is in the heart of the circle.

- 665 -

ॐ कम्बुतीर्थगायै स्वाहा

oṁ kambutīrthagāyai svāhā
She who goes on pilgrimage to the heart.

- 666 -

ॐ सर्वमन्त्रात्मिकायै स्वाहा

oṁ sarvamantrātmikāyai svāhā
She who is the capacity of all mantras.

- 667 -

ॐ विद्युते स्वाहा

oṁ vidyute svāhā
She who is the ambassador of knowledge.

- 668 -

ॐ यशोदायै स्वाहा

oṁ yaśodāyai svāhā
She who gives fame.

- 669 -

ॐ सर्वरञ्जिन्यै स्वाहा

oṁ sarvarañjinyai svāhā
She who gives all delight.

- 670 -

ॐ ध्वजच्छत्राश्रयायै स्वाहा

oṁ dhvajacchatrāśrayāyai svāhā
She who gives refuge under the flag-bearing umbrella.

- 671 -

ॐ भूम्यै स्वाहा

oṁ bhūmyai svāhā
She who is the land.

- 672 -

ॐ वैष्णव्यै स्वाहा

oṁ vaiṣṇavyai svāhā
She who is the energy of all-pervading consciousness.

- 673 -

ॐ सद्गुणोज्ज्वलायै स्वाहा

oṁ sadguṇojjvalāyai svāhā
She who shines with true qualities.

- 674 -

ॐ सुषेणायै स्वाहा

oṁ suṣeṇāyai svāhā
She who is an excellent doctor.

- 675 -

ॐ लोकविदितायै स्वाहा

oṁ lokaviditāyai svāhā
She who instructs the people.

- 676 -

ॐ कामसुवे स्वाहा

oṁ kāmasuve svāhā
She who exists in desire.

- 677 -

ॐ जगदादिभुवे स्वाहा

oṁ jagadādibhuve svāhā
She who is the existence of all in the perceivable world.

- 678 -

ॐ वेदान्तयोन्यै स्वाहा

oṁ vedāntayonyai svāhā
She who is the womb of wisdom.

- 679 -

ॐ जिज्ञासायै स्वाहा

oṁ jijñāsāyai svāhā
She who is the question.

- 680 -

ॐ मनीषायै स्वाहा

oṁ manīṣāyai svāhā
She who rules the mind.

- 681 -

ॐ समदर्शिन्यै स्वाहा

oṁ samadarśinyai svāhā
She who gives the vision of peace.

- 682 -

ॐ सहस्रशक्त्यै स्वाहा

oṁ sahasraśaktyai svāhā
She who has a thousand energies.

- 683 -

ॐ आवृत्त्यै स्वाहा

oṁ āvṛttyai svāhā
She who does not change.

- 684 -

ॐ सुस्थिरायै स्वाहा

oṁ susthirāyai svāhā
She who is completely still.

- 685 -

ॐ श्रेयसान्निधये स्वाहा

oṁ śreyasānnidhaye svāhā
She who remains in respect.

- 686 -

ॐ रोहिण्यै स्वाहा

oṁ rohiṇyai svāhā
She who shines with radiant light.

- 687 -

ॐ रेवत्यै स्वाहा

oṁ revatyai svāhā
She who is the energy of the sun.

- 688 -

ॐ चन्द्रसोदर्यै स्वाहा

oṁ candrasodaryai svāhā
She who is the energy of the moon.

- 689 -

ॐ भद्रमोदिन्यै स्वाहा

oṁ bhadramodinyai svāhā
She who is the excellent attachment.

- 690 -

ॐ आर्यायै स्वाहा

oṁ āryāyai svāhā
She who is purified by knowledge.

- 691 -

ॐ गव्यप्रियायै स्वाहा

oṁ gavyapriyāyai svāhā
She who is the beloved of cows.

- 692 -

ॐ विश्वभाविन्यै स्वाहा

oṁ viśvabhāvinyai svāhā
She who is the attitude of the universe.

- 693 -

ॐ सुविभाविन्यै स्वाहा

oṁ suvibhāvinyai svāhā
She who is excellent beyond attitudes.

- 694 -

ॐ सुप्रदृश्यायै स्वाहा

oṁ supradṛśyāyai svāhā
She who is the excellent cause of all perception.

- 695 -

ॐ कामचारिण्यै स्वाहा

oṁ kāmacāriṇyai svāhā
She who moves with desire.

- 696 -

ॐ अप्रमत्तायै स्वाहा

oṁ apramattāyai svāhā
She who is serious.

- 697 -

ॐ ललन्तिकायै स्वाहा

oṁ lalantikāyai svāhā
She who resides in the forehead.

- 698 -

ॐ जगद्योन्यै स्वाहा

oṁ jagadyonyai svāhā
She who is the womb of creation.

- 699 -

ॐ मोक्षलक्ष्म्यै स्वाहा

oṁ mokṣalakṣmyai svāhā
She who is the supreme goal of liberation.

- 700 -

ॐ सुदुर्लभायै स्वाहा

oṁ sudurlabhāyai svāhā
She who is the excellent one who is hard to attain.

- 701 -

ॐ भास्कर्यै स्वाहा

oṁ bhāskaryai svāhā
She who is radiant illumination.

- 702 -

ॐ पुण्यगेहस्थायै स्वाहा

oṁ puṇyagehasthāyai svāhā
She who resides in meritorious actions.

- 703 -

ॐ मनोज्ञायै स्वाहा

oṁ manojñāyai svāhā
She who knows the mind.

- 704 -

ॐ विभवप्रदायै स्वाहा

oṁ vibhavapradāyai svāhā
She who bestows existence.

- 705 -

ॐ लोकस्वामिन्यै स्वाहा

oṁ lokasvāminyai svāhā
She who is master of the worlds.

- 706 -

ॐ अच्युतार्थायै स्वाहा

oṁ acyutārthāyai svāhā
She who is the meaning of the infinite one.

- 707 -

ॐ पुष्कलायै स्वाहा

oṁ puṣkalāyai svāhā
She who is the residence of nourishment.

- 708 -

ॐ जगदाकृत्यै स्वाहा

oṁ jagadākṛtyai svāhā
She who is the uncreated world.

- 709 -

ॐ विचित्रहारिण्यै स्वाहा

oṁ vicitrahāriṇyai svāhā
She who takes away the varieties.

- 710 -

ॐ कान्तायै स्वाहा

oṁ kāntāyai svāhā
She who is beauty enhanced by love.

- 711 -

ॐ पाविन्यै स्वाहा

oṁ pāvinyai svāhā
She who is pure.

- 712 -

ॐ भूतभाविन्यै स्वाहा

oṁ bhūtabhāvinyai svāhā
She who is the attitude of the elements.

- 713 -

ॐ प्राणिन्यै स्वाहा

oṁ prāṇinyai svāhā
She who is the life force.

- 714 -

ॐ प्राणदायै स्वाहा

oṁ prāṇadāyai svāhā
She who gives life.

- 715 -

ॐ विद्वते स्वाहा

oṁ vidvate svāhā
She who is knowledge.

- 716 -

ॐ विश्वब्रह्माण्डवासिन्यै स्वाहा

oṁ viśvabrahmāṇḍavāsinyai svāhā
She who resides in the universal egg of God.

- 717 -

ॐ सम्पूर्णायै स्वाहा

oṁ sampūrṇāyai svāhā
She who is full, complete and perfect.

- 718 -

ॐ परमोत्साहायै स्वाहा

oṁ paramotsāhāyai svāhā
She who has great enthusiasm.

- 719 -

ॐ श्रीपत्यै स्वाहा

oṁ śrīpatyai svāhā
She who is the supreme food of respect.

- 720 -

ॐ श्रीमत्यै स्वाहा

oṁ śrīmatyai svāhā
She who is the supreme manifestation of respect.

- 721 -

ॐ श्रुत्यै स्वाहा

oṁ śrutyai svāhā
She who is that which is heard.

- 722 -

ॐ श्रयन्त्यै स्वाहा

oṁ śrayantyai svāhā
She who is the ultimate of that which is heard.

- 723 -

ॐ श्रयमाणायै स्वाहा

oṁ śrayamāṇāyai svāhā
She who is the thought about that which is heard.

- 724 -

ॐ क्ष्मायै स्वाहा

oṁ kṣmāyai svāhā
She who is forgiveness.

- 725 -

ॐ विश्वरूपायै स्वाहा

oṁ viśvarūpāyai svāhā
She who is the form of the universe.

- 726 -

ॐ प्रसादिन्यै स्वाहा

oṁ prasādinyai svāhā
She who is the consecrated offering.

- 727 -

ॐ हर्षिण्यै स्वाहा

oṁ harṣiṇyai svāhā
She who is pleased.

- 728 -

ॐ प्रथमायै स्वाहा

oṁ prathamāyai svāhā
She who is foremost.

- 729 -

ॐ सर्वायै स्वाहा

oṁ sarvāyai svāhā
She who is all.

- 730 -

ॐ विशालायै स्वाहा

oṁ viśālāyai svāhā
She who is great.

- 731 -

ॐ कामवर्षिण्यै स्वाहा

oṁ kāmavarṣiṇyai svāhā
She who is the plethora of desires.

- 732 -

ॐ सुप्रतीकायै स्वाहा

oṁ supratīkāyai svāhā
She who is the excellent representative.

- 733 -

ॐ पृश्निमत्यै स्वाहा

oṁ pṛśnimatyai svāhā
She who perceives the earth.

- 734 -

ॐ निवृत्त्यै स्वाहा

oṁ nivṛttyai svāhā
She who is involution.

- 735 -

ॐ विविधायै स्वाहा

oṁ vividhāyai svāhā
She who is various.

- 736 -

ॐ परायै स्वाहा

oṁ parāyai svāhā
She who is beyond.

- 737 -

ॐ सुयज्ञायै स्वाहा

oṁ suyajñāyai svāhā
She who is the excellent sacrifice.

- 738 -

ॐ मधुरायै स्वाहा

oṁ madhurāyai svāhā
She who is sweet.

- 739 -

ॐ श्रीदायै स्वाहा

oṁ śrīdāyai svāhā
She who gives respect.

- 740 -

ॐ देवरात्यै स्वाहा

oṁ devarātyai svāhā
She who is the night of the gods.

- 741 -

ॐ महामनसे स्वाहा

oṁ mahāmanase svāhā
She who is the great mind.

- 742 -

ॐ स्थूलायै स्वाहा

oṁ sthūlāyai svāhā
She who is the gross body.

- 743 -

ॐ सर्वाकृत्यै स्वाहा

oṁ sarvākṛtyai svāhā
She who is all that is uncreated.

- 744 -

ॐ सूक्ष्मायै स्वाहा

oṁ sūkṣmāyai svāhā
She who is subtle.

- 745 -

ॐ निम्नगव्यायै स्वाहा

oṁ nimnagavyāyai svāhā
She who is the diminished light.

- 746 -

ॐ तमोनुदायै स्वाहा

oṁ tamonudāyai svāhā
She who is the giver of darkness.

- 747 -

ॐ तुष्ट्यै स्वाहा

oṁ tuṣṭyai svāhā
She who is satisfied.

- 748 -

ॐ वागीश्वर्यै स्वाहा

oṁ vāgīśvaryai svāhā
She who is the supreme goddess of vibrations.

- 749 -

ॐ पुष्ट्यै स्वाहा

oṁ puṣṭyai svāhā
She who is nourishment.

- 750 -

ॐ सर्वायै स्वाहा

oṁ sarvāyai svāhā
She who is all.

- 751 -

ॐ आद्यायै स्वाहा

oṁ ādyāyai svāhā
She who is foremost.

- 752 -

ॐ स्वरुशोषिण्यै स्वाहा

oṁ svaruśoṣiṇyai svāhā
She who shines with Her own light.

- 753 -

ॐ शक्त्यात्मिकायै स्वाहा

oṁ śaktyātmikāyai svāhā
She who is the capacity of energy.

- 754 -

ॐ शब्दशक्त्यै स्वाहा

oṁ śabdaśaktyai svāhā
She who is the energy of words.

- 755 -

ॐ विशिष्टायै स्वाहा

oṁ viśiṣṭāyai svāhā
She who is special.

- 756 -

ॐ वायुमत्यै स्वाहा

oṁ vāyumatyai svāhā
She who is the spirit of the wind.

- 757 -

ॐ अमायै स्वाहा

oṁ amāyai svāhā
She who is immeasurable.

- 758 -

ॐ आन्वीक्षिक्यै स्वाहा

oṁ ānvīkṣikyai svāhā
She who illuminates all atoms.

- 759 -

ॐ त्रयीवार्तायै स्वाहा

oṁ trayīvārtāyai svāhā
She who knows the circumstances of the three world.

- 760 -

ॐ दण्डनीत्यै स्वाहा

oṁ daṇḍanītyai svāhā
She who gives strong discipline.

- 761 -

ॐ नियामिकायै स्वाहा

oṁ niyāmikāyai svāhā
She who is the capacity of all discipline.

- 762 -

ॐ व्याल्यै स्वाहा

oṁ vyālyai svāhā
She who performs all the appropriate behavior.

- 763 -

ॐ सङ्कर्षण्यै स्वाहा

oṁ saṅkarṣaṇyai svāhā
She who cultivates equality.

- 764 -

ॐ द्योतायै स्वाहा

oṁ dyotāyai svāhā
She who illuminates the heaven.

- 765 -

ॐ महादेव्यै स्वाहा

oṁ mahādevyai svāhā
She who is the great goddess.

- 766 -

ॐ अपराजितायै स्वाहा

oṁ aparājitāyai svāhā
She who is undefeatable.

- 767 -

ॐ कपिलायै स्वाहा

oṁ kapilāyai svāhā
She who has a natural color.

- 768 -

ॐ पिङ्गलायै स्वाहा

oṁ piṅgalāyai svāhā
She who is the path of the moon.

- 769 -

ॐ स्वस्थायै स्वाहा

oṁ svasthāyai svāhā
She who resides within Her own Self.

- 770 -

ॐ वलाक्यै स्वाहा

oṁ valākyai svāhā
She who expresses herself like a little girl.

- 771 -

ॐ घोषनन्दिन्यै स्वाहा

oṁ ghoṣanandinyai svāhā
She who is the daughter of the divine order.

- 772 -

ॐ अजितायै स्वाहा

oṁ ajitāyai svāhā
She who cannot be conquered.

- 773 -

ॐ कर्षण्यै स्वाहा

oṁ karṣaṇyai svāhā
She who is the producer of all that is created.

- 774 -

ॐ क्षान्त्यै स्वाहा

oṁ kṣāntyai svāhā
She who is patience.

- 775 -

ॐ गरुडायै स्वाहा

oṁ garuḍāyai svāhā
She who is the king of birds who carries Viṣṇu.

- 776 -

ॐ गरुडासनायै स्वाहा

oṁ garuḍāsanāyai svāhā
She who sits on the king of birds who carries Viṣṇu.

- 777 -

ॐ हलादिन्यै स्वाहा

oṁ halādinyai svāhā
She who plows the field.

- 778 -

ॐ अनुग्रहायै स्वाहा

oṁ anugrahāyai svāhā
She who appreciates.

- 779 -

ॐ नित्यायै स्वाहा

oṁ nityāyai svāhā
She who is eternal.

- 780 -

ॐ ब्रह्मविद्यायै स्वाहा

oṁ brahmavidyāyai svāhā
She who is the knowledge of the supreme.

- 781 -

ॐ हिरण्मय्यै स्वाहा

oṁ hiraṇmayyai svāhā
She who is the golden manifestation.

- 782 -

ॐ मह्यै स्वाहा

oṁ mahyai svāhā
She who is great.

\- 783 -

ॐ शुद्धविधायै स्वाहा

oṁ śuddhavidhāyai svāhā

She who is the discipline of purity.

\- 784 -

ॐ पृथ्व्यै स्वाहा

oṁ pṛthvyai svāhā

She who is the earth.

\- 785 -

ॐ शतानन्दायै स्वाहा

oṁ śatānandāyai svāhā

She who is a hundred forms of bliss.

\- 786 -

ॐ अंशुमालिन्यै स्वाहा

oṁ aṁśumālinyai svāhā

She who cultivates the parts.

\- 787 -

ॐ यज्ञाश्रयायै स्वाहा

oṁ yajñāśrayāyai svāhā

She who takes refuge in sacrifice.

\- 788 -

ॐ ख्यातिपरायै स्वाहा

oṁ khyātiparāyai svāhā

She who has the supreme fame.

\- 789 -

ॐ स्तव्यायै स्वाहा

oṁ stavyāyai svāhā

She who is expressed in songs of god.

\- 790 -

ॐ धृष्ट्यै स्वाहा

oṁ dhṛṣṭyai svāhā

She who is perception.

- 791 -

ॐ त्रिकालगायै स्वाहा

oṁ trikālagāyai svāhā
She who moves in the three times.

- 792 -

ॐ संवोधिन्यै स्वाहा

oṁ saṁvodhinyai svāhā
She who is all knowledge.

- 793 -

ॐ शब्दपूर्णायै स्वाहा

oṁ śabdapūrṇāyai svāhā
She who is the complete word.

- 794 -

ॐ विजयायै स्वाहा

oṁ vijayāyai svāhā
She who is victorious.

- 795 -

ॐ अंशुमत्यै स्वाहा

oṁ aṁśumatyai svāhā
She who is the light of all lights.

- 796 -

ॐ कलायै स्वाहा

oṁ kalāyai svāhā
She who is all attributes.

- 797 -

ॐ शिवायै स्वाहा

oṁ śivāyai svāhā
She who is the energy of the consciousness of infinite goodness.

- 798 -

ॐ स्तुतिप्रियायै स्वाहा

oṁ stutipriyāyai svāhā
She who loves song.

- 799 -

ॐ ख्यात्यै स्वाहा

oṁ khyātyai svāhā
She who is famous.

- 800 -

ॐ जीवयन्त्यै स्वाहा

oṁ jīvayantyai svāhā
She who is the ultimate life.

- 801 -

ॐ पुनर्वसवे स्वाहा

oṁ punarvasave svāhā
She who comes to earth again and again.

- 802 -

ॐ दीक्षायै स्वाहा

oṁ dīkṣāyai svāhā
She who is initiation.

- 803 -

ॐ भक्तार्तिहायै स्वाहा

oṁ bhaktārtihāyai svāhā
She who takes away the obstruction to devotion.

- 804 -

ॐ रक्षायै स्वाहा

oṁ rakṣāyai svāhā
She who is protector.

- 805 -

ॐ परीक्षायै स्वाहा

oṁ parīkṣāyai svāhā
She who gives the examination.

- 806 -

ॐ यज्ञसंभवायै स्वाहा

oṁ yajñasaṁbhavāyai svāhā
She whose whole being is in sacrifice.

\- 807 -

ॐ आर्द्रायै स्वाहा

oṁ ārdrāyai svāhā
She who is extremely subtle.

\- 808 -

ॐ पुष्करिण्यै स्वाहा

oṁ puṣkariṇyai svāhā
She who nourishes all the creation.

\- 809 -

ॐ पुण्यायै स्वाहा

oṁ puṇyāyai svāhā
She who is merit.

\- 810 -

ॐ गण्यायै स्वाहा

oṁ gaṇyāyai svāhā
She who has qualities.

\- 811 -

ॐ दारिद्र्यभञ्जिन्यै स्वाहा

oṁ dāridryabhañjinyai svāhā
She who removes affliction.

\- 812 -

ॐ धन्यायै स्वाहा

oṁ dhanyāyai svāhā
She who is wealthy.

\- 813 -

ॐ मान्यायै स्वाहा

oṁ mānyāyai svāhā
She who is contemplative.

\- 814 -

ॐ पद्मनेभ्यै स्वाहा

oṁ padmanebhyai svāhā
She who has a lotus navel.

- 815 -

ॐ भार्गव्यै स्वाहा

oṁ bhārgavyai svāhā
She who has all wealth.

- 816 -

ॐ वंशवर्धिन्यै स्वाहा

oṁ vaṁśavardhinyai svāhā
She who is the head of the family.

- 817 -

ॐ तीक्ष्णप्रवृत्यै स्वाहा

oṁ tīkṣṇapravṛtyai svāhā
She who evolves to the extreme.

- 818 -

ॐ सत्कीर्त्यै स्वाहा

oṁ satkīrtyai svāhā
She who has true fame.

- 819 -

ॐ निधिसेव्यायै स्वाहा

oṁ nidhisevyāyai svāhā
She who is served with discipline.

- 820 -

ॐ अघनाशिन्यै स्वाहा

oṁ aghanāśinyai svāhā
She who destroys the darkness.

- 821 -

ॐ संज्ञायै स्वाहा

oṁ saṁjñāyai svāhā
She who knows all.

- 822 -

ॐ निःसंशयायै स्वाहा

oṁ niḥsaṁśayāyai svāhā
She who is beyond doubt.

- 823 -

ॐ पूर्वायै स्वाहा

oṁ pūrvāyai svāhā
She who is in the east.

- 824 -

ॐ वनमालायै स्वाहा

oṁ vanamālāyai svāhā
She who wears a garland collected from the forest.

- 825 -

ॐ वसुन्धरायै स्वाहा

oṁ vasundharāyai svāhā
She who supports the earth.

- 826 -

ॐ पृथ्व्यै स्वाहा

oṁ pṛthvyai svāhā
She who is the earth.

- 827 -

ॐ महोत्कटायै स्वाहा

oṁ mahotkaṭāyai svāhā
She who is most complicated.

- 828 -

ॐ अहल्यायै स्वाहा

oṁ ahalyāyai svāhā
She who is uncultivated, pure as she is.

- 829 -

ॐ मण्डलायै स्वाहा

oṁ maṇḍalāyai svāhā
She who is the circle of existence.

- 830 -

ॐ आश्रितमानदायै स्वाहा

oṁ āśritamānadāyai svāhā
She who gives refuge to the mind.

- 831 -

ॐ सर्वस्यै स्वाहा

oṁ sarvasyai svāhā
She who is all.

- 832 -

ॐ नित्योदितायै स्वाहा

oṁ nityoditāyai svāhā
She who is always rising.

- 833 -

ॐ उदारायै स्वाहा

oṁ udārāyai svāhā
She who is in the digestion of all.

- 834-

ॐ जृम्भमाणायै स्वाहा

oṁ jṛmbhamāṇāyai svāhā
She who digests everything.

- 835 -

ॐ महोदयायै स्वाहा

oṁ mahodayāyai svāhā
She who rises with greatness.

- 836 -

ॐ चन्द्रकान्तोदितायै स्वाहा

oṁ candrakāntoditāyai svāhā
She who is the enchanting beauty of the rising moon.

- 837 -

ॐ सूर्यायै स्वाहा

oṁ sūryāyai svāhā
She who is the sun.

- 838 -

ॐ चतुरश्रायै स्वाहा

oṁ caturaśrāyai svāhā
She who is the refuge of the four.

- 839 -

ॐ मनोजवायै स्वाहा

oṁ manojavāyai svāhā
She who moves in the mind.

- 840 -

ॐ बालायै स्वाहा

oṁ bālāyai svāhā
She who is strong.

- 841 -

ॐ कुमार्यै स्वाहा

oṁ kumāryai svāhā
She who is eternally pure.

- 842 -

ॐ युवत्यै स्वाहा

oṁ yuvatyai svāhā
She who is young.

- 843 -

ॐ करुणायै स्वाहा

oṁ karuṇāyai svāhā
She who is compassionate.

- 844 -

ॐ भक्तवत्सलायै स्वाहा

oṁ bhaktavatsalāyai svāhā
She who loves devotees.

- 845 -

ॐ मेदिन्यै स्वाहा

oṁ medinyai svāhā
She who is the earth.

- 846 -

ॐ उपनिषन्मिश्रायै स्वाहा

oṁ upaniṣanmiśrāyai svāhā
She who is explained in the Upaniṣads.

- 847 -

ॐ सुमवीरवे स्वाहा

oṁ sumavīrave svāhā

She who is an excellent hero.

- 848 -

ॐ धनेश्वर्यै स्वाहा

oṁ dhaneśvaryai svāhā

She who is the supreme goddess of wealth.

- 849 -

ॐ दुर्मर्षण्यै स्वाहा

oṁ durmarṣaṇyai svāhā

She who is difficult to experience.

- 850 -

ॐ सुचरितायै स्वाहा

oṁ sucaritāyai svāhā

She who has excellent character.

- 851 -

ॐ वोधायै स्वाहा

oṁ vodhāyai svāhā

She who is well known.

- 852 -

ॐ शोभायै स्वाहा

oṁ śobhāyai svāhā

She who is pure.

- 853 -

ॐ सुवर्चलायै स्वाहा

oṁ suvarcalāyai svāhā

She who resides in excellent work.

- 854 -

ॐ यमुनायै स्वाहा

oṁ yamunāyai svāhā

She who is the Yamuna river.

- 855 -

ॐ अक्षौहिण्यै स्वाहा

oṁ akṣauhiṇyai svāhā
She who leads the army.

- 856 -

ॐ गङ्गायै स्वाहा

oṁ gaṅgāyai svāhā
She who is the Ganges.

- 857 -

ॐ मन्दाकिन्यै स्वाहा

oṁ mandākinyai svāhā
She who is the Mandākini river.

- 858 -

ॐ अमलाशयायै स्वाहा

oṁ amalāśayāyai svāhā
She who resides in the clean and pure.

- 859 -

ॐ गोदायै स्वाहा

oṁ godāyai svāhā
She who gives light.

- 860 -

ॐ गोदावर्यै स्वाहा

oṁ godāvaryai svāhā
She who is the Godāvari.

- 861 -

ॐ चन्द्रभागायै स्वाहा

oṁ candrabhāgāyai svāhā
She who is the part of the moon.

- 862 -

ॐ कावेर्यै स्वाहा

oṁ kāveryai svāhā
She who is Kāveri River.

- 863 -

ॐ उदन्वत्यै स्वाहा

oṁ udanvatyai svāhā
She who develops expression.

- 864 -

ॐ सिनीवाल्यै स्वाहा

oṁ sinīvālyai svāhā
She who wears the moon as Her crown.

- 865 -

ॐ कुह्वै स्वाहा

oṁ kuhvai svāhā
She who comes as a storm.

- 866 -

ॐ राकायै स्वाहा

oṁ rākāyai svāhā
She who comes into manifestation again and again.

- 867 -

ॐ वारणायै स्वाहा

oṁ vāraṇāyai svāhā
She who prohibits bad behavior.

- 868 -

ॐ सिन्धुमत्यै स्वाहा

oṁ sindhumatyai svāhā
She who is the Mother of the ocean.

- 869 -

ॐ अमायै स्वाहा

oṁ amāyai svāhā
She who is immeasurable.

- 870 -

ॐ पूर्तये स्वाहा

oṁ pūrtaye svāhā
She who grants fulfillment.

- 871 -

ॐ मायात्मिकायै स्वाहा

oṁ māyātmikāyai svāhā

She who is the capacity of the great measurement of consciousness.

- 872 -

ॐ स्फूर्तये स्वाहा

oṁ sphūrtaye svāhā

She who is delighted.

- 873 -

ॐ व्याख्यायै स्वाहा

oṁ vyākhyāyai svāhā

She who is all explanation.

- 874 -

ॐ सूत्रायै स्वाहा

oṁ sūtrāyai svāhā

She who is an abbreviated form of knowledge.

- 875 -

ॐ प्रजावत्यै स्वाहा

oṁ prajāvatyai svāhā

She who protects all beings born.

- 876 -

ॐ वृद्ध्यै स्वाहा

oṁ vṛddhyai svāhā

She who is all change and modification.

- 877 -

ॐ स्थित्यै स्वाहा

oṁ sthityai svāhā

She who is the circumstance of all beings.

- 878 -

ॐ ध्रुवायै स्वाहा

oṁ dhruvāyai svāhā

She who is truthful.

- 879 -

ॐ बुद्ध्यै स्वाहा

oṁ buddhyai svāhā
She who is intelligent.

- 880 -

ॐ त्रिगुणायै स्वाहा

oṁ triguṇāyai svāhā
She who embodies the three qualities of nature.

- 881 -

ॐ गुणगह्वरायै स्वाहा

oṁ guṇagahvarāyai svāhā
She who is the mine of all qualities.

- 882 -

ॐ अमोघायै स्वाहा

oṁ amoghāyai svāhā
She who has the best imperishable qualities.

- 883 -

ॐ शान्तिदायै स्वाहा

oṁ śāntidāyai svāhā
She who is the giver of peace.

- 884 -

ॐ सत्यायै स्वाहा

oṁ satyāyai svāhā
She who is truth.

- 885 -

ॐ ज्ञानदायै स्वाहा

oṁ jñānadāyai svāhā
She who is the giver of wisdom.

- 886 -

ॐ उत्कर्षिण्यै स्वाहा

oṁ utkarṣiṇyai svāhā
She who is most excellent.

- 887 -

ॐ शिवायै स्वाहा

oṁ śivāyai svāhā
She who is the energy of infinite goodness.

- 888 -

ॐ प्रकृत्यै स्वाहा

oṁ prakṛtyai svāhā
She who is nature.

- 889 -

ॐ भामिन्यै स्वाहा

oṁ bhāminyai svāhā
She who is illumination.

- 890 -

ॐ लोलायै स्वाहा

oṁ lolāyai svāhā
She who has a protruding tongue.

- 891 -

ॐ कमलायै स्वाहा

oṁ kamalāyai svāhā
She who is a lotus.

- 892 -

ॐ कामदुहे स्वाहा

oṁ kāmaduhe svāhā
She who fulfills all desires.

- 893 -

ॐ विद्ध्यै स्वाहा

oṁ viddhyai svāhā
She who is known in a special way.

- 894 -

ॐ प्रज्ञायै स्वाहा

oṁ prajñāyai svāhā
She who is the foremost wisdom.

- 895 -

ॐ रामायै स्वाहा

oṁ rāmāyai svāhā
She who is the perfect expression of the subtle body of consciousness.

- 896 -

ॐ परायै स्वाहा

oṁ parāyai svāhā
She who is supreme.

- 897 -

ॐ सन्ध्यायै स्वाहा

oṁ sandhyāyai svāhā
She who is the time of prayer.

- 898 -

ॐ सुभद्रायै स्वाहा

oṁ subhadrāyai svāhā
She who is the excellent among excellence.

- 899 -

ॐ सर्वमङ्गलायै स्वाहा

oṁ sarvamaṅgalāyai svāhā
She who is all welfare.

- 900 -

ॐ नन्दायै स्वाहा

oṁ nandāyai svāhā
She who is bliss.

- 901 -

ॐ भद्रायै स्वाहा

oṁ bhadrāyai svāhā
She who is excellent.

- 902 -

ॐ जयायै स्वाहा

oṁ jayāyai svāhā
She who is victorious.

- 903 -

ॐ रिक्तायै स्वाहा

oṁ riktāyai svāhā
She who is a total renunciate.

- 904 -

ॐ तिथिपूर्णायै स्वाहा

oṁ tithipūrṇāyai svāhā
She who is the full moon.

- 905 -

ॐ ऋतंभरायै स्वाहा

oṁ ṛtaṁbharāyai svāhā
She who supports the imperishable truth.

- 906 -

ॐ काष्ठायै स्वाहा

oṁ kāṣṭhāyai svāhā
She who is moments of time.

- 907 -

ॐ कामेश्वर्यै स्वाहा

oṁ kāmeśvaryai svāhā
She who is the supreme goddess of all desires.

- 908 -

ॐ निष्ठायै स्वाहा

oṁ niṣṭhāyai svāhā
She who is disciplined with sincerity.

- 909 -

ॐ काम्यायै स्वाहा

oṁ kāmyāyai svāhā
She who has desire.

- 910 -

ॐ राम्यायै स्वाहा

oṁ rāmyāyai svāhā
She who is beautiful.

- 911 -

ॐ धरायै स्वाहा

oṁ dharāyai svāhā
She who supports all.

- 912 -

ॐ स्मृत्यै स्वाहा

oṁ smṛtyai svāhā
She who is all rememberance.

- 913 -

ॐ शङ्किन्यै स्वाहा

oṁ śaṅkinyai svāhā
She who holds the conches.

- 914 -

ॐ चक्रिण्यै स्वाहा

oṁ cakriṇyai svāhā
She who holds the discus.

- 915 -

ॐ श्यामायै स्वाहा

oṁ śyāmāyai svāhā
She who is dark.

- 916 -

ॐ सामायै स्वाहा

oṁ sāmāyai svāhā
She who is song.

- 917 -

ॐ गोत्रायै स्वाहा

oṁ gotrāyai svāhā
She who is the lineage of wisdom.

- 918 -

ॐ रमायै स्वाहा

oṁ ramāyai svāhā
She who is playful.

- 919 -

ॐ द्युत्यै स्वाहा

oṁ dyutyai svāhā
She who illuminates all.

- 920 -

ॐ शान्तिदायै स्वाहा

oṁ śāntidāyai svāhā
She who is the giver of peace.

- 921 -

ॐ स्तुत्यै स्वाहा

oṁ stutyai svāhā
She who is praise.

- 922 -

ॐ सिद्ध्यै स्वाहा

oṁ siddhyai svāhā
She who is the attainment of perfection.

- 923 -

ॐ विराजायै स्वाहा

oṁ virājāyai svāhā
She who is always present.

- 924 -

ॐ अत्युज्ज्वलायै स्वाहा

oṁ atyujjvalāyai svāhā
She who is extremely bright.

- 925 -

ॐ अव्ययायै स्वाहा

oṁ avyayāyai svāhā
She who is infinite.

- 926 -

ॐ वाण्यै स्वाहा

oṁ vāṇyai svāhā
She who is all sound.

- 927 -

ॐ गौर्यै स्वाहा

oṁ gauryai svāhā
She who is rays of light.

- 928 -

ॐ इन्दिरायै स्वाहा

oṁ indirāyai svāhā
She who is all the senses.

- 929 -

ॐ लक्ष्म्यै स्वाहा

oṁ lakṣmyai svāhā
She who is the ultimate goal.

- 930 -

ॐ मेधायै स्वाहा

oṁ medhāyai svāhā
She who is the intellect of love.

- 931 -

ॐ श्रद्धायै स्वाहा

oṁ śraddhāyai svāhā
She who is faith.

- 932 -

ॐ अप्रमायै स्वाहा

oṁ apramāyai svāhā
She who is beyond measurement.

- 933 -

ॐ द्युतये स्वाहा

oṁ dyutaye svāhā
She who is illuminated.

- 934 -

ॐ स्वधायै स्वाहा

oṁ svadhāyai svāhā
She who is oblations of ancestral praise.

- 935 -

ॐ स्वाहायै स्वाहा

oṁ svāhāyai svāhā
She who is the proclamation, "I am one with God."

- 936 -

ॐ रतिरुषायै स्वाहा

oṁ ratiruṣāyai svāhā
She who is the dawn of spring.

- 937 -

ॐ वसवे स्वाहा

oṁ vasave svāhā
She who is the holder of wealth.

- 938 -

ॐ विद्यायै स्वाहा

oṁ vidyāyai svāhā
She who is knowledge.

- 939 -

ॐ धृत्यै स्वाहा

oṁ dhṛtyai svāhā
She who is constant.

- 940 -

ॐ सभायै स्वाहा

oṁ sabhāyai svāhā
She who is the assembly.

- 941 -

ॐ शिष्टायै स्वाहा

oṁ śiṣṭāyai svāhā
She who is ideal behavior.

- 942 -

ॐ इष्टायै स्वाहा

oṁ iṣṭāyai svāhā
She who is chosen.

- 943 -

ॐ शुच्यै स्वाहा

oṁ śucyai svāhā
She who is pure.

- 944 -

ॐ धात्र्यै स्वाहा

oṁ dhātryai svāhā
She who is the creator.

- 945 -

ॐ सुधारायै स्वाहा

oṁ sudhārāyai svāhā
She who is waves of excellence.

- 946 -

ॐ अक्षोण्यजायै स्वाहा

oṁ akṣoṇyajāyai svāhā
She who conquers every moment.

- 947 -

ॐ अमृतायै स्वाहा

oṁ amṛtāyai svāhā
She who is the nectar of immortal bliss.

- 948 -

ॐ रमण्यै स्वाहा

oṁ ramaṇyai svāhā
She who is beautiful.

- 949 -

ॐ एकायै स्वाहा

oṁ ekāyai svāhā
She who is the only one.

- 950 -

ॐ शारदाम्बायै स्वाहा

oṁ śāradāmbāyai svāhā
She who is the Mother of the ocean of all.

- 951 -

ॐ समेधायै स्वाहा

oṁ samedhāyai svāhā
She who is with the intellect of love.

- 952 -

ॐ आद्यायै स्वाहा

oṁ ādyāyai svāhā
She who is foremost.

- 953 -

ॐ शुभाक्षरायै स्वाहा

oṁ śubhākṣarāyai svāhā
She who is the pure manifestation.

- 954 -

ॐ रत्नावल्यै स्वाहा

oṁ ratnāvalyai svāhā
She who is all jewels.

- 955 -

ॐ भारत्यै स्वाहा

oṁ bhāratyai svāhā
She who shines with the light of wisdom.

- 956 -

ॐ ईडायै स्वाहा

oṁ īḍāyai svāhā
She who is the subtle part of the sun.

- 957 -

ॐ धीरायै स्वाहा

oṁ dhīrāyai svāhā
She who is consistent.

- 958 -

ॐ धियै स्वाहा

oṁ dhiyai svāhā
She who is contemplation.

- 959 -

ॐ केवलायै स्वाहा

oṁ kevalāyai svāhā
She who is the only one.

- 960 -

ॐ आत्मदायै स्वाहा

oṁ ātmadāyai svāhā
She who gives the soul.

- 961 -

ॐ यस्यै स्वाहा

oṁ yasyai svāhā
She who is one unto herself.

- 962 -

ॐ तस्यै स्वाहा

oṁ tasyai svāhā
She who is one unto all.

- 963 -

ॐ शुद्ध्यै स्वाहा

oṁ śuddhyai svāhā
She who is pure.

- 964 -

ॐ सोस्मितायै स्वाहा

oṁ sosmitāyai svāhā
She who has excellent memories.

- 965 -

ॐ कस्यै स्वाहा

oṁ kasyai svāhā
She who is Her own.

- 966 -

ॐ नीलायै स्वाहा

oṁ nīlāyai svāhā
She who is blue as the sky.

- 967 -

ॐ राधायै स्वाहा

oṁ rādhāyai svāhā
She who always gives love.

- 968 -

ॐ अमृतोद्भवायै स्वाहा

oṁ amṛtodbhavāyai svāhā
She who was born from the nectar of immortal bliss.

- 969 -

ॐ विभूत्यै स्वाहा

oṁ vibhūtyai svāhā
She who is manifestation.

- 970 -

ॐ निष्कलायै स्वाहा

oṁ niṣkalāyai svāhā
She who is beyond all attributes.

- 971 -

ॐ रम्यायै स्वाहा

oṁ ramyāyai svāhā
She who is always beautiful.

- 972 -

ॐ रक्षायै स्वाहा

oṁ rakṣāyai svāhā
She who protects all.

- 973 -

ॐ सुविमलायै स्वाहा

oṁ suvimalāyai svāhā
She who is excellent purity.

- 974 -

ॐ क्षमायै स्वाहा

oṁ kṣamāyai svāhā
She who is patient and forgiving.

- 975 -

ॐ प्राप्त्यै स्वाहा

oṁ prāptyai svāhā
She who attains Her desire.

- 976 -

ॐ वासन्तिकालेखायै स्वाहा

oṁ vāsantikālekhāyai svāhā
She who is celebrated with mantras in the spring time.

- 977 -

ॐ भूरिबीजायै स्वाहा

oṁ bhūribījāyai svāhā
She who is in all the seeds.

- 978 -

ॐ महाङ्गदायै स्वाहा

oṁ mahāṅgadāyai svāhā
She who gives the great body.

- 979 -

ॐ वरधुर्यायै स्वाहा

oṁ varadhuryāyai svāhā
She who gives the boon of tolerance.

- 980 -

ॐ स्वधायै स्वाहा

oṁ svadhāyai svāhā
She who is one's own spiritual discipline.

- 981 -

ॐ ह्रियै स्वाहा

oṁ hriyai svāhā
She who is always happy.

- 982 -

ॐ भुवे स्वाहा

oṁ bhuve svāhā
She who is the earth.

- 983 -

ॐ कामिन्यै स्वाहा

oṁ kāminyai svāhā
She who is all desires.

- 984 -

ॐ शोकनाशिन्यै स्वाहा

oṁ śokanāśinyai svāhā
She who destroys all sorrows.

- 985 -

ॐ मायायै स्वाहा

oṁ māyāyai svāhā
She who is the measurement of existence.

- 986 -

ॐ प्रीत्यै स्वाहा

oṁ prītyai svāhā
She who is beloved.

- 987 -

ॐ असहनायै स्वाहा

oṁ asahanāyai svāhā
She who is the source of all tolerance.

- 988 -

ॐ नर्मदायै स्वाहा

oṁ narmadāyai svāhā
She who is the Narmada River.

- 989 -

ॐ गोकुलाश्रयायै स्वाहा

oṁ gokulāśrayāyai svāhā
She who takes refuge in the family of light.

- 990 -

ॐ अर्कप्रभायै स्वाहा

oṁ arkaprabhāyai svāhā
She who is the light of the sun.

- 991 -

ॐ रसेभायै स्वाहा

oṁ rasebhāyai svāhā
She who experiences all taste.

- 992 -

ॐ श्रीनिलयायै स्वाहा

oṁ śrīnilayāyai svāhā
She who dwells in respect.

- 993 -

ॐ इन्दुप्रभायै स्वाहा

oṁ induprabhāyai svāhā
She who is the light of the moon.

- 994 -

ॐ अद्भुतायै स्वाहा

oṁ adbhutāyai svāhā
She who is wonderful and fantastic.

- 995 -

ॐ श्रियै स्वाहा

oṁ śriyai svāhā
She who is respect.

- 996 -

ॐ कृशानुप्रभायै स्वाहा

oṁ kṛśānuprabhāyai svāhā
She who is the light of the fire.

- 997 -

ॐ वज्रलम्बनायै स्वाहा

oṁ vajralambanāyai svāhā
She who wields the lightning.

- 998 -

ॐ सर्वभूमिदायै स्वाहा

oṁ sarvabhūmidāyai svāhā
She who gives all the land.

- 999 -

ॐ भोगप्रियायै स्वाहा

oṁ bhogapriyāyai svāhā
She who loves enjoyment.

- 1000 -

ॐ भोगवत्यै स्वाहा

oṁ bhogavatyai svāhā
She who is the spirit of all enjoyment.

- 1001 -

ॐ भोगीन्द्रशयनासनायै स्वाहा

oṁ bhogīndraśayanāsanāyai svāhā
She who is the seat of rest of the lord of enjoyment.

- 1002 -

ॐ अश्वपूर्वायै स्वाहा

oṁ aśvapūrvāyai svāhā
She who is the horses that come from the east (which pull the chariot of the sun).

- 1003 -

ॐ रथमध्यायै स्वाहा

oṁ rathamadhyāyai svāhā
She who is the pivot of the chariot.

- 1004 -

ॐ हस्तिनादप्रबोदिन्यै स्वाहा

oṁ hastinādaprabodinyai svāhā
She who is known to roar like an elephant.

- 1005 -

ॐ सर्वलक्षणलक्षिण्यायै स्वाहा

oṁ sarvalakṣaṇalakṣiṇyāyai svāhā
She who is the goal of all goals.

- 1006 -

ॐ सर्वलोकप्रियङ्कर्यै स्वाहा

oṁ saravalokapriyaṅkaryai svāhā
She who is the cause of love in all the worlds.

- 1007 -

ॐ सर्वमङ्गलमाङ्गल्यायै स्वाहा

oṁ sarvamaṅgalamāṅgalyāyai svāhā
She who is the welfare of all welfare.

- 1008 -

ॐ दृष्टादृष्टफलप्रदायै स्वाहा

oṁ dṛṣṭādṛṣṭaphalapradāyai svāhā
She who gives all fruit whether perceivable or imperceivable.

ॐ नामः इति

oṁ nāmaḥ iti
Oṁ and that is the end.

इति लक्ष्मीसहस्रनामावल्याः स्वाहाकारः समाप्तः ॥

iti lakṣmīsahasranāmāvalyāḥ svāhākāraḥ samāptaḥ ||
This ends the thousand names of Lakṣmī.

ॐ श्रीं लक्ष्म्यै नमः

oṁ śrīṁ lakṣmyai namaḥ
Oṁ I bow to the Goddess Lakṣmī

श्री लक्ष्मी चालीसा
śrī lakṣmī cālīsā

दोहा
dohā

मातु लक्ष्मी करि कृपा । करो हृदय में वास ।
मनोकामना सिद्ध करि । परुवहु मेरी आस ॥

mātu lakṣmī kari kṛpā | karo hṛdaya meṁ vāsa |
manokāmanā siddha kari | paruvahu merī āsa ||

Oh Mother Lakṣmī, bestow your grace and reside in my heart. Bring to perfection the desires of my mind, please fulfill this wish of mine.

सोरठा
soraṭhā

यही मोर अरदास । हाथ जोड विनती करुं ।
सब विधि करौ सुवास । जय जननि जगदम्बिका ॥

yahī mora aradāsa | hātha joḍa vinatī karuṁ |
saba vidhi karau suvāsa | jaya janani jagadambikā ||

This is my prayer, which I make with hands folded in humble supplication. Performing all appropriate forms of worship, victory to the Mother of the Perceivable Universe!

चौपाई
caupāī

सिन्धु सुता मैं सुमिरौ तोही । ज्ञान बुद्धि विद्या दो मोही ॥

sindhu sutā maiṁ sumirau tohī |
jñāna buddhi vidyā do mohī ||

I pray to you, oh Daughter of the Ocean, give me wisdom, intellect, and knowledge.

तुम समान नहिं कोई उपकारी ।
सब विधि पुरवहु आस हमारी ॥

tuma samāna nahiṁ koī upakārī |
saba vidhi puravahu āsa hamārī ||

There is no other who grants benefits as you do, you give complete fulfillment of all desires.

जय जय जगत जननि जगदम्बा ।
सबकी तुम ही हो अवलम्बा ॥

jaya jaya jagata janani jagadambā |
sabakī tuma hī ho avalambā ||

Victory, victory to the Mother of the Perceivable World, you are the support of all.

तुम ही हो सब घट घट वासी । विनती यही हमारी खासी ॥

tuma hī ho saba ghaṭa ghaṭa vāsī |
vinatī yahī hamārī khāsī ||

You reside within every form in creation, please accept my humble prayer.

जगजननी जय सिन्धु कुमारी ।
दीनन की तुम हो हितकारी ॥

jagajananī jaya sindhu kumārī |
dīnana kī tuma ho hitakārī ||

Victory to the Mother who is Daughter of the Ocean, you give the greatest benefit to the lowly and downtrodden.

विनवौं नित्य तुमहिं महारानी ।
कृपा करौ जग जननि भवानी ॥

vinavauṁ nitya tumahiṁ mahārānī |
kṛpā karau jaga janani bhavānī ||

Eternally we pray to you, oh Great Queen, bestow your grace upon us, Mother of the Universe.

केहि विधि स्तुति करौं तिहारी ।
सुधि लीजै अपराध बिसारी ॥
kehi vidhi stuti karauṁ tihārī |
sudhi lījai aparādha bisārī ||
With what words can I sing your praise? Please purify all of my transgressions.

कृपा दृष्टि चितववो मम ओरी ।
जगजननी विनती सुन मोरी ॥
kṛpā dṛṣṭi citavavo mama orī |
jagajananī vinatī suna morī ||
Please look at me with compassionate grace, oh Mother of the Universe listen to my prayer.

ज्ञान बुद्धि जय सुख की दाता । संकट हरो हमारी माता ॥
jñāna buddhi jaya sukha kī dātā |
saṁkaṭa haro hamārī mātā ||
You give victory and comfort to the wise and intelligent, the Mother who takes away all our difficulties.

क्षीरसिन्धु जब विष्णु मथायो । चौदह रत्न सिन्धु में पायो ॥
kṣīrasindhu jaba viṣṇu mathāyo |
caudaha ratna sindhu meṁ pāyo ||
When Viṣṇu churned the milk-ocean of pure consciousness, you were found among the fourteen jewels which arose from the ocean.

चौदह रत्न में तुम सुखरासी । सेवा कियो प्रभु बनि दासी ॥
caudaha ratna meṁ tuma sukharāsī |
sevā kiyo prabhu bani dāsī ||
Of the fourteen jewels you gave the greatest delight, and you served the Lord by becoming His servant.

जब जब जन्म जहां प्रभु लीन्हा ।

रुप बदल तहं सेवा कीन्हा ॥

jaba jaba janma jahāṁ prabhu līnhā |
rupa badala tahaṁ sevā kīnhā ||
Whenever, wherever the Lord takes birth, you change your form in order to serve Him.

स्वयं विष्णु जब नर तनु धारा ।

लीन्हेउ अवधपुरी अवतारा ॥

svayaṁ viṣṇu jaba nara tanu dhārā |
līnheu avadhapurī avatārā ||
When Vishnu Himself took a human body, and became an Avatar in the City of Ayodhya,

तब तुम प्रगट जनकपुर माहीं ।

सेवा कियो हृदय पुलकाहीं ॥

taba tuma pragaṭa janakapura māhīṁ |
sevā kiyo hṛdaya pulakāhīṁ ||
then you manifested in Janakpur (Miṭhilā), in order to serve Him with all your heart.

अपनाया तोहि अन्तर्यामी ।

विश्व विदित त्रिभुवन की स्वामी ॥

apanāyā tohi antaryāmī |
viśva vidita tribhuvana kī svāmī ||
You are Knower of the secrets in the hearts of all, Master of the three worlds, Knower of the universe.

तुम सम प्रबल शक्ति नहीं आनी ।
कहं लौ महिमा कहौं बखानी ॥

tuma sama prabala śakti nahīṁ ānī |
kahaṁ lau mahimā kahauṁ bakhānī ||
No other has such strength or energy as you, no one has capacity to describe your greatness.

मन क्रम वचन करै सेवकाई ।
मन इच्छित वाञ्छित फल पाई ॥

mana krama vacana karai sevakāī |
mana icchita vāñchita phala pāī ||
Who ever can serve you with mind, action, and word, will receive the appropriate fruit desired by their mind.

तजि छल कपट और चतुराई ।
पूजहिं विविध भांति मनलाई ॥

taji chala kapaṭa aura caturāī |
pūjahiṁ vividha bhāṁti manalāī ||
Renouncing cleverness, deceitfulness, and dishonesty, those who will worship you without other thoughts according to the prescribed procedure,

और हाल मैं कहौं बुझाई । जो यह पाठ करै मन लाई ॥

aura hāla maiṁ kahauṁ bujhāī |
jo yaha pāṭha karai mana lāī ||
and understand your presence in every circumstance, and keep this instruction in their mind,

ताको कोई कष्ट नोई । मन इच्छित पावै फल सोई ॥

tāko koī kaṣṭa noī | mana icchita pāvai phala soī ||
they will find no difficulties, and will attain the fruits of the desires of their mind.

त्राहि त्राहि जय दुःख निवारिणि ।
त्रिविध ताप भव बन्धन हारिणी ॥

trāhi trāhi jaya duḥkha nivāriṇi |
trividha tāpa bhava bandhana hāriṇī ||

Save me, save me, victory to She who takes away all pain, She who takes away the heat of affliction from the three worlds.

जो चालीसा पढ पढवै । ध्यान लगाकर सुनै सुनावै ॥

jo cālīsā paḍha paḍhavai |
dhyāna lagākara sunai sunāvai ||

Whoever will recite or cause others to recite these forty verses, whoever will meditate, listen or cause others to hear,

ताकौ कोई न रोग सतावै । पुत्र आदि धन सम्पत्ति पावै ॥

tākau koī na roga satāvai |
putra ādi dhana sampatti pāvai ||

they will not be bothered by disease, and will gain children and various other forms of wealth.

पुत्रहीन अरु सम्पति हीना । अन्ध बधिर कोढ अति दीना ॥

putrahīna aru sampati hīnā |
andha badhira koḍha ati dīnā ||

Those without children or without wealth, those who are blind, deaf, with leprosy, and other lowly and downtrodden

विप्र बोलाय कै पाठ करावै । शंका दिल में कभी न लावै ॥

vipra bolāya kai pāṭha karāvai |
śaṁkā dila meṁ kabhī na lāvai ||

who call upon you, or who have this recitation performed by knowledgeable people, will never entertain doubts in the hearts.

पाठ करावै दिन चालीसा । ता पर कृपा करैं गौरीसा ॥

pāṭha karāvai dina cālīsā | tā para kṛpā karaiṁ gaurīsā ||

Whoever will perform this recitation daily, will be illuminated with your grace.

सुख सम्पत्ति बहुत सी पावै । कमी नहीं काहू की आवै ॥

sukha sampatti bahuta sī pāvai |
kamī nahīṁ kāhū kī āvai ||

They will gain great comfort (happiness), and wealth, and will not experience any lack.

बारह मास करै जो पूजा । तेहि सम धन्य और नहिं दूजा ॥

bāraha māsa karai jo pūjā |
tehi sama dhanya aura nahiṁ dūjā ||

Whoever will worship in this way for twelve months, will be blessed, of this there is no doubt.

प्रतिदिन पाठ करै मन माही ।
उन सम कोइ जग में कहुं नाहीं ॥

pratidina pāṭha karai mana māhī |
una sama koi jaga meṁ kahuṁ nāhīṁ ||

Whoever will perform this recitation every day with one mind, there is no individual comparable in the world.

बहुविधि क्या मैं करौं बडई । लेय परीक्षा ध्यान लगाई ॥

bahuvidhi kyā maiṁ karauṁ baḍaī |
leya parīkṣā dhyāna lagāī ||

I praise you in every effort I produce, as you take examination of my capacity to pay attention (meditate).

करि विश्वास करै व्रत नेमा । होय सिद्ध उपजै उर प्रेमा ॥

kari viśvāsa karai vrata nemā |
hoya siddha upajai ura premā ||

Whoever will perform this vow of worship with faith, will attain perfection and be filled with love.

जय जय जय लक्ष्मी भवानी ।

सब में व्यापित हो गुण खानी ॥

jaya jaya jaya lakṣmī bhavānī |
saba meṁ vyāpita ho guṇa khānī ||

Victory, victory, victory to Lakṣmī, Mother of the Universe, who defines the qualities within all individuals.

तुम्हरो तेज प्रबल जग माहीं ।

तुम सम कोउ दयालु कहुं नाहिं ॥

tumharo teja prabala jaga māhīṁ |
tuma sama kou dayālu kahuṁ nāhiṁ ||

You are the light and strength of the expansive creation, there is no one as compassionate as you.

मोहि अनाथ की सुधि अब लीजै ।

संकट काटि भक्ति मोहि दीजै ॥

mohi anātha kī sudhi aba lījai |
saṁkaṭa kāṭi bhakti mohi dījai ||

Now save me from being an orphan, Mother, destroy my troubles and give me pure devotion.

भूल चूक करि क्षमा हमारी । दर्शन दजै दशा निहारी ॥

bhūla cūka kari kṣamā hamārī |
darśana dajai daśā nihārī ||

Forgive our transgressions from having forgotten you, give the intuitive vision of your being, oh you who take away unfortunate circumstances.

बिन दर्शन व्याकुल अधिकारी ।
तुमहि अछत दुःख सहते भारी ॥

bina darśana vyākula adhikārī |
tumahi achata duḥkha sahate bhārī ||

Without your intuitive vision we deserve sadness (longing), only you can save us from (repress) unlimited pain.

नहिं मोहिं ज्ञान बुद्धि है तन में ।
सब जानत हो अपने मन में ॥

nahiṁ mohiṁ jñāna buddhi hai tana meṁ |
saba jānata ho apane mana meṁ ||

Well you know in your mind that in this body I am devoid of wisdom and intelligence.

रुप चतुर्भुज करके धारण । कष्ट मोर अब करहु निवारण ॥

rupa caturbhuja karake dhāraṇa |
kaṣṭa mora aba karahu nivāraṇa ||

Display your form with four arms, and take away from me all of my difficulties.

केहि प्रकार मैं करौं बडई ।
ज्ञान बुद्धि मोहि नहिं अधिकाई ॥

kehi prakāra maiṁ karauṁ baḍaī |
jñāna buddhi mohi nahiṁ adhikāī ||

Understanding that I am devoid of wisdom and intelligence, I have sung your praises in this way.

दोहा
dohā

त्राहि त्राहि दुःख हारिणी । हरो वेगि सब त्रास ।
जयति जयति जय लक्ष्मी । करो शत्रु को नाश ॥
trāhi trāhi duḥkha hāriṇī | haro vegi saba trāsa |
jayati jayati jaya lakṣmī | karo śatru ko nāśa ||
Save me, save me, oh you who take away all pain, destroy all that torments. Be victorious, be victorious, victory to Lakshmi, destroy all enmity!

रामदास धरि ध्यान नित । विनय करत कर जोर ।
मातु लक्ष्मी दास पर । करहु दया की कोर ॥
rāmadāsa dhari dhyāna nita | vinaya karata kara jora |
mātu lakṣmī dāsa para | karahu dayā kī kora ||
This Servant of God (name of the singer) regularly performs meditation with humility. Oh Mother Lakṣmī, bestow your compassion upon your servant.

ॐ विश्वरूपस्य भार्ज्यासि पद्मे पद्मालये शुभे ।
सर्वतः पाहि मां देवी महालक्ष्मि नमोऽस्तु ते ॥
oṁ viśvarūpasya bhārjyāsi padme padmālaye śubhe
sarvataḥ pāhi māṁ devī mahālakṣmi namo-stu te
Oṁ The form of the universe, you are the wife of the universe, Lotus One, She Who Resides in Lotuses, Pure One; always protect me, oh Goddess. Oh Great Goddess of True Wealth, I bow to you.

shree maa pūjā

worship of shree maa

ॐ सनातनी माया विद्महे ज्ञान प्रकाशायै धीमहे ।

तन्नो श्री माँ प्रचोदायत् ॥

oṁ sanātanī māyā vidmahe
jñāna prakāśāyai dhīmahe
tanno śrī māṁ pracodāyat

Oṁ we meditate on the Eternal Measurement of Consciousness, we contemplate She who illuminates wisdom. May that Shree Maa grant us increase.

ॐ श्री सनातनी मायै नमो नमः

oṁ śrī sanātanī māyai namo namaḥ

oṁ again and again I bow to the Eternal Shree Maa.

मन्त्रपुष्पाञ्जली समर्पयामि

mantrapuṣpāñjalī samarpayāmi

I offer these handfuls of flowers with mantras and the highest respect.

puṣpāñjalī
offer flowers

सर्वमङ्गल मङ्गल्ये शिवे सर्वार्थ साधिके ।
शरण्ये त्र्यम्बके गौरि नारायणि नमोऽस्तु ते ॥

sarvamaṅgala maṅgalye śive sarvārtha sādhike
śaraṇye tryambake gauri nārāyaṇi namo-stu te

To the Auspicious of all Auspiciousness, to the Good, to the Accomplisher of all Objectives, to the Source of Refuge, to the Mother of the Three Worlds, to the Goddess Who Is Rays of Light, Exposer of Consciousness, we bow to you.

ॐ श्रीं लक्ष्म्यै नमः मन्त्रपुष्पाङ्जली समर्पयामि

oṁ śrīṁ lakṣmyai namaḥ mantrapuṣpāñjalī samarpayāmi

I offer these handfuls of flowers with mantras and the highest respect Oṁ I bow to the Goddess Lakṣmī.

सृष्टिस्थितिविनाशानां शक्तिभूते सनातनि ।
गुणाश्रये गुणमये नारायणि नमोऽस्तु ते ॥

sṛṣṭisthitivināśānāṁ śaktibhūte sanātani
guṇāśraye guṇamaye nārāyaṇi namo-stu te

You are the Eternal Energy of Creation, Preservation and Destruction in all existence; that on which all qualities depend, that which limits all qualities, Exposer of Consciousness, we bow to you.

ॐ श्रीं लक्ष्म्यै नमः मन्त्रपुष्पाङ्जली समर्पयामि

oṁ śrīṁ lakṣmyai namaḥ mantrapuṣpāñjalī samarpayāmi

I offer these handfuls of flowers with mantras and the highest respect Oṁ I bow to the Goddess Lakṣmī.

शरणागतदीनार्त परित्राण परायणे ।
सर्वस्यार्ति हरे देवि नारायणि नमोऽस्तु ते ॥

śaraṇāgatadīnārta paritrāṇa parāyaṇe
sarvasyārti hare devi nārāyaṇi namo-stu te
For those who are devoted to you and take refuge in you, you save from all discomfort and unhappiness. All worry you take away, Oh Goddess, Exposer of Consciousness, we bow to you.

ॐ श्रीं लक्ष्म्यै नमः मन्त्रपुष्पाङ्जली समर्पयामि

oṁ śrīṁ lakṣmyai namaḥ mantrapuṣpāñjalī samarpayāmi
I offer these handfuls of flowers with mantras and the highest respect Oṁ I bow to the Goddess Lakṣmī.

praṇām

दुर्गां शिवां शान्तिकरीं ब्रह्माणीं ब्रह्मणः प्रियाम् ।
सर्वलोक प्रणेत्रीञ्च प्रणमामि सदा शिवाम् ॥

durgāṁ śivāṁ śāntikarīṁ brahmāṇīṁ brahmaṇaḥ priyām
sarvaloka praṇetrīñca praṇamāmi sadā śivām
The Reliever of Difficulties, Exposer of Goodness, Cause of Peace, Infinite Consciousness, Beloved by Knowers of Consciousness, all the inhabitants of all the worlds always bow to Her, and I am bowing to Goodness Herself.

मङ्गलां शोभनां शुद्धां निष्कलां परमां कलाम् ।
विश्वेश्वरीं विश्वमातां चण्डिकां प्रणमाम्यहम् ॥

maṅgalāṁ śobhanāṁ śuddhāṁ niṣkalāṁ paramāṁ kalām
viśveśvarīṁ viśvamātāṁ caṇḍikāṁ praṇamāmyaham
Welfare, Radiant Beauty, Completely Pure, Without Limitations, the Ultimate Limitation, the Lord of the Universe, the Mother of the Universe, to you Caṇḍi, to the Energy that Tears Apart Thought, I bow in submission.

सर्वदेवमयीं देवीं सर्वरोगभयापहाम् ।
ब्रह्मेशविष्णुनमितां प्रणमामि सदा शिवाम् ॥

sarvadevamayīṁ devīṁ sarvarogabhayāpahām
brahmeśaviṣṇunamitāṁ praṇamāmi sadā śivām

Composed of all the Gods, removing all sickness and fear, Brahma, Maheśwara and Viṣṇu bow down to Her, and I always bow down to the Energy of Infinite Goodness.

विन्ध्यस्थां विन्ध्यनिलयां दिव्यस्थाननिवासिनीम् ।
योगिनीं योगजननीं चण्डिकां प्रणमाम्यहम् ॥

vindhyasthāṁ vindhyanilayāṁ divyasthānanivāsinīm
yoginīṁ yogajananīṁ caṇḍikāṁ praṇamāmyaham

The dwelling place of Knowledge, residing in Knowledge, Resident in the Place of Divine Illumination, the Cause of Union, the Knower of Union, to the Energy that Tears Apart Thought we constantly bow.

ईशानमातरं देवीमीश्वरीमीश्वरप्रियाम् ।
प्रणतोऽस्मि सदा दुर्गां संसारार्णवतारिणीम् ॥

īśānamātaraṁ devīmīśvarīmīśvarapriyām
praṇato-smi sadā durgāṁ saṁsārārṇavatāriṇīm

The Mother of the Supreme Consciousness, the Goddess Who Is the Supreme Consciousness, beloved by the Supreme Consciousness, we always bow to Durgā, the Reliever of Difficulties, who takes aspirants across the difficult sea of objects and their relationships.

ॐ महादेव महात्रान महायोगि महेश्वर ।
सर्वपाप हरां देव मकाराय नमो नमः ॥

oṁ mahādeva mahātrāna mahāyogi maheśvara
sarvapāpa harāṁ deva makārāya namo namaḥ

Oṁ The Great God, the Great Reliever, the Great Yogi, Oh Supreme Lord, Oh God who removes all Sin, in the form of the letter "M," which dissolves creation, we bow to you again and again.

ॐ नमः शिवाय शान्ताय कारणत्राय हेतवे ।
निवेदायामि चात्मानं त्वं गति परमेश्वर ॥

oṁ namaḥ śivāya śāntāya kāraṇatrāya hetave
nivedāyāmi cātmānaṁ tvaṁ gati parameśvara

Oṁ I bow to the Consciousness of Infinite Goodness, to Peace, to the Cause of the three worlds, I offer to you the fullness of my soul, Oh Supreme Lord.

ॐ नमः शिवाय

oṁ namaḥ śivāya

oṁ I bow to the Consciousness of Infinite Goodness.

aśīrbād

blessings

ॐ श्रीर्वर्चस्वमायुष्यमारोग्यमाविधात् पवमानं महीयते ।

धान्यं धनं पशुं बहुपुत्रलाभंशतसंवत्सरं दीर्घमायुः ॥

oṁ śrīrvarcasvamāyuṣyamārogyamāvidhāt pavamānaṁ mahīyate

dhānyaṁ dhanaṁ paśuṁ bahuputralābhaṁ śatasaṁvatsaraṁ dīrghamāyuḥ

Oṁ You are blessed with the Highest Respect, with Wealth, with Life, with Freedom from disease and freedom to be One with the Greatness; with food, with wealth, with animals and with many children, and with a long life of one hundred years.

मन्त्रार्थाः सफलाः सन्तु पूणाः सन्तु मनोरथाः ।

शत्रूणां बुद्धिनाशोऽस्तु मित्राणामुदयस्तव ॥

mantrārthāḥ saphalāḥ santu pūṇāḥ santu manorathāḥ

śatrūṇāṁ buddhināśo-stu mitrāṇāmudayastava

May the meanings of the mantras bring excellent fruit, and may the journey of your mind be full and complete. May all enmity be removed from your intellect, and may friendship continuously rise.

आयुष्कामो यशस्कामो पुत्र-पौत्रस्तथैव च ।

आरोग्यं धनकामश्च सर्वे कामा भवन्तु मे ॥

āyuṣkāmo yaśaskāmo putra-pautrastathaiva ca

ārogyaṁ dhanakāmaśca sarve kāmā bhavantu me

May you enjoy life; may you enjoy fame, children and grandchildren throughout the generations; may you all live without disease, with abundance of wealth; and may all your disires be fulfilled.

visārjaṇa

removing the divine energy to the unmanifest

ॐ ईतः पूर्व प्राणबुद्धिदेह धर्माधिकारतो ।
जाग्रत् स्वप्नशुषुप्तयवस्थाशु मनसा ॥

oṁ ītaḥ pūrva prāṇabuddhideha dharmādhikārato jāgrat svapnaśuṣuptyavasthāśu manasā

Oṁ Thus the full and complete intelligence of the Life Force, the Cause of Dharma, the Way of Truth to Perfection, has been given. Waking Consciousness, Dreaming (or thinking) Consciousness, and Consciousness in Dreamless Dleep (intuitive Consciousness) in which all thoughts are situated.

वाचा कर्मणा हस्ताभ्यां पध्भ्यामूदरेण शिश्ना ।
यत् कृतं यदुक्तं यत् स्मृतं तत् सर्वं ब्रह्मार्पणं भवतु स्वाहा ॥

vācā karmaṇā hastābhyāṁ padhbhyāmūdareṇa śiśnā yat kṛtaṁ yaduktaṁ yat smṛtaṁ tat sarvaṁ brahmārpaṇaṁ bhavatu svāhā

All speech has been offered with folded hands raised in respect while bowing to the lotus feet. That activity, that speech, that memory, all of that has been offered to the Supreme Divinity. I am One with God!

मां मदीयञ्च सकलं श्री चण्डिका चरणे समर्पये ।
ॐ तत् सत् ॥

māṁ madīyañca sakalaṁ śrī caṇḍikā caraṇe samarpaye oṁ tat sat

All of me and all that belongs to me entirely, I surrender to the feet of the respected caṇḍikā, She Who Tears Apart Thought. The Infinite, That is Truth.

ॐ ब्रह्मार्पणं ब्रह्म हविर्ब्रह्माग्नौ ब्रह्मणा हुतम् ।
ब्रह्मैव तेन गन्तव्यं ब्रह्मकर्मसमाधिना ॥

oṁ brahmārpaṇaṁ brahma havirbrahmāgnau
brahmaṇā hutam
brahmaiva tena gantavyaṁ brahmakarmasamādhinā

Oṁ The Supreme Divinity makes the offering; the Supreme Divinity is the offering; offered by the Supreme Divinity, in the fire of the Supreme Divinity. By seeing the Supreme Divinity in all actions, one realizes that Supreme Divinity.

ॐ पूर्णमदः पूर्णमिदं पूर्णात् पूर्णमुदच्यते ।
पूर्णस्य पूर्णमादाय पूर्णमेवावशिश्यते ॥

oṁ pūrṇamadaḥ pūrṇamidaṁ
pūrṇāt pūrṇamudacyate
pūrṇasya pūrṇamādāya pūrṇamevāva śiśyate

Oṁ That is whole and perfect. This is whole and perfect. From the whole and perfect, the whole and perfect becomes manifest. If the whole and perfect issue forth from the whole and perfect, even still only the whole and perfect remain.

ॐ शान्तिः शान्तिः शान्तिः

oṁ śāntiḥ śāntiḥ śāntiḥ

Oṁ Peace, Peace, Peace

क्षमास्य (visārjaṇ mudrā)

kṣamāsya

Please forgive me.

More Books by Shree Maa and Swami Satyananda Saraswati

Annapurna Sahasranam
Before Becoming This
Bhagavad Gita
Chandi Path
Cosmic Puja
Cosmic Puja Bengali
Devi Gita
Devi Mandir Songbook
Durga Puja Beginner
Ganesh Puja
Hanuman Puja
Kali Dhyanam
Kali Puja
Lakṣmī Sahasranam
Sahib Sadhu, The White Sadhu
Shiva Puja Beginner
Shiva Puja and Advanced Yajna
Shree Maa Cookbook
Shree Maa: The Guru and the Goddess
Shree Maa: The Life of a Saint
Sundar Kanda
Swami Purana

CDs and Cassettes

Chandi Path
Dark Night Mother
Durga Puja Beginner (Instructional)
Goddess is Everywhere
Lalita Trishati
Mahamrtyunjaya Mantra
Mantras of the Nine Planets
Navarna Mantra
Om Mantra
Sadhu Stories from the Himalayas
Shiva is in My Heart
Shiva Puja Beginner (Instructional)
Shiva Puja & Advanced Yajna
Shree Maa in the Temple of the Heart
Shree Maa on Tour 1998
Songs of Ramprasad
Thousand Names of Kali

Videos

Across the States with Shree Maa & Swamiji
Meaning and Method of Worship
Shree Maa: Meeting a Modern Saint
Visiting India with Shree Maa and Swamiji

Please visit us at www.shreemaa.org
Our email is info@shreemaa.org

www.ingramcontent.com/pod-product-compliance
Lightning Source LLC
Chambersburg PA
CBHW021051080526
44587CB00010B/215
* 9 7 8 1 8 7 7 7 9 5 0 5 3 *